Catholicism and the Making
of Politics in Central Mozambique,
1940–1986

Rochester Studies in African History and the Diaspora

Toyin Falola, Series Editor
The Jacob and Frances Sanger Mossiker Chair in the Humanities
and University Distinguished Teaching Professor
University of Texas at Austin

Recent Titles

*Islam, Power, and Dependency in the Gambia River Basin:
The Politics of Land Control, 1790–1940*
Assan Sarr

Living Salvation in the East African Revival in Uganda
Jason Bruner

On Durban's Docks: Zulu Workers, Rural Households, Global Labor
Ralph Callebert

*Mediators, Contract Men, and Colonial Capital:
Mechanized Gold Mining in the Gold Coast Colony, 1879–1909*
Cassandra Mark-Thiesen

Muslim Fula Business Elites and Politics in Sierra Leone
Alusine Jalloh

Race, Decolonization, and Global Citizenship in South Africa
Chielozona Eze

Plantation Slavery in the Sokoto Caliphate: A Historical and Comparative Study
Mohammed Bashir Salau

African Migration Narratives: Politics, Race, and Space
Edited by Cajetan Iheka and Jack Taylor

Ethics and Society in Nigeria: Identity, History, Political Theory
Nimi Wariboko

Catholicism and the Making of Politics in Central Mozambique, 1940–1986
Eric Morier-Genoud

A complete list of titles in the Rochester Studies in African History and the
Diaspora series may be found on our website, www.urpress.com.

Catholicism and the Making
of Politics in Central Mozambique,
1940–1986

Eric Morier-Genoud

UNIVERSITY OF ROCHESTER PRESS

First published 2019

University of Rochester Press
668 Mt. Hope Avenue, Rochester, NY 14620, USA
www.urpress.com
and Boydell & Brewer Limited
PO Box 9, Woodbridge, Suffolk IP12 3DF, UK
www.boydellandbrewer.com

ISBN-13: 978-1-58046-941-8
ISSN: 1092-5228

Library of Congress Cataloging-in-Publication Data

Names: Morier-Genoud, Eric, author.
Title: Catholicism and the making of politics in central Mozambique, 1940–
    1986 / Eric Morier-Genoud.
Other titles: Rochester studies in African history and the diaspora ; v. 84.
Description: Rochester : University of Rochester Press, 2019. | Series: Roches-
    ter studies in African history and the diaspora ; v. 84 | Includes bibliograph-
    ical references and index.
Identifiers: LCCN 2019019156 | ISBN 9781580469418 (hardcover : alk. paper)
Subjects: LCSH: Catholic Church—Mozambique—History—20th century. |
    Catholic Church—Clergy—Political activity—Mozambique. | Clergy—Politi-
    cal activity—Mozambique. | Religion and politics—Mozambique. | Church
    and state—Mozambique. | Mozambique—Politics and government—20th
    century.
Classification: LCC BX1682.M85 M67 2019 | DDC 282.6790904—dc23 LC
    record available at https://lccn.loc.gov/2019019156

This publication is printed on acid-free paper.
Printed in the United States of America.

To my parents, Jacques and Janet
To my wife and son, Esperança and Guillaume

Contents

Illustrations

Figures

Tables

Acknowledgments

Research for this book has spanned across three continents over numerous years. Starting with institutional support, for generous grants, I thank the Luso-American Foundation (with the Instituto dos Arquivos Nacionais/ Torre de Tombo) and the Gulbenkian Foundation that enabled research in Portugal as well as the Société Académique Vaudoise in Switzerland. I also thank the State University of New York at Binghamton, its Department of Sociology and its library for providing me with an assistantship for several years, a stimulating intellectual environment, and great research facilities. Over the past ten years, Queen's University Belfast, Northern Ireland, afforded me support and encouragement as I worked on this book while teaching African history.

In Mozambique, I express my gratitude to the Arquivo Histórico de Moçambique; to the late Bishop Jaime Gonçalves who allowed me to do research in the archive of the Diocese of Beira; and to Bishop Hilario Massinga who allowed me to work in the archives of the Franciscan Custodia in Maputo. In Portugal, I thank the Arquivo Histórico do Ultramar, the Arquivo do Ministério dos Négocios Estrangeiros, and the Instituto dos Arquivos Nacionais/Torre de Tombo where I conducted much of my research in excellent conditions. In Rome, I acknowledge the invaluable help that the late Ivan Page and Dominique Arnauld gave me as the archivists of the Archives Générales des Missionnaires de l'Afrique; and the Institut Suisse de Rome where I stayed most comfortably. In the Netherlands, the Picpus society generously offered me accommodation as I worked in their archives in Breda. In Madrid, the Spanish province of the White Fathers most kindly opened up its archive and helped me with interviews. Fathers Gust Beeckmans and Joe Eberle graciously provided me with photographs from the White Fathers' provincial archives in Germany and the Netherlands.

In Spain, Luis G. Corral and Father Antonio González Mohíno-Espinosa provided material on the Burgos fathers, and the late Father Molina Molina of the White Fathers kindly granted me time and access to his personal pictures. In Oporto, Portugal, the late José Soares Martins and his brother Father Sebastião Braz kindly gave me advice and unrestricted access to the private papers of their uncle, the first bishop of Beira (these papers are now held at the University of Oporto). In Lisbon, Zélia Pereira generously shared photocopies of documents from the archives of the Portuguese province of the Jesuits. Also in Lisbon the Franciscans, and particularly Bishop Antonio Montes Moreira, received me graciously and allowed me to work in their library. I thank all of them sincerely.

An important component of my research was formed by the interviews I conducted with members of the church and beyond. Conducting this kind of research is about gathering testimonies and information, but affords the researcher much more than that: people share parts of their lives, invite one for a meal or to stay over, all without demanding any return. I deeply thank everyone who granted me an interview: Laurinda Baptista; Nicolau da Barca; André de Bels; Miguel Buendia; António Dina Cardos; Father Filipe José Couto; Father Francisco Augusto da Cruz Correia; Paulo Cuvaca; Father José Maria Moreira Pereira de Faria; Manuel João Favor; Bishop Jaime Gonçalves; Father Guilherme da Costa Gonçalves; Lawe Laweki; Margarita Rodrigues Lopes; Abel Mabunda; Benjamin Tomocene Majambe; Benjamin Taramba Manhoca; Father Antonius Petrus Joseph Martens; José Chicuara Massinga; Alfredo Arnaldo Matsinhe; Father Antonio Molina Molina; Bishop António Montes Moreira; Gustavo Lukas and Maria Mozinho; the late Father Samuel Abudo Mucauro; Agostinho Cufa dos Muchangos; Bishop Januário Machaze Nhangumbe; João Sozinho Nhongo; the late Bishop Custódio Alvim Pereira; Father Fernando Pietro Perez; the late Father Charles Maurice Pollet; Lukas Bizeque Quembo de Raposo; Vitorino Mendes dos Reis; Júlio Meneses Rodrigues Ribeiro; Sister Fernanda Jesus Rodrigues; Sister Margarida Lopes Rodrigues; Father Mateus Carbonell Rodrigues; Sister Maria Joana Araujo Rosa; Father Rogier van Rossum; Benjamin Serapião; Marcelino dos Santos; the late Bishop Alberto Setele; Alberto Jequessene Soro; the late Father José Augusto Alves de Sousa; Henriquetta Teixeira; Father José Verhoeven; Lukas Alfandegas Zingue; and Father André van Zon.

Special mention goes to Júlio Meneses Rodrigues Ribeiro who took days if not weeks to explain the functioning and history of the Catholic Church, tell me stories, and find documents in his private archive. The late Father Pollet, the mythical Catholic figure in Beira, was as charismatic, enthusiastic, and passionate at eighty as he had been in Mozambique in his younger days. André de Bels narrated his life history, which he had not yet told his own family; and jointly Gustavo and Maria Lukas Mozinho patiently recalled their life in Dondo for me. I wish for this book to be a return on all their investments, even if some details and smaller truths had to be dropped because of the need to trace larger processes over time. My acknowledgment of their help is therefore even more sincere.

On the editorial side, I wish to thank my colleague Caroline Jeannerat for editing and proofreading the manuscript. I thank the team at the

University of Rochester Press who were most patient and professional. I am grateful to Maura Pringle and Valérie Alfaurt for drawing the maps. I acknowledge the contribution of two anonymous external reviewers; and I express my gratitude to Toyin Falola for believing in this project and accepting it for publication in this series at the University of Rochester Press.

Finally, I would like to mention the deep support, stimulation, and friendship that Martin Murray, Anne Pitcher, and Eric Allina have showed me. The late Patrick Harries was an inspiration and a unique mentor. In Mozambique, I have received kind friendship and generous support from Yussuf Adam, Miguel Buendia, Teresa Cruz e Silva, Joel das Neves Tembe, and Amélia Neves de Souto; as well as from the late Dom Jaime Gonçalves, Father Diamantino Guapo Antunes, Frei Gabriel Guiterez Ramirez, Frei Victor Manuel Gomes Rafael, Bishop Hilário da Cruz Massinga, and Lawe Laweki. In Europe, I would like to mention the untiring and stimulating support of Michel Cahen, the help and friendship of António Matos Ferreira, and the motivation and support of Jean-Francois Bayart and the late Klauspeter Blaser. I would also like to mention the friendship and support of Paulo F. de Oliveira Fontes, Corrado Tornimbeni, and João Miguel Almeida. In Switzerland, acknowledgment is due to my old accomplice Didier Péclard, to Nicolas Monnier, and my friends Jean-Michel Henchoz, Alain de Bernardis, and Pierre Willa. Last but not least, my biggest debt is to my family who have patiently seen me through this long project.

Note on Translations

Translations of excerpts from other works, from archival documents, and from interviews have been done by the author, except where official translations are available. Some terms do not translate into English because they are culturally or historically specific. In these situations, I have chosen to use the original term. In relation to racial categories, I have followed administrative and common practice in Mozambique whereby four key groups were deemed to exist before independence—africans, whites, indians, and misto (mixed race). In the volume, I use the term "mestiço" as it has supplanted the term "misto" and is generally used in English.[1]

Regarding subnational administrative units, because of the different meanings of terms such as "district" or "province" in the world and the change of these terms after independence in Mozambique, I have made a compromise for the purpose of clarity and consistency. Following colleagues working on Mozambique, I have opted to use the term "district" and "province" across the volume, applying these categories retrospectively to the colonial times. Before independence, a province was called a "district" and a district was called a "circumscrição." Just before independence, Mozambique had nine districts or provinces while it had ten after independence, following the separation of Manica and Sofala into two distinct provinces. To give an idea of scale, in 1964 Manica and Sofala had twelve districts (*circumscrições*) whereas Tete had eight.[2] The provinces of Manica and Sofala and Tete, which constitute the area under consideration here, have a total area of 228,632 square kilometers.

Finally, to make reading easier, I use the title "bishop of Beira" across the book, even though, from 1962, the Diocese of Beira became an archdiocese and the bishop of Beira became an archbishop. I also use the name "Polícia Internacional e de Defesa do Estado" for the Portuguese security police throughout, even though it was renamed "Direcção-Geral de Segurança" in 1969.

Abbreviations

CEM	Conferência Episcopal de Moçambique (Episcopal Conference of Mozambique)
COREMO	Comité Revolucionário de Moçambique (Revolutionary Committee of Mozambique)
FIRM	Federação dos Institutos Religiosos de Moçambique (Federation of [Male] Religious Institutes of Mozambique)
Frelimo	Frente de Libertação de Moçambique (Mozambique Liberation Front)
GE	Grupo Especiais (military units)
GEP	Grupos Especiais Paraquedistas (military units)
IEME	Instituto Español de Misiones Extranjeras (Spanish Institute of Foreign Missions)
MANC	Mozambique African National Congress (formerly Kilimane Freedom Party)
MANU	Mozambique African National Union
NATO	North Atlantic Treaty Organization
PCN	Partido da Convenção Nacional (National Convention Party)
PIDE	Polícia Internacional e de Defesa do Estado (International and State Defense Police)
RENAMO	Resistência Nacional Moçambicana (Mozambican National Resistance)
TANU	Tanganyika African National Union
UDENAMO	União Democrática Nacional Moçambique (National Democratic Union of Mozambique)
UNAMI	União Nacional Africana de Moçambique (African National Union of Mozambique)
USAREMO	União dos Sacerdotes e Religiosas de Moçambique (Union of Priests and Religious Women of Mozambique)
UISG	International Union Superiors General (International Union of [Female] Congregations)
USG	Union of Superiors General (International Union of [Male] Congregations)
ZANU	Zimbabwean African National Union

Introduction

In 1971 the war of liberation in Mozambique entered its seventh year. It had not reached the Diocese of Beira yet, but the church there was facing a deep crisis all the same. The clergy was profoundly divided over theology and politics. An increasing number of religious and lay individuals condemned the alliance between the Vatican and the Portuguese colonial state (an alliance formalized in 1940 by a concordat and a Missionary Accord) and favored African nationalism and the independence of Mozambique. Some missionaries were even helping Africans join the liberation struggle and fight the war in the neighboring Diocese of Tete. At the same time, other missionaries in Beira diocese, mostly of Portuguese nationality, opposed African nationalism and remained faithful to the Portuguese colonial state and project. They believed in the Portuguese Empire, or its reform, and supported its fight to keep "terrorism" and "communism" at bay. When the war finally reached the Diocese of Beira in 1973, these missionaries increased their collaboration with the authorities, and some of them went on to actively support the army and the state security police.

The division of the clergy in Beira in the 1970s was not just political in nature. It was theological too, with heated debates about what kind of pastoral approach the Catholic Church and its clergy should adopt, which church model it should favor, and to whose benefit. Most of the Portuguese missionaries (primarily Jesuits and Franciscans) were in favor of a pastoral approach that focused on converting Africans to a Portuguese-centered Catholicism. They wished for a religious *and* cultural conversion, and their means remained classic, focused on infrastructure and schooling. In contrast, many foreign missionaries, particularly the White Fathers and the Picpus fathers, as well as some secular Portuguese priests and some sisters, tried to build a locally centered Mozambican church, linked to the Vatican, relying on the laity, and using African forms of liturgy—following the lead of the Second Vatican Council. A few missionaries from the Instituto Español de Misiones Extranjeras (Spanish Institute of Foreign Missions, also called "Burgos fathers") went further. They promoted a theology of liberation, inspired by the work of their institute in Latin America. They wanted small base communities and not a hierarchical administration or Vatican-centered institutions.

In the face of divisions and infighting, the recently nominated bishop of Beira struggled to keep on top of his clergy and eventually lost both his calm and the control of the diocese. After several blunders and many difficulties following his appointment in 1967 (including a request from some of the clergy for him to resign), in 1969–70 Dom Manuel Ferreira Cabral chose to side openly with the "conservative" elements of his clergy, aligned with the colonial state and favoring a Portuguese-centered church. In this manner, he fanned the flames in an already divided church. The existing tensions between priests and sisters turned into an ugly internal battle for faith, power, and politics, some priests relying on the state security police to resolve internal church affairs and others threatening to leave Mozambique if the church's alliance with the colonial state did not end. Unable to resolve the crisis, and suffering from stress, the bishop fled his diocese in January 1971 and took refuge in Portugal—never to return to Mozambique. Seeing that their concerns were not being addressed, the White Fathers decided in April 1971 to withdraw from Mozambique *as a whole* in protest—a Catholic first. Yet, before they could implement their decision, the Portuguese administration expelled the society *manu militari*. This created a worldwide scandal and drew the attention of the international press and community on the war for independence in Mozambique and the deep divisions prevalent in the Catholic Church there.

The crisis in the Diocese of Beira in the early 1970s was exceptional for its depth and violence. It saw priests and religious congregations pitted against one another and against the head of the diocese, and drawing on support from outside of the church. Members of the church leadership as well as of religious congregations left the diocese under pressure, in protest, or having been expelled by the state. Differences and tensions between congregations are normal in the Catholic Church, but this kind of crisis is exceptional. What is particularly interesting in this crisis is that it revealed, in an amplified form, the complex internal dynamics at play in the Catholic institution. It made obvious not just the different currents, groups, and organizations at work in the Catholic institution at the time but also the reason for their disagreement, and demonstrated how such groups (often based in religious congregations) compete for influence within the church, to the point that they can engage in notable fights with each other and draw on resources outside of the church to gain more traction. The crisis thus reveals that there are not only different *levels* of authority inside the church (between the Vatican, the dioceses and their bishops, and the clergy on the ground) but also different *centers* of power at each level. Religious congregations coalesce around and structure many of these differences. These centers of power run parallel to each other and compete with one another for influence in the overall church. Sometimes, they clash and fight.

Catholicism and the Making of Politics is concerned with the internal diversity and complexity of the Roman Catholic Church. It examines the way in which the Roman Catholic institution works, the formation of its politics, and its wider influence. All too often, analysts reduce the Roman Catholic Church to its hierarchical dimension, focusing on the official face of the church (the pope, an episcopal conference, or a bishop) in a classic top-down approach. Against such a point of view, the coming pages analyze the intermediary level of the religious congregations and their multiple and decentered top-down *and* bottom-up roles in the making of Catholic politics. Much of the diversity in the Roman institution is structured by religious congregations, orders, societies, and institutes, yet hardly any studies have analyzed their role and influence in shaping the policies of the overall institution. The Diocese of Beira is a perfect case for exploring such a problematic. For one, many congregations worked in the diocese, both before and after independence, with significant change over time. For another (and as already seen above), these congregations competed with each other over the orientation of the institution. The period under consideration is from 1940 to 1986, four and a half decades that cover high colonialism, independence, and postindependence. It is a period during which the church experienced both the full support of the (colonial) state and opposition and even violence by the (postcolonial) state. It is also a period during which the church underwent substantial transformation, not least during and after national independence. This opens a series of questions about the nature of the church, the changes it underwent, and its political orientation.

Politics beyond the "Political Paradigm"

For decades, the literature about religion and politics in Africa has been locked in a "political paradigm." A paradigm, according to Thomas Kuhn, is an explanatory scheme that provides achievements that are sufficiently unprecedented to attract researchers away from competing modes of scientific activity and sufficiently open-ended to leave all sorts of problems to resolve.[1] The political paradigm I refer to here has been locked into the question of whether Christianity has historically been located on the side of colonialism or that of African nationalism; on the side of the empire or that of a locally representative church; on the side of a genuine faith-sharing exercise or that of cultural imperialism. In some investigations, the question of "on whose side was the church" is raised explicitly, in the title of the book or article, and drives the author's narrative—such as in Ado

Tiberondwa's *Missionary Teachers as Agents of Colonialism* or Andrew Porter's *Religion versus Empire?*[2] In others, the question lurks in the background as a more or less explicit framework—think of Jean Comaroff and John Comaroff's two-volume work *Revolution and Revelation*.[3] This "political paradigm" has directly and indirectly dominated the historiography, and remains prevalent in much of the research and writing on religion and politics in Africa today. It has led authors not to ask certain questions, not to consider alternative angles, and not to make allowance for competing scientific explanations. It also keeps authors asking the same superficial question, if in different ways. Discussing the referendum in Guinea in 1958, Fred Cooper made a remark that applies perfectly to this subject: "It is not clear that asking who was the most uncompromisingly radical, [and] the most genuinely anticolonial, is a fruitful historical question."[4]

We can distinguish two phases in the literature on religion dominated by this political paradigm. The first, roughly spanning the 1950s to the 1970s, debated the political positioning of churches and religious men and women, missionaries in particular. Authors like Nosifo Majeke (pen name for Dora Taylor) and Ado Tiberondwa showed that Christian missionaries were active and direct collaborators of the European imperial powers in Africa: they helped establish colonialism by discovering new territories, working with the army, and teaching Christian morals in times of war. After the implementation of colonial regimes, missionaries worked as intermediaries between the administration and Africans, disseminated imperial values, and provided a moral superstructure for the colonial system.[5] Against this line of argument, authors like Bolaji Idowu defended the missionaries by arguing that, in spite of their failings, the missionaries had had good intentions.[6] More substantially, authors like Jonna-Lynn Mandelbaum explained that churches and missionaries were also "cultural brokers": they taught Africans new skills and helped them gain new connections and ideas, which facilitated the adaptation of Africans to colonial times and contributed to African resistance, if not African nationalism.[7]

A second phase in the literature dominated by the political paradigm came in the 1990s. Building on Edward W. Said's work,[8] the Comaroffs wrote two volumes in which they argued that missionaries were agents not just of imperialism but of *cultural* imperialism. The authors explained that, apart from politics, missionaries had brought a "revolution in the habits of the people," transforming their ways of thinking, their notions of value and wealth, their notions of space, their building and housing, their farming, dressing, medicine, and even their conception of cleanliness.[9] Adding to and echoing earlier Marxist analyses, the Comaroffs concluded that the missionary had played a role as "agent, scribe and moral alibi" of the

colonizing project.[10] Their argument led to a lively debate and strong critique. Porter, for example, contended that the Comaroffs understood "culture" as something discrete and fixed, with the unchanging wholes of "the
British" and "the Africans" engaged in an exchange that could only result
in gains or in losses.[11] Instead, Porter proposed that culture is fragmented,
dynamic, and continuously exchanged, therefore always changing. He thus
presented Africans as actors in their encounter with the British missionaries, and posited that missionaries cannot be understood solely as agents or
allies of imperialism.

The historiography of Christianity in the Portuguese African empire
developed an added twist. The scholarship set up a sharp distinction
between Protestant and Catholic institutions. Scholars have argued that
the Catholic Church was closely allied, if not subservient, to the Portuguese
colonial state while Protestants were opposed to the colonial state and thus
close to Africans. In this view, Catholics helped the Portuguese imperial
state colonize Africans due to their formal alliance with Portugal (though
some exceptions were recognized) while Protestants respected Africans,
fostered their political consciousness, and promoted African nationalism
and independence.[12] Teresa Cruz e Silva, for example, wrote that the Swiss
Protestant missionaries in Mozambique

> based their methods of education and evangelization on the retention of
> Mozambican "national" rather than Portuguese culture, which was a fun-
> damental contribution to the education of the "native" population and
> development of its political consciousness. Operating in the opposite
> direction, and contrasting with the Portuguese "nationalist" [i.e., Catho-
> lic] education which transmitted state-approved moral and ideological
> principles, the Protestants' and particularly the Swiss Mission's education
> took on a stronger political significance, as the general question of Afri-
> can decolonization and nationalism came to the fore in the 1950s.[13]

Working on Angola, Benedict Schubert argued against this contrast
between Protestants and Catholics, which is equally strong in that former
Portuguese colony. He even contended that it promoted a "propagandis-
tic vision" of history, which transformed "tendencies into facts" to wrongly
assert "that Protestants would have sided with the liberation movements
while the Catholics would have continued to bless the Portuguese colonial
system."[14]

In the past two decades several authors have attempted to move away
from this "political paradigm." Some abandoned the issue of politics to
focus on religion while others asked broader political questions about conversion, intellectual debates, and identity formation. Derek Peterson, for

example, explored the intellectual works and debates of African Christians during the East African Revival, analyzing their writings, debates, and ethnic identity formation that he contends operated on a tangent from "the dialectics of the colonial encounter."[15] Along similar lines, the coming pages move away from narrow political questions to ask what the Catholic Church in central Mozambique did *in spite of*, or *due to*, its political positioning. Contrary to the historiography on the Portuguese African colonies that has primarily focused on Protestant churches, I look at the Roman Catholic institution. I do not engage in a comparison between the Protestant and the Catholic, nor do I assume as given that Catholics would have been less supportive of African nationalism. Instead, I explore the history of the Roman Catholic Church in its full breadth and depth to understand its development. In relation to politics, I displace the narrow political question by investigating the underlying question of how Catholic politics was made and deployed and what influence it had. This should help us better understand the Catholic institution and add to a historiography where analyses of the Roman institution are rare outside of the church's own historiography.[16]

The Historical Formation of the Church

The Catholic Church in southeast Africa dates back to the late fifteenth century. This book looks only at the period from 1940 to 1986. It is a comparatively recent and short period but represents a foundational moment in more than one way. The institution had totally collapsed in the area in the nineteenth century, with a short revival between the 1880s and 1911. While it recovered somewhat after 1927, when the Portuguese colonial state was again interested in having a religious ally in its colonies, it only began to grow significantly after it entered a formal alliance with the Portuguese state in 1940, gaining in importance across the whole territory. Between 1940 and 1974, the institution witnessed a major expansion of its infrastructure and proselytizing, and saw double-digit rates of conversions across the land, both phenomena leading to the definitive embedding of the Catholic Church and faith in Mozambique. Independence in 1975 forced major changes upon the church, including a political realignment and an adaptation of its personnel and identity. By the 1980s, the Catholic Church had developed a new position and identity. Although technically the outcome of five hundred years of evangelization, as the church likes to say,[17] it is really between 1940 and 1986 that the Catholic institution became a fully organized, autonomous, and self-sustaining religious organization in its own right.

By analyzing the period from 1940 to 1986, *Catholicism and the Making of Politics* adopts a diachronic approach. It breaks with the convention of looking at either the colonial or the postcolonial period and examines both as a single unit. Instead of focusing on the closure of the colonial period and the beginnings of the postcolonial period, the volume looks at the continuities and ruptures across both periods. This allows for a deeper analysis of continuity and change across the so-called turning point of independence. Instead of characterizing individual periods, the book focuses on understanding and identifying the *historical trajectory* of the church.[18] This diachronic approach allows a fine-grained examination of the changes that took place during the transition period (between 1974 and 1975), when many dynamics that had developed inconspicuously during the colonial period came to the surface and erupted into critical debates (for example, issues of race and political pluralism), after which some subsided again once a new political order had established itself.

I approach the history of the Catholic institution in terms of "historical formations." History is not made by "great men" nor is it the simple outcome of structures. As Fred Cooper reminds us, history is the result of the interplay between "possibility and constraint," or the interaction between structure and agency. Under the Portuguese, the Catholic Church in Mozambique operated within a structure formed by colonialism and capitalism, and after independence one determined by authoritarian socialism, yet it still had space to make choices that had a significant influence not just on its believers but also on the very structures that constrained the institution. Similarly, members of the church were constrained by the church–state agreements, by the Catholic Church itself, and by the existing Catholic culture, yet they still remained agents in their own right. They were both actors and agents, that is to say, they were "structuring agents," as Christopher Lloyd calls them, contributing both to the making and the changing of the structures that constrained them.[19] Needless to say, there is not a single agency within one structure, but rather many agencies within many structures (church, state, colonialism, etc.). History is not the result of the sum of all individual actions (as rational choice theorists would have it) but rather the intended and unintended consequences of the interaction of agencies and structures, both dialectically and tangentially, with many resulting "creative derivations," as Jean-François Bayart reminds us.[20]

For heuristic purposes, *Catholicism and the Making of Politics* distinguishes between an "imperial church" and an "African church." What I call the imperial church is the institution that was set up from outside of Mozambique to evangelize the people of southeast Africa, while the "African church" is the institution that developed internal to Mozambique from indigenous elements. This heuristic device allows a consideration not only of the dimension of the Africanization of the church (as a policy) but also of the growth and eventual blossoming of the African elements nestled within the imperial institution. This allows a view of the Africanization that took place in earlier periods and opens up space for an analysis of the trajectory of the African institution in its own right, something that is important since this became the dominant stream of the church at independence in 1975. This approach prevents the discussion from ending up as yet another narrow political debate about whether the church was imperial or African or, after independence, neocolonial. As my double characterization suggests (and as the coming pages show), the church was *both* imperial *and* African, at the same time and from very early on, if not from the very beginning. While the imperial dimension dominated until independence, the African dimension became the prevailing one afterward. Yet both existed and worked together, before and after independence, in unequal partnerships. Finally, distinguishing between these two dimensions allows an analysis of the interaction between the two elements of the church (cut across by religious orders, class, and other factors) whose dialectical outcome, and its creative derivation, led to the formation of a singular Mozambican Catholic Church and culture.

The approach of this book is resolutely multidisciplinary. Conjoining history, political science, and the sociology of religion allows a deeper analysis of the history of the tensions and struggles within and around the Roman Catholic Church and its politics in Mozambique. Philip Abrams argues that "history and sociology are and always have been the same thing. Both seek to understand the puzzle of human agency and both seek to do so in terms of the process of social structuring."[21] Just as importantly, I would argue that sociology is a particularly strong field in relation to the subject of religion, with authors, theories, and models that cannot be ignored when engaging with a history of religion. The same applies to political science when we look at the topic of politics. The point here is not to combine these three disciplines to get a perfect meta-approach. Rather, it is an issue of developing something of a toolbox approach that is theoretically better informed so as to develop a more plausible explanation and narrative.

Religious Institutes and Catholic Politics

The dominant approach to understanding the Catholic institution, its orientation and politics has been a *vertical* one. It looks at the hierarchical structure of the institution and focuses on how the top-down chain of command operates: how the pope, the Vatican, and bishops make decisions; how priests, brothers, and sisters apply them in the field; and how the laity receives (or resists) them. Accordingly, many authors focus their analysis on the pope, the Vatican, or the bishops. Thomas Reese, for example, analyzes the politics and organization of the Catholic Church "inside the Vatican."[22] His assumption is that rulings and guidelines from the Vatican are passed on and executed faithfully at the lower levels. If and when there is opposition, this is often considered to be "dissidence" or "deviance" by the religious personnel and the believers. Thus, the presence of Jesuits in the Sandinista government in Nicaragua is explained not as a decision by a group of men or a congregation, but as an "exception" from the church's official stance against the left-wing government—an exception that would somehow confirm the overall reactionary nature of the church.[23] Closer to our interest, most scholars of the Portuguese colonies present any "progressive" clergy in Portugal or Mozambique as "exceptions" or "dissidents" in a top-down institution wholly compromised with colonialism and imperialism.[24] An alternative explanation presents internal contradictions as the result of explicit strategies or conspiracies on the part of the hierarchy. Thus, some authors explain the development of liberation theology in Latin America (at a time when the hierarchy did not promote it officially) as a secret move on the part of the official church to retain its influence in the face of religious rivals in a context favorable to left-wing politics.[25]

There are several problems with such a top-down approach. First, it presumes the Catholic institution to be united and solely hierarchical, when it is diverse, complex, and not solely vertical in structure. It is multifaceted primarily because the church comprises hundreds of congregations, orders, and societies that represent a great variety of social, religious, and intellectual currents within the global institution.[26] Second, these Catholic religious organizations (congregations, orders, and societies) are *autonomous* within the Catholic institution and relatively independent from the top-down Catholic hierarchy. There are today about 1,400 different religious orders in the church (officially now called "Institutes of Consecrated Life" or Societies of Apostolic Life). They employ the overwhelming majority of the church's personnel—over 1.3 million individuals.[27] These organizations have their own leadership hierarchies and have full freedom of organization; their leaders are responsible primarily to the Vatican and not to any local or national church hierarchy. At the diocesan level, the personnel of the congregations answer as much to their organization's superior as to the local bishop—usually an agreement is signed between a bishop and a congregation to regulate their respective areas of competence.[28] Religious orders and congregations thus cut through the much-discussed hierarchical top-down structuring of the Roman Catholic Church and constitute what Eric Hanson has called "parallel hierarchical structures" and Ralph della Cava a "horizontal structuring."[29]

Max Weber developed some useful (and rarely used) insights about this "dual nature" of the Catholic Church. Weber distinguished between what he called a "hierocracy" and charismatic movements. Hierocracies are "groups in which the power of domination relies on a monopoly to dispense salvation goods."[30] A hierocracy exists, says Weber, when a body of professional priests develops; they aim at a universal domination; dogma and cults are rationalized and consigned in sacred writings; and all these developments take place in a single institutionalized community.[31] In a hierocracy, charism becomes separated from any individual, and therefore the greatest threats to a hierocracy are "charismatic movements" that develop their own charism, separate from any institution.[32] Monasticism is one example of charismatic movements where men "refuse to compromise with the 'world' and remain attached to the original postulates of the charismatic founder." Another example are the "virtuosi" (virtuous monks) who appeared in the Middle Ages when they "left their convents for an 'interior mission' realized systematically in the streets," such as the Franciscans and Dominicans.[33] Now, the particularity of the Catholic Church as an institution is that these charismatic movements did not split away to form new churches but became historically institutionalized *within* the institution as autonomous religious orders or, in today's terms, "institutes of consecrated life." This is the fundamental characteristic of the Catholic institution: it embodies both hierocracy and institutionalized charismatic movements.[34]

If the Catholic Church has a dual or double structure, the question follows as to who determines the religious and political orientation of the institution: the hierocracy or the horizontal structures constituted by the religious orders and congregations? We noted earlier that most studies look at the hierarchy to understand how the institution operates and chooses to position itself toward issues and the world. They look at the Vatican, the bishops, and the priests. In this study, I look at the question from the angle of the religious orders. I investigate the extent to which, and the manner in which, religious congregations shape Catholic history and policy. My argument is that religious congregations play an important, unrecognized, and largely unstudied role in determining the Catholic Church's history and politics. On the one hand, religious orders can shape church policy and positioning through their personnel on the ground. Often, what is seen as deviance and dissidence from within the church hierarchy is in reality a religious order's legitimate choice to take issue with a policy passed by the Catholic hierarchy. On the other hand, religious orders can shape policies,

not least through their representatives that sit in church bodies at the diocesan level and that of the Vatican. The church is thus influenced by religious orders much more than is presently acknowledged. By resistance and
by proactive influence, religious orders have a fundamental role in shaping
the orientation and history of the Roman Catholic Church.

What do we know about religious orders and their influence within
the Roman Catholic Church and the making of its politics? The literature on the subject is thin, and mostly theological and legal. Historical,
sociological, and political science works on the subject emerged in the
1950s but have not proliferated since. I examine these works here to better understand religious orders and to frame some of the discussions in
the coming pages, in particular in chapter 2 on the internal makeup and
dynamics of the imperial church. I also review this literature to understand how far social scientists and historians have gone in unpacking the
relationship between religious orders, the church hierarchy, and church
politics, and to identify where this book contributes new insights. Before
I do so, let me note that there are many works on religious orders or
congregations that I do not consider here because they do not relate to
the concern of this book. There are, for example, many studies of single
congregations in particular countries that, as excellent as they may be,
do not look at how the religious organization relates to other congregations in the area or how it articulates itself with the church hierarchy.[35]
In addition, a multitude of works investigate the history or sociology of *all*
religious orders and congregations in the church, but their concern with
the "rise and fall" of these orders over time does not correlate with the
present concerns.[36]

Within the relevant literature, one can distinguish between two types of
works: one in which authors study and compare religious orders, and the
other in which authors unpack the relationship between religious orders
and the hierarchy. In the first category, a significant author is Emerich
K. Francis who, in an article of 1950, compared religious orders in terms
of Ferdinand Tönnies's distinction between *Gemeinschaft* (community)
and *Gesellschaft* (society). Francis developed a spectrum of organizations,
with monastic orders at one end and religious orders at the other end.
On the *Gemeinschaft* side, the monastic orders are made of "face-to-face
groups that, in the extreme case, perform practically all the functions
of the natural family short of biological procreation." On the *Gesellschaft*
side, religious orders tend "to substitute more impersonal, segmental, and
abstract relationships among the members of its local establishment, more
properly called 'convents,' that is, gathering places rather than communities."[37] Twenty years later, Michael Hill reworked the typology using Erving

Goffman's analysis of a "total institution."[38] Hill argued that religious orders do not separate between the normally distinct spheres of sleep, work, and play, nor do they place these spheres under the administration of different authorities. Instead, they are all merged and fall under a single authority. All activities are done in common and are tightly scheduled as well as structured by formal rules. In that sense, Hill argued, religious orders are like "total institutions," though they are normative rather than coercive ones—hence not fully "total institutions." Adherence to the organization is voluntary and there is no distinctive and separate elite within a religious order (in contrast to a prison).[39] Hill thus added the new dimension of the total institution to Francis's ideal-typical spectrum. Chapter 2 tests the applicability of these models in the case of the Diocese of Beira.

The second sociological current studying religious orders also emerged in the 1950s, though with a stronger political angle. Its main author is Léo Moulin who has written significantly about power within Catholic congregations. He noted, first, that the "diversity of vocations corresponds to no smaller a variety of forms of government": there are congregations with democratic, aristocratic, and monarchic forms of government.[40] Yet all of them, even the most hierarchical ones, have checks and balances that are reduced to written constitutions and rules, thus confirming Weber's distinction between monasteries and religious orders/virtuosi.[41] Second, Moulin argued that religious orders were the source of many modern electoral and deliberative techniques. He showed that while the democratic techniques of Roman or Greek polities were idealized as "sources" of democracy, in reality these had disappeared as models by the Middle Ages. The democratic government that inspired the "communes" was, in reality, that of the religious orders.[42] As insightful as this analysis may be, Moulin does not extend his examination to discuss how religious orders relate to the Catholic hierarchy and what role, if any, they have in influencing or shaping Catholic politics. The closest he gets to this is a section in his book *Le monde vivant des religieux* where he studies the reactions of the Vatican to the emergence of new congregations. He explains that the Vatican has historically had a very liberal approach toward new congregations and that it is only in the late sixteenth century that it instituted a Congregation for the Religious to monitor and control this section of the church.[43]

The only author who developed a concern similar to my own is Robert Soullard. In an article published in 1981 under the title "Le pouvoir des religieux dans l'église" (The power of the religious in the church), Soullard looked at the place of congregations in the Catholic institution. He noted, to start with, that religious men and women make up a major part of the personnel of the church and that religious orders have real autonomy. He posed the question whether, "in relation to the ecclesiastical hierarchy, the religious are not as much partners as subjects."[44] The question is somewhat rhetorical, though it does put forward that religious orders hold power. Soullard then examined three difficulties that religious orders create for the church. First, the charismatic nature of religious life introduces a zone of autonomy in the church. Second, religious orders do not correlate with the territorial divisions of the church and do not always fit in easily with the structures of the local churches. Third, religious superiors (called "generals" and "provincials") have powers equivalent to "ordinaries" (bishops) in terms of managing their personnel; bishops therefore do not have total authority over religious staff working in their areas. Soullard identified several solutions that Catholic legislators devised to control these difficulties. The main one seems to have been the Codex passed in 1917 in Rome that clearly separated the powers of the religious from the diocesan power under the control of a bishop. The Codex made religious congregations formally autonomous, and answerable to Rome only.[45] What Soullard did not investigate is how, on that basis, congregations shape the making of politics in the Roman Catholic Church.

Defining and Historicizing the Horizontal Church

What I interchangeably call "religious orders" and "congregations" (and at times also "religious societies" and "institutes") are organizations that form an integral part of the Roman Catholic Church. That means that they are recognized by the Vatican. They are made up of religious men or women who live together in a community, have taken vows or made an oath, and follow the rules of association set up by the founder of their group. They have a constitution and traditions that define a spirit, a way of functioning, and the minutiae of each member's life.[46] Before 1983, when a revised canon law came into force, these structures were known as "religious orders," "congregations," "societies," or "institutes." As these were the terms used during the period under study here, I use them in the coming pages. At the time, the organizations were distinguished between those that required their members to take vows (congregations and orders) and those who did not (societies and institutes), as well as between those who demanded permanent vows (orders) and those with simple vows (congregations).[47] In 1983, a revision of canon law simplified the categories and classified these organizations into two groups, with "Institutes of Consecrated Life" representing those requiring vows and "Societies of Apostolic Life" for those that do not.

The pre-1983 distinctions between the terms "order," "congregation," "society," and "institute" are problematic because they developed over centuries, are primarily legal or religious, and are based on a single criterion (vows). Tellingly, the authoritative *Dizionari degli Istituti di Perfezione* (Dictionary of the institutes of perfection), written in the 1990s by specialists in their fields, faced its biggest problem when it composed the entry on Catholic religious institutes. It aimed to present a typology of institutions, but the authors disagreed profoundly over the criteria to be used. The only agreement they could find was that no typology fitted all cases. The editors found a compromise by adding an introduction to the entry in which a different expert explored the possibilities of other typologies.[48] The solution adopted for the present book is different: I have chosen to use the terms of the period under consideration (irrespective of present-day canon law) and to use them interchangeably (in particular, the terms "religious orders" and "congregation") in order to make the reading easier.

In a last step, it is worth looking at the development of the different types of religious organizations within the Catholic Church; it allows us to better understand their contemporary diversity and forms (chapter 2 then analyzes the different religious congregations in the Diocese of Beira specifically). The first orders to emerge within the Catholic Church were monastic organizations. *Monachism*, as it came to be known, emerged in the fourth century when groups of men or women secluded themselves in monasteries in order to retreat from public life and dedicate themselves to the celebration of God. In the thirteenth century, new forms of religious organizations emerged, called the *mendicants* (represented today by the Franciscans and Dominicans): the members of these societies left the cloister to practice their faith and respect their vows within society. In the sixteenth century, and as a consequence of the Protestant Reformation and the Catholic Counter-Reformation, two new types of Catholic congregations appeared: the *orders of clerics regular* (for example, the Jesuits and the Barnabites) and *societies of priests* (such as the Lazarists and the Spiritans).[49] Like the mendicants, they are not cloistered and live and work among the wider society. What was new was that they dropped the elements of uniformity in prayer, penitence, and dress (which had been retained by the mendicants), though they maintained discipline as a collective element. Toward the end of the eighteenth century, yet newer forms of religious association arose with the emergence of *clerical congregations* and *lay congregations*. Clerical congregations (such as the Montfortians or Redemptorists) accept lay brothers (men who are not priests) whereas lay congregations (such as the Christian Brothers) are made up of lay brothers only.[50]

The newer forms of Catholic organizations have been most successful. Statistically, in the 1970s almost half (78) of a total of 177 male organizations were clerical congregations. However, while there were only 9 mendicant orders, they had the highest number of members with some 78,000 men in 1965, thus 25 percent of a total of 310,500 religious men globally.[51] While there are not as many types of female associations, due to the fact that they cannot take on higher authority in the church,[52] there are more female congregations and sisters in total than male congregations and religious men. While there were 201 male religious communities worldwide with 310,500 members in 1965, there were 1,116 female organizations with 900,000 members.[53] In the Diocese of Beira, there were more than 15 male and female religious orders between 1940 and 1960. Some were congregations, some were religious orders and societies of priests, and one was a mendicant order. Chapter 2 examines in detail their specific histories and cultures, and how they related to each other and to the bishop of Beira. Subsequent chapters look at how they relate to the church hierarchy, collectively and individually, and how they contribute to the making of Catholic politics.

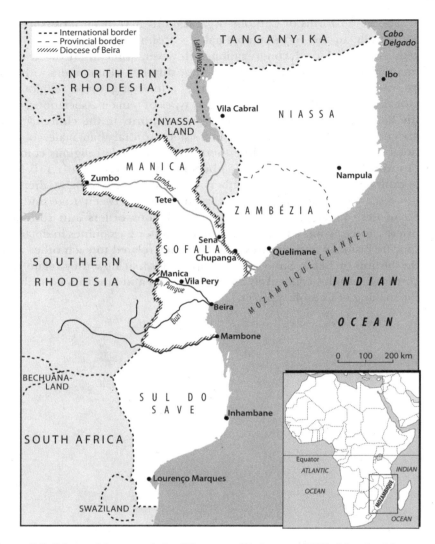

Figure 1.1. Mozambique and the Diocese of Beira, ca. 1950. Map by Maura Pringle.

1

The Making of the Diocese of Beira

The Vatican established the Diocese of Beira in 1940. Its founding marked a rupture in the way the church had been organized in the area until then and opened up a new era of Catholic development. It was the direct result of the signing of a Concordat and a Missionary Accord between the Vatican and the Portuguese government that same year. These international agreements aimed at establishing a harmonious relationship between church and state, both in the metropole and in the colonies. They set up a framework that allowed the church to expand but also controlled the way it could operate. Among others, they stipulated that the Catholic Church had to be structured into dioceses (and not vicariates) in the Portuguese colonies and that all bishops had to be Portuguese.

The coming pages aim to explicate the context and structuring of the Diocese of Beira as well as reveal the personality and orientation of the bishop of Beira beyond the "political paradigm." Rather than investigate who benefited most from the alliance between church and state, the chapter analyzes the nature of the alliance between the two and investigates what the Catholic Church did thanks to (or in spite of) it. It looks at the the history and unfolding of the post-1940 church–state alliance, it investigates the training, personality, and inclinations of the first bishop of Beira, and it analyzes the overall achievements of the Catholic institution in Central Mozambique in terms of occupation, infrastructure, and personnel.[1]

The Vatican, Portugal, and Beira

The history of the Catholic Church in Mozambique is one of grandeur in the sixteenth and seventeenth centuries, decline in the eighteenth century, and collapse by the mid-nineteenth century. The church set foot in southeast Africa in 1498 when a priest accompanying Vasco de Gama on his way to India disembarked on the Island of Mozambique. As the Portuguese proceeded to build forts in the region in the following decades, the Catholic institution built churches next to these fortresses and sent clergymen to serve there. Soon Jesuits and Dominican friars engaged in a broader evangelization drive. The Dominicans rapidly claimed success with thousands of conversions along the Zambezi River while the Jesuits converted the court of the key and dominant Monomotapa Empire (based in what is present-day Zimbabwe and extending into the center of present-day Mozambique). These conversions did not last, however. As the geopolitics of the area changed and new wars began, the Jesuit priest posted at the Monomotapa court was assassinated (1562) and the Dominicans, like the Jesuits, faced such difficulties that around 1590 they were no longer able to expand. The missionaries consolidated their hold on the area by establishing huge church properties along the Zambezi River, where they worked with the white and Afro-Portuguese populations as well as with small nuclei of Africans settled on their properties.

While the church in Mozambique did not expand in the sixteenth and seventeenth centuries, the coming to power in Lisbon of the Marquis of Pombal initiated its decline. The marquis energetically implemented a policy to separate church and state—*régalisme à outrance* (excessive regalism), as Charles Boxer put it.[2] In 1759, the Marquis expelled the Jesuits from Portugal and with that the church lost half its missionaries in Mozambique. Over the following decades the Catholic institution went further into decline, with the anticlericalism triggered by the "liberal wars" in Portugal in the late 1820s and early 1830s leading to the eventual collapse of the church in Mozambique in the second half of the nineteenth century. By 1855 only five priests were left in the whole of Mozambique and no prelate.[3]

Two broad processes in the second half of the nineteenth century enabled the Catholic Church to make a return. First, the elite in Portugal (including religious men and women) began to focus on the African continent again after Brazil became independent from Lisbon in the 1820s. Portugal began a concerted effort at colonizing African territories and thus built the basis for the "Third Portuguese empire."[4] This took place in parallel with the wider colonial "scramble for Africa," so that to some extent world politics drove the Portuguese enterprise. Yet, being short of money, Lisbon struggled to occupy the whole of Mozambique, effectively controlling only the coast and the Zambezi valley. The colonial power decided to draw on the Catholic Church and private chartered companies, among others, to assist it in its efforts. It lent about half of the territory of Mozambique to chartered companies under renewable twenty-five-year licenses in exchange for capital investment and the effective occupation of the area.

One of these was the Companhia de Moçambique, which was given control over the center of the country.[5] Second, the latter half of the nineteenth century saw a marked improvement in the relationship between the church and the Portuguese state.[6] This resulted in the return of missionaries to Africa, including to the territories under the control of the chartered companies. The growth was so strong that by 1909 there were no less than seventy-one fathers (both members of religious orders and secular priests) and ten sisters in Mozambique—a figure never reached in Mozambique before.[7]

This renewed Catholic growth came to an abrupt end in 1910 when a coup d'état in Lisbon brought to power an anticlerical regime. It expelled the Jesuit order as well as several other congregations from Portugal and from Mozambique, and opposed religious works.[8] Because of the First World War and pressure from the Vatican, Germany, and Britain,[9] the anticlerical attitude of the first Portuguese republic did not last. From 1916, the government allowed religious orders to return to Portugal. In 1918, after a coup d'état by Sidónio Pais, the new government reestablished relations with the Vatican and took measures to subsidize the church in the colonies. Between 1916 and 1926, the government improved the conditions for the church, even if it did so selectively by favoring secular priests, who were considered as being more nationalist, over religious clergy. Eventually, another coup d'état in 1926 brought military officers to power who, lacking leaders, entered into an alliance with Catholic men who soon dominated the government.[10] As a consequence, church-state relations improved yet further. In 1926 the Catholic institution was again granted the status of juridical person while Catholic missions overseas were attributed "organic status," which enabled them to receive financial and ideological support from the state, as confirmed in the Colonial Act of 1930. Lisbon also allowed the church to reopen seminaries in Portugal. In this climate, a number of religious orders returned to Portugal and the number of missionaries to the colonies increased. It was not to be a return to the pre-1910 situation, however. As the regime developed from 1926 onward, it crystalized into the Estado Novo, a corporatist, nationalist, and authoritarian state. Its republican approach meant, however, that it wanted an alliance with the church that kept the spiritual and temporal spheres well separated.[11]

To establish a long-lasting alliance, the Holy See and Lisbon opened negotiations in the late 1920s for the establishment of a concordat. The post-1926 government was interested in resolving the "religious question" and integrating the Catholic institution into its hegemonic quest.[12] The Catholic Church, in turn, wished to ensure that anticlericalism would never return to Portugal and wanted to achieve an "effective missionization" of the Portuguese colonies. Negotiations opened in the mid-1920s and preliminary accords were signed in 1928 and 1929: they confirmed and prolonged a series of prerogatives that the state had acquired in the fifteenth century in terms of the Padroado,[13] and in turn gave increased space to the Catholic institution to work in education, health, and social works.[14]

In 1929, negotiations to establish a concordat and a missionary accord began in earnest. The situation of the church in the colonies was an important part of the discussions. The Vatican refused to sign a concordat separate from, or before, a missionary accord. In turn, Lisbon wanted to make sure the state's prerogatives in terms of the Padroado would be preserved, not least that the Sacred Congregation for the Propagation of the Faith (aka Propaganda Fide), the Vatican's body responsible for missionary work, would not have any jurisdictions over its colonies. Indeed, António Salazar, who came to power in 1932, saw Propaganda Fide as showing "a sort of imperialism on the part of the church against the nationalism of states in colonial matters."[15] Among others Lisbon wanted to ensure that Portuguese nationals would be in control of the Catholic institution in its territories.

After eleven years of negotiations and some major concessions by the church, the Vatican and Lisbon finally signed in 1940 a concordat and a missionary accord.[16] An additional and more detailed agreement, the Missionary Statute, was signed in 1941. Together these accords closed the period of anticlericalism and strong regalism, and opened a new era intended to benefit both church and state. For their part, the Portuguese bishops wrote in 1941 that these accords were finally bringing "religious peace" to Portugal.[17]

The Concordat, an international agreement signed between the Holy See and nation-states, is typical of the period: the Vatican signed no less than twenty-eight such accords in Europe in the early twentieth century. Yet the Portuguese one was singular in that it was particularly extensive and encompassing, as well as double-stranded, applying different principles in Portugal than in the colonies. While it stipulated a clear "agreed separation" ("separação concordata") between church and state in Portugal, it established a close alliance between the two in the colonies.[18] In the metropole, the Catholic institution renounced its ambitions to receive any reparation for the nationalization of its properties during the First Republic, agreed to the limitation of its political ambition, notably in relation to Catholic Action (the association organizing the work of the laity), and accepted that its personnel should not receive salaries from the state. In exchange, the Portuguese government agreed to give up many of its regalist pretensions, accorded the church legal status, and gave it free rein to organize socially and religiously. In the colonies, by contrast, the state was to invest massively in missionary activities, by subsidizing the dioceses, paying the salaries of missionary personnel, allocating land and granting tax exemption to the church, and paying for Catholic health and educational facilities. The church, in turn, accepted that the Catholic hierarchy had to be of Portuguese nationality, consented to develop educational and health facilities for Africans, and agreed not only to evangelize but to *civilize* and *Portugalize* Africans, thus to turn Africans into Portuguese subjects.

The details and modalities of the alliance in relation to the colonies were registered in the Missionary Accord and in the Missionary Statute published by the government in 1941. In general terms, these accords considered missions as "institutions of imperial utility, with an utmost civilizing importance."[19] Specifically, they recognized Catholic weddings as official; attributed and specified the subsidies to be paid per congregation and per diocese (see table 1.1 for the overall figures from 1940 to 1960); and detailed the salaries and additional perks, such as retirement funds and travel subsidies, which the clergy were to be granted by the state. The accords specified the quantity of land to be given free of charge to each mission (up to two thousand hectares) and stipulated that foreign missionaries would only be allowed into the colonies if not enough Portuguese missionaries were available. Religious orders were only allowed to work in the colonies if they registered with the state and had a presence in Portugal itself, and if their personnel submitted to Portuguese law. Lisbon was granted a say in the nomination of bishops in the colonies and the choice of mission teachers, and it gained a restriction of the use of non-Portuguese personnel. And the Missionary Statute obliged all missionaries to do all secular teaching in the Portuguese language.[20]

Another element that the Concordat and the Missionary Accord specified was the Catholic division and organization of the Portuguese colonies.

Table 1.1. State subsidies to the church in Mozambique (constant US$), 1940–1962.

Year	1940–1942	1943–1945	1946–1948	1949–1951	1952–1954	1955–1957	1958–1960	1961–1962*
US$	878,848	1,384,597	1,952,396	2,582,698	3,091,882	3,587,566	4,672,545	4,140,822
Constant	878,848	1,120,483	1,401,720	1,519,234	1,633,447	1,874,101	2,263,516	1,938,846

*This period comprises only two years.

Source: E. dos Santos, *L'état portugais*, 121–23.

Note: The constant dollar amount is calculated on the basis of the consumer price index.

Like most other Portuguese overseas territories, from 1783 onward the church in Mozambique was structured as a prelacy and placed under the authority of a nonresident "bishop *in partibus infidelium*" (bishop in the lands of the unbelievers). After 1930, the Vatican wanted to modernize its structures in the colony. The initial plan was to create a single Apostolic prefecture in Mozambique, directed by a specific group of missionaries from a single congregation in view of later establishing several vicariates. The prelate of Mozambique in the 1930s, Dom Rafael da Assunção, a Franciscan friar who had worked in Beira for many years, favored this option and actively promoted it in Lisbon.[21] He hoped that his order, the Franciscans, would thus gain control of about two-thirds of Mozambique.[22] Yet, though Dom Rafael was very influential in the Vatican and with the government in Lisbon, his efforts were eventually unsuccessful: the Concordat signed between the Holy See and the Portuguese government established that Mozambique, like Angola, would be divided into dioceses—initially Nampula, Beira, and the archdiocese Lourenço Marques. This was a surprising choice since the preparatory discussions had been about vicariates and since a diocesan structure was usually only adopted for countries with "mature Christianities." While the reasons behind this decision are not all clear, four elements stand out. First, there was competition between congregations for access to and control over Mozambique. The adoption of dioceses avoided having one congregation, such as the Franciscans, control and exclude other congregations from large swathes of the territory.[23] Second, vicariates are more tightly linked than dioceses to Propaganda Fide. Choosing a diocese thus allowed Lisbon to keep at bay Propaganda Fide which it saw as working against the Portuguese Padroado. Third, having dioceses in the colonies was more prestigious for Portugal as a colonial power since the diocesan form was normally reserved for territories with mature Christianities. Fourth, it is probable that the Holy See was ready to accept one form of organization or the other as long as it was sure that there would be a growth in the church.

After agreeing to the structure of the church in Mozambique, the Vatican began to appoint the clergy for the new posts. In 1940 it nominated Dom Teodósio Clemente de Gouveia, a Lazarist, as archbishop of Lourenço Marques and as interim apostolic administrator of the dioceses of Beira and Nampula. In 1941, it nominated the Franciscan friar Teófilo de Andrade as bishop of Nampula.[24] For Beira, the Vatican aimed to install a secular priest as bishop rather than a religious prelate, but it struggled to find an adequate person. When the Vatican had still not appointed a bishop in 1943, Lisbon became impatient and Salazar suggested nominating a Franciscan as bishop but granting the Jesuit congregation (that worked in the area) a special dispensation so that it would not have to submit to a bishop from another congregation.[25] This was not to the Holy See's taste and, a few days later, the nuncio in Portugal proposed Sebastião Soares de Resende to the Portuguese government as bishop of Beira. A secular priest, thirty-seven years old, Dom Sebastião was professor and vice-rector of the Major Seminary in Oporto. The government accepted the proposal (on April 6), whereupon the Holy See officially nominated Dom Sebastião to the position on April 21, 1943. On August 15, Dom Sebastião was ordained as bishop in Oporto by the former prelate of Mozambique and the bishops of Coimbra and Oporto. Arriving in his diocese three months later, on December 1, 1943, he wrote the following words in his diary:

> At nine [o'clock], Monsignor Santos, the Governor and the President of the Municipality came to fetch me at the ship and took me to a pavilion next to the jetty where the Governor and the President greeted me. Followed a procession to the Cathedral where I took power solemnly. There was much Franciscan clergy, Father Sarreira SJ, etc. I had lunch at the Episcopal residence where were present: secretary Monsignor Santos, Father Lobo who is his secretary, Father António Ribeiro OFM, Father Sarreira SJ and the Father Superior of the FF [?]. The day was very hot. My body was distilling water. In the afternoon, we went to breathe some air at the Lighthouse of Macuti, at Manga where we saw the tile factory of the mission and at the boarding house of the Franciscan Sisters of Maria. That's how my first day in the Diocese of Beira took place.[26]

The First Bishop of Beira

Sebastião Soares de Resende was born in 1906 in Milheirós de Poiares, a village close to the city of Oporto in northern Portugal (see fig. 1.2). He was the son of a reasonably rich farmer, owner of the land he worked on, and had two sisters and a brother. The family was religious but lacked a tradition of clerics—only one uncle was a priest. In 1923 Soares de Resende entered the seminary of Vilar, and in 1926, the Major Seminary of Oporto. He was one of the best students, receiving various prizes during the course of his school career. He finished the seminary in October 1928 and was ordained soon thereafter.[27] In 1932 Dom Sebastião went to Rome to continue his studies. He completed a doctorate in philosophy at the Gregorian University and began one in theology, though he did not finish it. He then took a course in social sciences in Bergamo, in northern Italy, after which he returned to Portugal and, in 1934, became professor and

Figure 1.2. Dom Sebastião Soares de Resende, n.d. Photograph courtesy of Father Mollina.

vice-rector of the Major Seminary of Oporto. In 1936 he was chosen to be part of the chapter (i.e., advisory college) of the Diocese of Oporto. In those years, Dom Sebastião continued with the study of neo-Thomism and the renewal and modernization of Portuguese theology, the topic of his doctorate, not least through articles in Catholic journals and presentations at conferences.[28]

In terms of Salgado de Matos's model, Dom Sebastião's life followed the typical trajectory or *cursus honorum* of a Portuguese bishop before 1975.[29] He was born in a rural and Catholic district of Portugal; his family displayed an above-average religiosity; he studied at the Gregorian University in Rome; he taught at and was vice-rector of a major seminary; and he was part of a diocesan chapter. Yet, if Dom Sebastião's biography was conventional in terms of social origin, education and religious career, what distinguished him was the generation he belonged to. He was part of what Salgado de Matos calls the "seminarians of the Law of Separation," the group of bishops who were trained in the 1910s and 1920s when the fight between the church and Portuguese state was at its highest.[30] This generation lived through, and suffered under, the anticlerical regime of the First Republic and this influenced their worldview. Many seminarians of this generation experienced the government's anticlericalism as a form of trauma and developed a militant vision of the church. The Portuguese historian José Barreto goes as far as to speak of a "mentality of the catacombs" as well as one of antipluralism.[31] Another characteristic of Dom Sebastião's age group was that it was very Roman in orientation. Most bishops of this generation studied at the Gregorian University in Rome, one of the best Catholic universities, which was under the pedagogic guidance of the Jesuits. As a result, these bishops tended to be ultramontane, believing that the papacy should be at the center of the church, and inclined to be more Rome-centric than Lisbon-centric.[32]

Dom Sebastião's thinking can be characterized as ultramontane, neo-Thomist, and nationalist. Dom Sebastião was *ultramontane* in that he always placed the objectives of the Catholic Church above those of the national state, and the aspirations of Rome above those of the local church or the congregations.[33] As shown in his doctoral studies, he was a *neo-Thomist*: this is a theological approach based on the writings of Saint Thomas of Aquinas and promoted by the Vatican after 1878 as a way to overcome the stalemate of "intransigent Catholicism," which argued for an ontological unity between the spiritual and material realms and between the monarchy and the church. Intransigent Catholicism opposed the Enlightenments and liberalism and wanted to keep, or return to (as in the case of France), a system of hereditary monarchies where the church had both spiritual and temporal power. In contrast, neo-Thomism distinguished between the field of life of the church, which deals with grace and predestination, and that of the state, which deals with nature and material things. In this theological approach, the temporal realm of the state is subordinate to the spiritual one since it is the latter that gives meaning to the former. Dom Sebastião thus argued in his dissertation that science could not be an end in itself but needed theology or faith, else it would be an "immoral art of thinking."[34] Neo-Thomism followed intransigent Catholicism in its disdain for modernity, but rather than rejecting it completely, it tried to shape it so as to make it Christian. It also promoted a degree of church involvement in politics since the religious sphere was meant to give meaning to both social and political life. Accordingly neo-Thomists recommended a threefold strategy for the church to influence society: implementing ultramontanism;

shaping the political system through the creation of Christian democratic political parties (a process called *ralliement*); and developing a Catholic social doctrine. Since *ralliement* was not permitted under Salazarism and the 1940 Concordat, Dom Sebastião vigorously promoted only ultramontanism and the social doctrine of the church.[35]

The third characteristic of the bishop's thinking was *nationalism*. Ultramontanism and nationalism are strange bedfellows. But Dom Sebastião was a systematic and ambitious thinker and tried to reconcile these two supposedly incompatible systems of thought. He first did so in his doctoral dissertation in which he proposed renewing and modernizing Portuguese theology by aligning it with the official Vatican position and thus reconciling the church's national with its ultramontane dynamics. He explained:

> I know very well that there cannot exist a national science or theology. The activity of pure intelligence, or of intelligence served by faith, ignores particular temperaments and does not know the specific climate of countries to embrace truth. . . . But what exists, or can exist, are humans who belong to certain countries and serve the cause of science or theology. In this classified activity of intelligence, there is always a group of characteristics that, without affecting the universal doctrine, give each author or collectivity of authors certain traits so that they can be classified into schools, regions, or countries.[36]

This attempt at reconciling ultramontanism and Portuguese nationalism was quite unique among Portuguese clergy of the time. Most bishops in Mozambique and elsewhere in the Portuguese world were simply not ultramontane or were split between ultramontanism in religious affairs and nationalism in the political realm. Over time, however, Dom Sebastião would become increasingly ultramontane and from 1958 evolved to drop his support for the Portuguese state so as to better protect the interests of the church in Mozambique (see chapter 4). Up to then, however, the bishop was nationalist in approach and quite passionately so in his early years. In his third pastoral letter in December 1946, Dom Sebastião ardently wrote that Portuguese colonization is

> the restless and generous, thrilling, and orderly manifestation of the exciting life of a people who—after having conquered, pacified, and organized a portion of the continent where they live, [now] intoxicated by expansion—throw themselves into an encounter with a new continent to infuse other people, their brothers, with the benefits of the fertilizing seeds that overflow from its chest. It is a beautiful ideal, all made of love and sacrifice, of sanctity and heroism, which decorates the sky of

Portugal with glorious constellations and embellishes the most glorious chapters of our history with the perfume of flowers.[37]

In the view of the bishop, colonization was a juridical and a historical right drawn from all Portuguese activities since the crusades. Dom Sebastião's enthusiasm sprang from the conception that the Portuguese Empire had been, and remained, at the service of God. The expansion of the empire thus went hand in hand with the expansion of faith, and therefore was beautiful. The Portuguese state promoted a Christian civilization, "hence colonization also means Christianization."[38] One needs to understand, the bishop argued, that some countries were minors, like individuals were minors, and that imperial states therefore had the right to colonize and engage in mission to bring these countries to adulthood—like a father or godfather had the responsibility of raising his son or godchild. Dom Sebastião acknowledged that mistakes could happen in the colonizing process and that different methods could be used. But the right of colonization was *absolute*, he claimed, and anyone who opposed it could *not* be genuine in intention. To him, criticizing the colonial system could only mean that one was trying to substitute one colonizing power with another.[39] Not only were these writings nationalist and procolonial, therefore, but they echoed an explicitly politico-religious messianism typical of Portuguese nationalism.[40]

If colonization was a right, according to Dom Sebastião, it entailed duties, regulating norms, and limits. He considered the social doctrine of the church to form these regulating norms and limits. The prime duty of colonization was to bring colonized countries to adulthood and to work for the good of the indigenous people. This meant not just occupying and exploring a territory's wealth for the good of Portugal but also developing the economy and people of the colony. Civilization was central in this task: "Our civilizing mission will justify the occupation of our overseas countries," explained the bishop.[41] One can easily guess the central role he foresaw for the church in the colonies: it was not just one factor but the prime factor of civilization. The church had a specific function "to save all human values, to better them, and to bring them to their highest destiny through the communication of the divine values that Christianity is worth of."[42] The bishop was aware that, to fulfill its function, the church had to enter a "compromise" with the state when it signed the 1940 Concordat and Missionary Accord. He wrote in one of his pastoral letters:

Catholic missions have entered a solemn compromise with the state by which they are bound to apply all of their apostolic zeal to evangelize the Portuguese territory. There is no doubt about this. Missions are by divine precept part of the works of the church that are Catholic, Apostolic, and Roman, and they have as their aim the beautiful ideal of Christianization of the people without allowing themselves to be drawn into partisan ideologies, national limits, ethnic groups, or whatever other criteria there may be that are not those of absolute universalism. By virtue of the Missionary Accord, however, missions fit into the general organization of the state services, in-line with the law, without ever losing their supranational character that is inalienable.[43]

As already indicated, the bishop's thinking changed over time, a development that is traced in the course of the next chapters. For now, we need to note that, upon Dom Sebastião's arrival in Beira, we can see an immediate dissonance between his nationalism and enthusiasm and the realities he discovered on the ground in his diocese. This led him to adjust his standpoint and, over time, even alter some of his views. In two domains the bishop faced particular tension: in relation to the church's social doctrine and in relation to politics. I discuss these in turn.

The first domain where the bishop faced tension is the dissonance he experienced between the social realities on the ground in the colony and the church's social doctrine. While Portugal had abolished slavery in the second half of the nineteenth century, forced labor was commonplace in the colony, practiced not least by the state and applied in particular in the forced cultivation of cotton and rice.[44] The bishop's diary is replete with comments about social, racial, and labor abuses. On October 19, 1944, for example, he noted that "Portuguese indigenous policy has still not lost its sting from the time of slavery—only its name has changed but little more. This is the greatest problem of the colony."[45] His diary entry for June 22, 1945, reads similarly:

> There is, behind this civilization, the most absurd barbarism that stinks to high heaven and calls responsible men to demand vengeance. The law says there is no forced labor. But the reality is that all, or almost all of those who work are forced to work in conditions that do not respect freedom, justice and social conventions. This is not civilizing. It is crushing some so as to build temples of vice for others. Thus barbarism continues.[46]

In the face of such realities, the bishop eventually decided to go public with his criticism. In early 1950, six years after his arrival, he published a pastoral letter titled "Anti-communist Order" (dated to December 1949). Here he laid out the social doctrine of the church and used it to condemn the forced cultivation of cotton and rice in his diocese. He criticized the abuse committed and the benefits drawn by concessionary companies on the basis of permissive colonial law, and pointed out the dramatic social consequences of forced labor, such as the exploitation of African workers, the destruction of their families, and population exodus to neighboring Malawi and Southern Rhodesia.[47] Unsurprisingly, the colonial adminis-tration rapidly prohibited the pastoral letter from being sold.[48] When the provincial governor asked the bishop for the names of the companies responsible for abuse, Dom Sebastião refused to provide them, saying it was not his job to give names. He commented in his diary: "I pointed to the rabbit, they have to hunt it down."[49] The state's inquiry into the scandal, launched a few days later, brought no notable results. The affair remains important as it marked the first time the bishop intervened publicly to criti-cize the government.

The second domain where the bishop faced tension is the dissonance between his ideals and the politics he found in the colony. When he arrived, Dom Sebastião enthusiastically supported the empire and colo-nialism, and had a positive view of state support of the church. With time he realized, however, that the alliance between church and state was more complicated and not as beneficial as (and possibly more harmful than) he had first thought. For one, the bishop realized that whereas the Catholic Church had many friends in the state, it also had powerful enemies there. He found anticlerical and Freemasonic elements in the local administra-tion and colonial government as well as in the metropole. Up to the 1950s, the bishop's diary is full of references to Freemasonic conspiracies and attacks. In part, this reflected his (and more widely the church's) paranoia in relation to Freemasonry in those days. In part, it also reflected real fac-tional fights that took place secretly within the authoritarian regime. While the Estado Novo had prohibited Freemasonry, it had not eliminated it fully: rather, it co-opted some elements as it was repressing others, even within the government. Thus President Óscar Carmona was a Freemason and so were some government ministers, right up to 1974.[50] For another, his enthusiasm for the regime and the church–state alliance thinned over time as the bishop felt that the state did not deliver what it had promised in the alliance. For example, on many occasions Dom Sebastião felt that the colonial administration invested less than it should in Catholic works, in particular in missions and schools. Similarly, he experienced several occa-sions where the state's interests conflicted with those of the church. For example, the state was reluctant to allow foreign missionaries entry into Mozambique, and for a while in 1950 even prohibited access to Dutch, German, and Italian priests.[51] This militant and enthusiastic bishop did not allow his dissatisfaction to stop his work. But by the late 1950s it did lead him to criticize the state even more, privately and publicly, as he grew increasingly concerned about the location of the church in the colony within a quickening movement toward decolonization, both nationally and internationally (see chapter 4).

The evolution of the bishop's thinking was not linear and the tension between ultramontanism and nationalism continued for a long time. As an ultramontane, the bishop subscribed to and avidly read journals such as the *Civilitá catolica* and the *Revue du clergé africain* as well as the latest books in vogue in Rome. Ideas from his reading flowed into his pastoral letters and led him to be at the forefront of Catholic trends nationally, if not worldwide. In the late 1950s, for example, he promoted the role of the laity, and in the 1960s he attended the Second Vatican Council where he was the most active Portuguese bishop in terms of the number of interventions made.[52] But such views also set the bishop on a collision course with several of his episcopal colleagues, as we will see in the coming chapters. In relation to politics, in the 1950s Dom Sebastião became a follower of Lusotropicalism, a theory developed by Brazilian sociologist Gilberto Freyre suggesting that the Portuguese had a singular understanding of, and capacity for, tropical life, people, and societies. Supporters of Lusotropicalism envisioned that the Portuguese colonies would first achieve autonomy and then gradual independence (with settlers staying) to eventually give way to a Lusophone federation centered in Portugal. In 1951, Dom Sebastião met Gilberto Freyre in Brazil, and the latter visited Beira the following year at the invitation of the Portuguese government. Indeed, in the early 1950s, the Portuguese government tried to co-opt Freyre's theory in order to bolster the legitimacy of its colonial enterprise.[53] Lusotropicalism reached its zenith in Portugal in the early 1960s when Adriano Moreira became subsecretary of state for Overseas Territories and, soon after, minister of Overseas Territories. By that time, however, the bishop (who was close to Moreira) had begun to think beyond Lusotropicalism toward the direct and full independence of Mozambique as a nation.[54] Again, Dom Sebastião was at the forefront of new thinking and, in this case, his ultramontane perspective led him to see beyond Lusoptropicalism.

Strategy for the Diocese of Beira

The Diocese of Beira was created in 1940 when the prelacy of Mozambique was divided into three units. At 360,645 square kilometers in area, it spanned half of the colony of Mozambique (four times the size of Portugal itself) and had a population of two million individuals. It had twenty-eight priests, eight religious brothers, and twenty-one religious sisters, many of whom had arrived in Mozambique after the church–state agreements of 1940.[55] The missionaries were Franciscans and Jesuits from Portugal with a few secular priests from Goa. Many lived in the provincial capital of Beira and worked with the city's settler population rather than with the African population in the rural hinterland. The rate of Catholics in the population was extremely low, reaching a mere 1.9 percent in 1943. This means that at the time of Dom Sebastião's arrival in Beira, the diocese was young and the church still very weak. Everything had to be done, or redone if we think of the earlier, more dynamic times. This raises a number of questions: How did the bishop organize his diocese to increase the number of Catholics, to "educate" them, and try to create Christendom in Beira? What was his strategy and who did he target? How did he manage to attract more missionaries and how did he coordinate their work? What Catholic structures and organizations did he set up, for whom, and how did he do so?

The first preoccupation of the bishop upon arriving in Beira was, unsurprisingly, a missionary one, namely, the conversion of the African population. This entailed two broad aspects: the recruitment of missionaries to come and work in Beira, and the creation of mission stations all over the diocese. First, as soon as he was nominated to the position of bishop, Dom Sebastião wrote to religious orders around Europe to invite them to send their personnel to Mozambique. According to the Concordat and Missionary Accord, the Catholic Church was required to prioritize Portuguese personnel. But there were not enough missionaries available in Portugal, partly because the colonies were so much bigger than the homeland and partly because the anticlerical First Republic had led to a major fall in religious recruitment. As a result, the bishop had no choice but to turn his attention to other European nations. He contacted a wide range of missionary orders to attract religious workers for his diocese, including the White Fathers, the Montfort fathers, the Dominicans, the Capuchins, the Burgos fathers, the Congregation of the Sacred Hearts of Jesus and Mary (also called the Picpus fathers), the Carmelites, and even the controversial Opus Dei. His primary criteria were not political or national; his concern was to get (preferably qualified) religious men and women who would be useful to the diocese. During the first two years of his appointment, the Second World War was still ongoing and very few religious personnel were available in Europe. After the war, Lisbon was reluctant to allow foreign missionaries into the colonies. It feared Italian, German, and Dutch Catholic missionaries in particular because their countries had just lost their colonies and it thought they might undermine the Portuguese Empire out of national jealousy—in 1950 Lisbon even banned them outright.[56] Yet Dom Sebastião persisted in his quest for missionaries, writing to the minister of colonies and traveling to Lisbon and Rome on several occasion. In this way he managed to build up an ever-growing collective of religious men and women, as figure 1.3 indicates.

For the bishop of Beira, evangelization required men as well as mission stations to house the missionaries, establish health and educational facilities, occupy and mark the landscape, and to evangelize. Dom Sebastião was explicit about the need for this infrastructure, as exemplified in his first annual report of 1944 to the Portuguese administration:

> One of the first steps to be taken in the missionary work of the Diocese of Beira is what we can call its occupation. By occupation I mean the establishment of a mission station in each administrative area. If we want to work with intelligence and method to succeed in the fields of instruction,

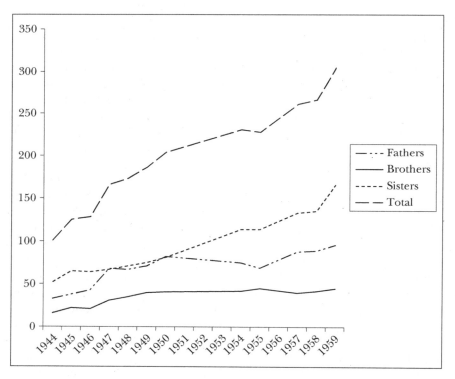

Figure 1.3. The number of missionaries from 1944 to 1959. A slight fall in numbers occurred in 1955 when the new Diocese of Zambezia was split off from the Diocese of Beira. Source: Yearly reports of the bishop of Beira to the state (Fundo do Governo da Beira, Arquivo Histórico de Moçambique; and Fundo dos Ministério do Ultramar, Overseas Historical Archives, Lisbon).

catechization, assistance, and nationalization, then we have to allocate each administrative area a group of at least two fathers, properly trained, motivated by an intense zeal, and equipped with at least a minimum of infrastructure to work among the infidels. Later, they will expand from this center to the extremes of the administrative area and establish secondary mission stations in places seen as appropriate to that end, in-line with the services the indigenous masses require and the possibilities of the personnel at our disposal.[57]

Such occupation required personnel as well as funds. The state was meant to finance the expansion and the running of the Catholic institution, but it could not, or did not want to, invest as much as the church desired. Like his colleagues, Dom Sebastião was impatient to "occupy" his diocese, so he soon started to complain about the lack of funds. He also felt that his diocese was receiving less than other religious administrative units considering its size and population.[58] While he regularly complained about this in his annual reports, Dom Sebastião worked on an alternative, namely, to gather funds, labor, and material for the construction of mission stations and churches from local administrations and the private sector. He regularly asked for free wood from sawmills, free cement from the local factory in Beira, and free material or even the construction of church buildings from local administrators.[59] In this manner his diocese did well and by 1953 the bishop considered his territory to be "minimally occupied," a status he had defined in 1949 as being achieved once each district had a mission station.[60]

At this point, with the initial occupation and installation of a minimum number of mission stations, expansion from these centers outward could begin. The number of substations expanded proportionally to the mission stations founded, and so did the number of schools (see fig. 1.4). As a result, the church needed an ever-increasing number of catechists and teachers. The diocese decided to go ahead with plans drafted before the arrival of the bishop to open a catechist and teachers' training college at Boroma in Tete province. The idea had been proposed by the prelate of Mozambique in partnership with the Jesuits who were to run the college. It opened in 1944, after a few minor delays and it offered three-year courses for teachers and catechists. The first class graduated in 1947. Over the first years, the college housed some fifty students; by the 1960s, between seventy and one hundred students were enrolled at any one time. One problem the church faced was that the private companies and the colonial state paid higher salaries than the church was able to afford, so that many graduates eschewed becoming teachers and catechists after completing their

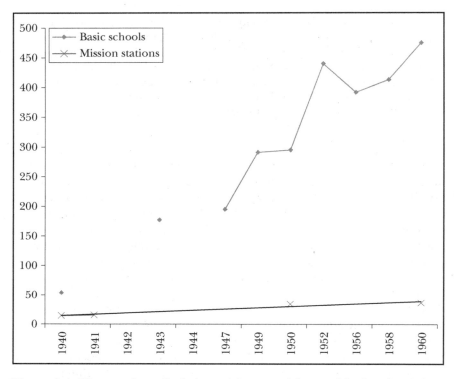

Figure 1.4. The number of mission stations, parishes and basic schools in the Diocese of Beira, 1940–60. The fall in 1955 is caused by the split off of the Diocese of Zambezia, which takes along about half of the personnel. Source: Annual reports of the Bishop of Beira to the state (Fundo do Governo da Beira, Arquivo Histórico de Moçambique; and Fundo do Ministério do Ultramar, Overseas Historical Archives, Lisbon).

training and went instead to work for the state or private businesses.[61] Year after year the bishop complained to the colonial administration, asking the state for more money so that the church could pay better salaries to its employees.[62] In 1950 he proposed a law by which teachers would need to commit to work ten to twelve years for the church if they were trained at a Catholic college.[63] This proposal does not seem to have been taken up and the church's problem in relation to its African personnel continued right up to independence.

Another preoccupation of the bishop after his arrival was the Christian "reconquest," that is, the reconversion of white settlers and "assimilated" Africans (*évolués*) who had stopped practicing their faith or even given it up. To this end, Dom Sebastião opened new schools and colleges to cater to their children. Three new institutions were opened in the decade after his arrival (three already existed): the Instituto D. Gonçalo da Silveira (1948) for white boys, the secondary college of Tete (1950) for white boys and girls, and the Colégio Nossa Senhora da Conceição in Vila Pery (1952) for white and *mestiço* (mixed race) girls. He also launched or expanded on a series of new Catholic structures for adults. Prime among these was the Catholic Action organization promoted by the Vatican, particularly after 1922, to counter the secularization of society. (Outside of Portugal, Catholic Action was also used to implement the church's policy of political *ralliement*, a policy that could not be implemented in Portugal as agreed in the Concordat.)[64] The church exported the organization to its colonies without any alteration or adaptation. When Dom Sebastião arrived in Beira, the Catholic Action had already been founded in some cities, among which were Tete and Beira. In Beira, however, only a women's branch was active, the Liga da Acção Católica Feminina. The bishop thus actively worked to create a number of additional branches: the Liga dos Homens da Acção Católica for men, the Juventude Católica for the youth, the Liga Opéraria Católica for workers, and the Juventude Operaria Católica for young workers.[65] From Beira, the Catholic Action expanded to various parishes of the diocese. Yet, by 1964, only four mission stations had Catholic Action branches, which is to say that the organization never took off well among Africans and largely remained a settler organization.

To help drive the "reconquest," the bishop of Beira also decided to found a newspaper. He imagined a publication that would have "a common title page" that could "penetrate all social milieus" and make inroads "even among those indifferent or hostile" to religion.[66] Initially, Dom Sebastião wanted to call it *Adeante* (Ahead), but eventually decided on the more neutral *Diário de Moçambique* (Mozambique daily).[67] The newspaper was registered as a private business (thus not as part of the diocese) and given a neutral, non-Catholic design (see fig. 1.5). Hampered by various difficulties, not least financial problems, the newspaper was launched on December 24, 1950, and quickly became a standard in Beira, if not in the whole of Mozambique.[68] There was only one other newspaper in Beira, the Portuguese/English *Notícias da Beira*, which closed in 1951.[69] The bishop appointed Father Francisco Nunes Teixeira as editor in chief of the newspaper. When the Vatican nominated Teixeira as head of the Diocese of Quelimane in 1955, Júlio Meneses, a lay Portuguese missionary, took over for a short period until José Soares Martins, the bishop's nephew, was appointed in 1959. Martins stayed at the helm of the

Quarta-feira
2 de Abril de 1952

DIÁRIO
de Moçambique

ANO II N. 449
Preço 2$50

REDACÇÃO E ADMINISTRAÇÃO — RUA CORREIA DE BRITO — Telefones: 2701-2700 // DIRECTOR — DR. A. MATIAS FERREIRA // OFICINAS — RUA MOUSINHO DE ALBUQUERQUE — Telefone 2701

PROPRIEDADE DO «CENTRO SOCIAL, LDA.» /// ENDEREÇO TELEGRÁFICO «DIÁRIO-BEIRA» /// CAIXA POSTAL 643 /// BEIRA — ÁFRICA ORIENTAL PORTUGUESA

O Jogo da Rússia
e a Unificação Alemã

Por CORREIA MARQUES

Melhor seria terem acertado que de tal maneira se trabalije entre a Rússia durante a batalha, que se ganhem a guerra, mas se perdea a paz. Ainda dir-vos-ei a prelito «estudando a Rússia a terem paifacia criminosa. O crime catastrofico-será os Estos irto que ode se querta tanter durante aquêa mas e durante os primeiros anos subsequentes à União, mas asora do qual se está agora falado-os impantas...

Dois ministros
TUNISIANOS

do antigo Gabinete seguem para a América dispostos a apresentar a causa da Tunísia perante o Conselho de Segurança da O. N. U.

CAIRO, 1 — Os dois ministros tunisianos do antigo gabinete de Chenick, que vieram para esta cidade, procederam-se de lida para...

O trágico desastre ferroviário da linha de Cascais
O desabamento de terras deu-se numa extensão de quinze metros

Causou profunda impressão em todo o país o terrível desastre ocorrido registado no linha de Oeiras, perto da...

AS BODAS DE PRATA
SACERDOTAIS
do Red.° Pároco de Quelimane

EISENHOWER
CONFESSA QUE O OCIDENTE POSSUI AINDA RESERVAS MORAIS E ECONÓMICAS
SUFICIENTES PARA ENFRENTAR O PERIGO SOVIÉTICO

PARIS, 1 — No relatório sôbre o primeiro aniversário da criação do supremo comando da Europa, declarou o General Eisenhower que, apesar da grande crise...

Num conflito
entre a polícia e populares
ficaram mortos dois marroquinos

CASA BRANCA, 1 — No conflito que houve ontem en Saft, na costa oeste do país, entre os populares e a polícia...

Presidência da República

LISBOA, 1 — O sr. Presidente da República recebeu o Ministro das Obras Públicas, e os directores da Companhia Nacional de Navegação e da Associação dos Bombeiros Voluntários de Carcavelos. — (L.)

Começou a lavrar
o vulcão submarino das Filipinas

MANILA, 1 — O vulcão submarino «Diderot» das Filipinas expele lavas e rochedos a 150 metros de altura. — (L.)

ESTE NÚMERO FOI VISADO PELA COMISSÃO DE CENSURA.

No 7.° aniversário do desembarque das Forças Aliadas na Normandia e França, durante a segunda grande guerra. O Supremo Comandante das Forças, General Eisenhower, diante da cruz que marca a sepultura de soldado desconhecido dos Estados Unidos.

(Continua na 2.ª pág.)
(Continua na 2.ª página)
(Continuação da 2.ª página)

newspaper until 1968.[70] Dom Sebastião kept oversight of the newspaper, yet rarely intervened in its editorial work or in the functioning of the press—though he did write columns and editorials. Thanks to the newspaper's quality and independence, it rapidly gained clout. It dared address sensitive issues such as labor relations or famine, and was soon challenged by the colonial state (which temporarily suspended the publication several times),[71] though this only augmented its prestige and circulation. In the early 1960s, the diocese decided to expand its media presence: in 1962, it took over the weekly *Voz Africana*, the newspaper of the mestiços' African Center of Manica and Sofala, and in 1963 launched the *Economia de Moçambique* magazine.[72]

The last major issue of concern to the bishop of Beira after his arrival in Mozambique was the reproduction of the local church. To address the issue, he founded a minor seminary. In his first official report to the state in 1944, Dom Sebastião wrote, in-line with Vatican guidelines: "What is normal is that the posts of leadership of the church are filled with persons of the same region. The life of the church in Africa will only become normal when the priests are Africans. Besides, in spite of all the goodwill there may be, the metropolis will never be able to provide enough missionaries to ensure a regular assistance of all inhabitants."[73]

In 1945 Dom Sebastião bought a farm on a plateau near the town of Zobuè (in a remote corner of the diocese, close to the border with Malawi), where he began construction for the facilities of the seminary in 1946. It officially opened its doors in August 1949 with classes starting for the academic year of 1950/51. Originally, the bishop wanted the Jesuits to run the seminary, but the latter refused because of a lack of personnel and resources and their prior commitment to running the Boroma teacher training college.[74] The bishop then approached the White Fathers who were just moving into the diocese and had extensive experience across Africa in training indigenous clergy, who accepted.

Within a decade of his arrival in central Mozambique, the bishop of Beira had managed to set up a full modern Catholic Church in his diocese. The alliance between church and state (formalized in the Concordat and Missionary Accord) made this possible even if it structured and constrained to some extent the activities and options of the Catholic institution. The contradictions inherent in the Catholic-Portuguese imperial hegemonic project were rapidly clear to Dom Sebastião and he soon began to denounce the practices that went against the social doctrine of the church. With time he would begin to think about alternative colonial projects and eventually abandon his support for the state so as to save the church. Between 1940 and 1960, however, the church grew steadily and the bishop was happy enough with Portuguese colonialism. His ultramontane and militant vision of the church was being realized thanks to an everincreasing number of missionaries. It is to these men and women that we now turn.

2

Diversity and Dynamics of the Imperial Church

When Dom Sebastião Soares de Resende arrived in Beira in 1943, there were only four religious orders working in his diocese, alongside some secular priests. By 1960, there were fifteen congregations in the diocese (see table 2.1 for the distribution of the congregations) and by 1974 yet another three, bringing the total to eighteen missionary organizations by the time of independence.[1] This increase was the result of the bishop's energetic national and international recruitment drive to attract more religious orders and missionaries to Beira. For Dom Sebastião, their enlistment was a way to strengthen the church and build Christendom in Beira, by opening up and staffing mission stations, occupying the extent of the diocese, and converting the population. Yet, while the arrival of these congregations did indeed lead to significant results—the rate of Catholics in the population increased fivefold between 1944 and 1964—the multiplication of religious congregations also fostered intra-Catholic diversity. The congregations came with their own traditions, histories, and charismas, with distinct types of personnel from a range of countries, and with various training, sent to Mozambique for disparate aims and for different lengths of time. While the diversity of the church in Beira might have been rather unique (most dioceses only had a few congregations), it is representative of the church worldwide and makes for a perfect case to study the church's internal diversity and dynamics.

To explore the dynamics and internal diversities of the church in central Mozambique—imperial in nature since there was no local clergy until the 1960s—this chapter looks at the origins of the different congregations, compares them with each other, and investigates how the bishop managed this diversity. As we saw in the introduction, in theory, things are relatively clear and regulated by canon law: the bishop rules over all clergy in his diocese while the heads of the congregations rule over the internal affairs

Table 2.1. Catholic congregations in Beira, 1960s.

Male congregations	Female congregations
Order of Friars Minor ("Franciscans") (1898)	Sisters of Saint Joseph of Cluny (1890)
Society of Jesus ("Jesuits") (1881/1941)	Franciscan Sisters of Mary ("White Franciscans") (1897)
Missionaries of Africa ("White Fathers") (1946)	Franciscan Sisters of Calais (since 1964 Franciscan Missionaries of Our Lady) (1935)
Little Brothers of Mary ("Marist Brothers") (1948)	Franciscan Sisters of Our Lady of Victories/ Irmãs da Nossa Senhora das Vitorias, ("Madeirense" or "Vitorianas") (1938)
Instituto Español de Misiones Extranjeras ("Burgos Fathers") (1954)	Franciscans Hospitaller of the Immaculate Conception/Franciscanas Hospitaleiras da Imaculada Conceição ("Irmãs Hospitaleiras" or "Irmãs da Caridade") (1948)
Congregation of the Sacred Hearts of Jesus and Mary ("Picpus Fathers") (1956)	Franciscan Missionaries of the Mother of the Divine Shepherd/Franciscanas Missionárias da Mãe do Divino Pastor (1953)
Comboni Missionaries of the Heart of Jesus (1968)	Repairing Missionaries of the Sacred Heart of Jesus/Missionárias Reparadoras do Sagrado Coração de Jesus (1956)
	Missionary Daughters of Calvary (1958)
	Mercedarian Missionary Sisters (1959)
	Instituto do Sagrado Coração de Maria (Sisters of the Sacred Heart of Mary) (1961)
	Daughters of Charity of Saint Vincent de Paul (commonly known as Pauline sisters) (1969)

Source: Pinheiro, *Na entrega do testemunho 1975.*

of their congregations. In practice, however, things are more complicated as both authorities rule over the same individuals, the affairs of the diocese and those of a congregation overlap, and the distinction between them is uncertain. In this context, the relations between religious orders and the prelate of the diocese had to be negotiated: first, in a contract between the bishop and the congregation, signed before the religious order is allowed to move into the diocese; and second, in daily practice.

Congregations Moving to Beira

The timing of a congregation's arrival in Beira is important analytically because certain claims, if not rights, were associated with being first- or latecomers. The way they arrived is also important because this determined how they managed to set themselves up in Beira, how they were permitted to operate, and what geographical area they worked in. This section describes the mission societies that came to work in the Diocese of Beira, both before and during the tenure of Dom Sebastião.

Arriving in 1881, the Society of Jesus was the first congregation to come to central Mozambique in modern times. As we saw in the introduction, the Jesuits were in the area in the early sixteenth century. They were among the first religious orders to come to southeast Africa and, with the Dominican friars, one of only two congregations in the area until 1759, when it was expelled from both Portugal and Mozambique. In 1773 the order was abolished by Pope Clement XIV.[2] In 1814 it was reestablished by Pope Pius VII and, fifteen years later, made its way back to Portugal. It was another fifty-two years before the Jesuits managed to return to the Zambezi area in 1881. The reason for this delay was the weakness of the Jesuits' Portuguese province that focused its energies on its restoration in Portugal rather than on overseas expansion. It is not this restoration per se that led the Jesuits to return to Mozambique, however. This came about on request by the Portuguese government, which feared the British might take over its colonies, particularly the area where the Jesuit missionaries had previously worked and which was deemed to hold much gold (see chapter 1 for the general dynamics). Although the Portuguese Jesuits lacked personnel to move to Mozambique, they agreed to the request and began their work with mostly foreign personnel.[3] Their work was interrupted again by the anticlerical and Masonic First Republic of 1910 in Portugal that, yet again, expelled all Jesuits from the country and its colonies. The society tried to return to Mozambique as soon as it was allowed back into Portugal in the early 1930s, but the government prohibited this for as long as there was no valid concordat and missionary accord between the government and the Vatican; it was thus using the Jesuits as a pawn in its negotiations with the Vatican. The Jesuits finally made their way back to Mozambique in 1941, a year after the Concordat was signed, yet this time with only Portuguese missionaries.[4] They returned to their former mission stations (Lifidzi, Boroma, Marara, and Fonte Boa) in the Tete region of the Diocese of Beira and thus began what they termed the "fourth period" of their mission in Mozambique.[5]

The Franciscan fathers of the Order of Friars Minor arrived in Mozambique in 1898.[6] Their arrival took place soon after they were allowed to reestablish their province in Portugal in 1891 and in the same year that the Vatican appointed a Franciscan as prelate of Mozambique.[7] Following on the Jesuits, the Franciscans were the second religious order to come to southeast Africa since the prohibition of religious orders in Portugal and Mozambique in 1834. Their arrival in Beira took place in a new social and political context, namely, the return to grace of the church and the establishment of the Companhia de Moçambique in the area of Manica and Sofala. The Franciscans established themselves in the city of Beira itself, which had begun as a commercial post a decade earlier (1887) and had become the official seat of the province in 1892—having moved there from Chiloane, farther south, to avoid encroaching on the Gaza empire in southern Mozambique and to respond to the economic developments in the Manica area, in particular the construction of the Beira–Rhodesia railway line.[8] The arrival of the Franciscans thus coincided with the launch of a new imperial period in the region, of which they became an integral part. The fathers took responsibility for the parish of Beira city (the town and a huge territory around it) for which they called on the Franciscan Sisters of Mary. They built the cathedral in Beira, opened a mission station in Matundo and launched a technical school in Beira for mestiço and African students, inaugurated in 1905 as the Escola de Artes e Ofícios. By 1910 the Franciscans had 9 missionaries, 7 auxiliary brothers, 10 sisters, and 8 schools with 1,300 students in their schools in Central Mozambique.[9]

The Franciscans were much less affected than the Jesuits by the Portuguese First Republic of 1910. For one, the anticlerical stance by the new government in Lisbon was aimed particularly at the Jesuits (similar to the stance the Marquis of Pombal took against them in the eighteenth century).[10] For another, the Companhia de Moçambique protected the church against anticlerical decisions from Lisbon to some extent as the governor of Mozambique refused to execute some of Lisbon's new policies.[11] Critically, while the Franciscans were expelled from Portugal, they were allowed to remain in Mozambique, only having to accept the curtailment of their expansion in Manica and Sofala and a reduction in their subsidy. This was a minor obstruction, and by 1917 the restrictions diminished in the wake of Sidonio Pais's coup d'état in Portugal. After 1926 the position of the church in Mozambique not only normalized but was promoted again, and the Franciscans were well placed to benefit fully from this new predisposition of the state—while the Jesuits were kept away until 1941. Another factor favorable to the Franciscans was the nomination in 1920 of Rafael da Assunção, one of their former missionaries in Beira, as prelate of Mozambique. After his return to Portugal in 1935, Dom Rafael became an adviser to the Portuguese government in the negotiations of the Concordat and Missionary Accord.[12]

Since the First Republic only affected the Franciscans briefly and moderately, the congregation could soon grow again. The number of Franciscan missionaries expanded anew already in the 1920s, in spite of a lack of personnel in Portugal resulting from the closure of their novitiates there. Between 1919 and 1926, the number of Franciscan men in Mozambique thus rose from seven to twenty-two.[13] During the same period, these missionaries expanded their work in central Mozambique by taking over the (formerly Jesuit) mission of Chupanga, on the Zambezi River, and opening mission stations in Macequece and Amatongas in the Manica region. In all these places, the Franciscans applied for, and generally succeeded in gaining, the title deeds for the land they were working on. In this way (and despite their principle of poverty), they wanted to guarantee their autonomy from the state as well as from the Catholic hierarchy.[14] To extend their autonomy, they launched a Franciscan seminary for Africans in Amatongas in 1934. As a result, by 1943 the Franciscan fathers were solidly established in the area that had just become the Diocese of Beira. They dominated numerically and had built up a complete set of institutions so as to be autonomous. It is no wonder that Dom Rafael Assunção tried to influence the government in Lisbon and the Vatican to create vicariates in Mozambique rather than dioceses: his congregation was well placed to take control of such vicariates, in particular in central Mozambique, and it could thus become wholly autonomous, depending only on the Vatican. Unfortunately for him, not only were dioceses the preferred structure for Beira, but a diocesan bishops was chosen and new religious orders were soon allowed to move into the diocese. The Franciscans reluctantly accepted this new reality, and well into the 1950s, up to the early 1960s, actively fought against any attempts by the diocese and the Vatican to reduce their autonomy.

The White Fathers, members of the Missionaries of Africa congregation, came to Mozambique in 1946. Before that date, they had had a short presence in the area in the late 1890s. Indeed, in 1889 they had been invited by the Portuguese authorities to establish a mission station at Mponda, on the southern tip of Lake Malawi, in a territory over which the English were trying to gain sovereignty. The Portuguese claimed the region for themselves in-line with the rights given to them by the Padroado and they wished for the White Fathers to assist them in consolidating this claim.[15] The White Fathers were well aware of the diplomatic game that was going on, but as it was in the Vatican's interest as well as their own to set foot in the area, they accepted the invitation. This background made establishment of the Mponda mission station highly political and, unsurprisingly, it lasted only as long as the Portuguese had the upper hand in the region. In 1891, after various maneuvers, the English government issued an ultimatum to the Portuguese government demanding it give up its claim over the area. Portugal had to cave in (leading to major political crisis): the country lost the area and the missionaries had to leave after months of work.[16] They left behind what Ian Linden calls a "diplomatic storm."[17]

Interestingly, and paradoxically, the White Fathers never made any reference to this event when they prepared to move to Mozambique again decades later. Hence, their official "arrival" in Mozambique (rather than a "return") came after the bishop of Beira made a request to the headquarters of the society in Rome in 1944. At the time, the superior of the White Fathers was reluctant to accept this invitation because of the Second World War. Traveling was difficult and many fathers were working as military chaplains so that the society was experiencing a shortage of personnel. Dom Sebastião did not give up, and asked the Vatican to put pressure on the society. In 1945 the White Fathers decided to accept the invitation, but informed the bishop that they would send only a few fathers at this point and more only after the war ended.[18] Thereafter the first White Fathers sent to Mozambique (two of Italian and two of Belgian nationality) only arrived in Beira in June 1946.

In 1949 the bishop of Beira engaged in a "violent exchange of letters" with the Portuguese minister of colonies when the latter forcefully rejected all applications for permission for Italian, Dutch, and German missionaries to be allowed into Mozambique. As we saw earlier, the government opposed German and Italian fathers because it feared these would oppose Portuguese colonialism in a situation where their own nations had lost their colonies. While Dom Sebastião's engagement in the matter led to permission for a few of these "prohibited" missionaries to be allowed in, the Portuguese government made clear that this was a one-off authorization; it also did not yet sufficiently alleviate the bishop's need for missionaries in Beira.

Thereafter Dom Sebastião had to think of an alternative, and in 1950 began to consider the Spanish missionaries of the Instituto Español de Misiones Extranjeras (IEME, Spanish Institute of Foreign Missions, founded in the town of Burgos in Spain, after which it is also often called).[19] Two points spoke in their favor: Burgos missionaries were already working in neighboring Rhodesia (since 1949), and the bishop considered that their nationality might "slightly dissipate the morbid fantasies" of the Portuguese government.[20] In 1953 Dom Sebastião visited the Burgos seminary in Spain, after which he wrote a formal request to the institute.[21] After receiving approval from Rome in September 1953 (the IEME was regulated by the Vatican's Congregation of Faith) and formal acceptance from the institute itself in October 1953, IEME's first missionary (in the person of Victor Cenera) arrived in Beira in mid-1954, having moved there from across the border in Rhodesia. A second group of Burgos fathers arrived in November 1954, prompting Dom Sebastião to comment in his diary: "I received two Spanish fathers who are coming to this diocese. They are two men, young, and the way they present impressed me favorably."[22]

The Congregation of the Sacred Hearts of Jesus and Mary, also called the Picpus fathers (for the Picpus Road where they had their headquarters in Paris), arrived in Mozambique in 1956. The Dutch province of the order had moved to Portugal in 1931 on instruction of the Vatican to improve the moral and pastoral quality of the Portuguese clergy and thus modernize the church there. It was put in charge of the Major Seminary of Cristo Reis and ran some popular mission stations in northern Portugal.[23] Its decision to move to Mozambique came in 1953, when the priests resolved to establish themselves permanently in Portugal and open their own Portuguese seminary in order to recruit men for the congregation. Yet, to be recognized officially and be able to receive subsidies from the state in Portugal, the Picpus congregation, like all Catholic organizations, had to have missions in the overseas territories (the Portuguese state dropped the term "colony" in 1951). Looking for a place to do mission work, the Picpus were offered two options: Timor and Beira. Due to the uncertainty over the future of Timor, the order's provincial superior and his men in Lisbon chose Dom Sebastião's diocese.[24] A Picpus delegate visited Beira in 1955 and returned with enthusiastic reports. In early 1956 two Dutch Picpus missionaries were sent to Portugal for six months to learn the Portuguese language. From there they traveled to Beira, arriving in November 1956. This was the first time a priest from the Congregation of the Sacred Hearts of Jesus and Mary went to work in Africa.[25]

Smaller groups of missionaries worked in Beira too. The Marist brothers (of the Little Brothers of Mary congregation) arrived in Mozambique in 1948 with the sole mission to work at the Institute D. Gonçalo da Silveira, a white-only secondary school in Beira. The Comboni Missionaries of the Heart of Jesus expanded from Nampula (where they had been since 1946) to Tete and Beira in 1967, inaugurating a new teachers' school near Beira and working in different missions in the Tete area.[26] In 1969 they had three men in Beira and three in Tete; by 1974 they had six men in Beira and six in Tete.[27] Finally, there were some secular priests (who did not belong to religious congregations). Some were already working in the Diocese of Beira when the bishop arrived in 1943 (particularly priests from Goa); others came with the bishop. Their number remained stable after 1943 at around five to ten priests, most of them working directly with the bishop as secretary of the diocese, vicar-general, or staff on the diocesan newspaper.

A significant number of female congregations also worked in Beira—eleven by 1974. Most arrived around the time of the nomination of the first bishop of Beira, but two came a few decades earlier. The Sisters of Saint Joseph of Cluny moved to central Mozambique in 1890 at the request of the Jesuits, were expelled with them in 1910–12, and only returned in 1943 to work in the Tete region.[28] The Franciscan Sisters of Mary (commonly known as "White Franciscans" because of their white religious habit) arrived in 1897 at the request of the Franciscan fathers to work in Beira city.[29] The next congregations arrived in the 1930s: they were the Franciscan Sisters of Calais in 1938, who settled on mission stations in the central and southern areas of the diocese alongside their male Franciscan counterparts, and the Franciscan Sisters of Our Lady of Victories (Irmãs da Nossa Senhora das Vitorias, also known as "Madeirense," as they originate from Madeira) in 1938, who worked in Beira at the Macuti Hospital and as linotypists at the newspaper, as well as at the hospital of Chimoio. Together the Sisters of Calais and the Madeirense represented half of the total number of sisters in Beira.[30]

The Portuguese Franciscan Hospitaller of the Immaculate Conception congregation (Franciscanas Hospitaleiras da Imaculada Conceição, commonly known as "Irmãs da Caridade") moved to central Mozambique in 1948 and worked with Franciscan fathers in the areas of Manica and Mossurize.[31] The Franciscan Missionaries of the Mother of the Divine Shepherd arrived in 1953 and worked alongside the White Fathers in the area of Sena and Gorongosa as well as with Jesuit missionaries in Angonia.[32] Finally, the Repairing Missionaries of the Sacred Heart of Jesus (Missionárias Reparadoras do Sagrado Coração de Jesus) moved to the diocese in 1956 to work in Beira city; the Missionary Daughters of the Calvary arrived in 1958 to work in Tete and Moatize areas, alongside the Burgos fathers;

the Mercedarian Missionary Sisters came in 1959 and worked with the Burgos fathers in Marávia and Zumbo; the Sisters of the Sacred Heart of Mary arrived in 1961 and worked with the Picpus fathers in Dondo; and the Daughters of Charity of Saint Vincent de Paul came to Beira in 1969 to open a bookshop.[33]

Geographically, male religious orders worked in distinct and separate areas of the diocese, along principles similar to the Protestant "comity agreements" that ensured that the work of the various orders did not overlap.[34] The spatial distribution of religious orders in the Diocese of Beira followed a historic, pragmatic, and functional logic. At first the area of the diocese was divided between the Jesuits and Franciscans fathers. Soon after his arrival, Bishop Soares de Resende called in new religious orders and allocated parts of the area under Jesuit and Franciscan control to them. The bishop's approach was pragmatic: the Jesuits and Franciscans did not have the manpower to missionize all of the area they had been given. The new congregations took over Franciscan and Jesuit mission stations that had been without personnel, or areas that did not yet have a mission station and required one—usually in consideration with what the Jesuits and Franciscans considered as their "traditional" or "historic" areas or mission stations. The distribution that was reached in the late 1950s remained largely the same until independence (see fig. 2.1).

The "comity" principle was not applied to female congregations: they worked alongside the male orders and were distributed based on what was required on the ground and how many sisters were available. Because the Jesuits traditionally worked with the Sisters of Cluny, the latter worked in Jesuit areas only. Similarly, for a long time the Sisters of Calais worked exclusively with the Franciscans. Other female congregations usually worked with more than one male congregation: the Franciscan Missionaries of the Mother of the Divine Shepherd worked, for example, with the White Fathers and the Jesuits, whereas the Madeirense worked with the Franciscans, White Fathers, and Picpus fathers.

Comparing Religious Orders

There were many other differences between congregations in Beira besides their date of arrival, their reason for coming to central Mozambique, and the geographical location they worked in. History is one such dimension. Two extreme examples illustrate this point. On the one hand were the Franciscans, a congregation that placed high significance on times past. They saw themselves as the first congregation to have come to the Diocese

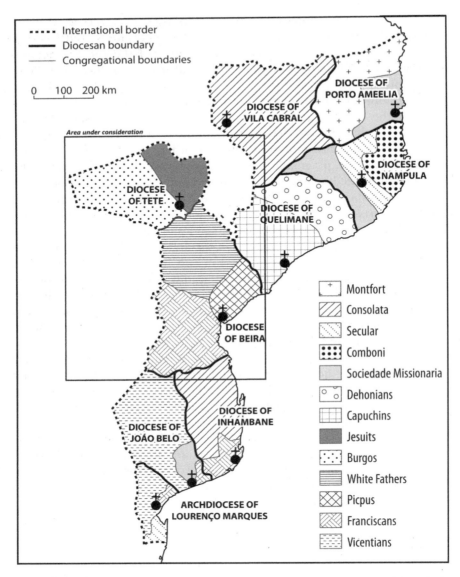

Figure 2.1. Distribution of religious orders in Mozambique, ca. 1964. Map by Maura Pringle, designed on the basis of data (slightly simplified) from Pedro, *Anuário católico do ultramar português 1964*.

of Beira (leaving aside the earlier work of the Jesuits between 1881 and 1910) and felt that the diocese (at least the part that constituted the province of Manica and Sofala) was "theirs." They had come to central Mozambique under the auspices of a Franciscan prelate, which they hoped would mean that they would be able to create a vicariate in Beira under their control. This profoundly shaped the Franciscan approach in central Mozambique, leading them to a "reactionary outlook": they resented having to give up areas to newer congregations and hoped to return to a past when they had controlled most of the diocese's area. Typically, the fathers idealized the time before 1940, were not keen for new congregations to arrive, and resisted what they considered as centralizing decisions by the bishops (this is further examined below).

On the other hand were the Picpus fathers who arrived in Mozambique with no previous missionary history in the area and no connection to the African continent at all. Their involvement in Beira was a calculated strategy by the congregation in Portugal that wished to receive state subsidies, thus requiring that it build up a missionary engagement overseas.[35] Not only was Africa wholly new to the Picpus fathers, but they had a limited interest in it, investing little energy in the venture. According to the official Picpus historian, "The first missionaries of 1956 were literally 'dumped' in Mozambique"; they were not trained for missionary work, and were not provided with money, transport, or accommodation in Beira.[36] In the 1960s, the provincial still spoke about the lack of experience of his men in Mozambique.[37] In an interview in the 2000s, a former Picpus missionary to Beira reflected that he had received no missionary training before coming to Mozambique in 1962. This only began to change in the decade before independence—until then it was as if the Picpus fathers went to Beira backward, keeping their eyes focused on Portugal and on their future there.[38]

The second difference between religious congregations was their structure, the way they were organized and the way they operated internally. The Jesuits and White Fathers are very centralized organizations: as examined in the introduction, the models of E. K. Francis and Michael Hill suggest that they oscillate between a *Gesellschaft* and a "total institution." The Jesuits (popularly known as the pope's "light brigade" or "grenadiers") are very hierarchical, with a special charism of total dedication to the papacy.[39] The White Fathers are similarly hierarchical but possibly even more centralized than the Jesuits. They owe complete obedience to their superiors who regulate the tiniest details in their lives, including wine drinking, bedtime, and permissible hairstyles.[40] This included the requirement not only that the regional and provincial superiors had to report to the superior-general in Rome on a regular basis, but that *all* missionaries had to submit regular written reports to their superiors who in turn kept statistics on the number and regularity of these letters.[41] The Franciscans, in contrast, are among the most decentralized, if not the most democratic, Catholic congregations. Not only is the order not directly subject to the pope (the head of the congregation has to give account to the Vatican's Congregation for Religious, today called Congregation for the Institutes of Consecrated life and the Societies of Apostolic Life), but power within the congregation is also strongly decentralized. Decisions are made at the provincial level and in general chapters at which representatives are *elected* by the fathers and brothers at the grassroots level.[42] This structuring means significant autonomy for each province and even for each mission station.[43] In terms of Francis's and Hill's models, we can say that the Franciscan congregation leans toward a *Gemeinschaft* model. In more than one way, the three congregations just discussed constitute the extremes on a spectrum of structuring types, with many of the other congregations located between them. In Beira, our focus here, the Picpus order leaned toward the Jesuit model while the Burgos fathers as well as most female congregations leaned toward the Franciscan model.

Tied to history and structure is the third difference, culture. In this respect, a first element is the charism of each congregation, namely, the inspirational purpose that gives each organization its official and foundational aim and identity. As mentioned above, the Jesuit order was created to serve the pope; it also had the task of educating elites, just as the Sisters of Cluny did. While the Jesuits had difficulties in realizing the latter objective in Mozambique (unable to take up the offer of running the minor seminary of Zobuè due to a lack of personnel, for example), it was a constant preoccupation and objective nonetheless.[44] The Franciscan charism, in turn, was (and still is) to work for the poor and to remain poor themselves—their dress intending to reflect this. In Mozambique this commitment to poverty was blurred by the Franciscans' preoccupation with title deeds in order to ensure their autonomy, but it was a key element of their identity nonetheless. The charism of the White Fathers is missionary work on the African continent and, in particular, among Muslims. This led them to adopt a habit that blended in with Muslim dress, and a pastoral approach particular to this mission situation (of which more below). The Picpus fathers' charism is evangelization, particularly of the poor, building up "popular missions" in the Netherlands and Portugal. As the Burgos fathers were secular missionaries, their society was not guided by a charism. The organization had been launched by the Diocese of Burgos as a diocesan seminary for missions, which the Vatican transformed—by imposition—into a national organization for missionaries in the 1920s, which it made dependent on the Propaganda Fide. Thus, while the Spanish society had no charism to speak of, it developed a particular identity and culture based on its secular and diocesan character, adopting a rather anti-ultramontane attitude in reaction to the Vatican's imposition in the 1920s.[45] Finally, all female congregations in Beira were Franciscans and thus shared the charism to serve the poor and vulnerable. Within that broad framework, however, they had areas of specialization. The Sisters of Calais and the Sisters of Mary both ran health posts, maternities, nursery schools, disability care centers, and boarding houses for African girls. The Sisters of Cluny ran the secondary college in Tete, the Sisters of Mary that in Beira, and the Sisters of Calais that in Vila Pery. The Sisters of Our Lady of Victories worked as nurses and as linotypists at the diocesan newspaper.[46]

A second cultural element of difference relates to the social and national makeup of each congregation. As mentioned before, after 1943 all Jesuits and Franciscans in Beira were of Portuguese nationality. Similarly, the missionary sisters in the Diocese of Beira were nearly exclusively Portuguese: in 1957 only 10 percent of sisters were not Portuguese against 50 percent for male clergy.[47] In contrast, the Picpus fathers were all Dutch, the Burgos fathers were all Spanish (interestingly, many men were from the Basque country, something that would become an important factor in the 1960s), and the White Fathers recruited men from many nationalities. In Beira, the White Fathers' members were mostly German, Belgian, Italian, Swiss, Spanish, and French (see table 2.2). The society considered it important that people from different nationalities were mixed in order to avoid any national interest prevailing and interfering with the work of the church. With nationality came specific attitudes and cultural traits, most obviously in relation to the Portuguese imperial project. While the Jesuits and Franciscans fully

Table 2.2. Nationality of the White Fathers in Mozambique, 1953.

	Fathers	Brothers
German	9	8
Belgian	6	—
Italian	4	—
Swiss	1	1
Spanish	1	—
French	1	—
Total	22	9

Source: Statistics December 31, 1953, 548(8), Archives Générales des Missionnaires de l'Afrique (White Fathers).

supported the Portuguese colonial project, other national groups were more critical of it and developed different political positions in relation to colonialism and decolonization in the 1960s, a point we take up later.

The last element differentiating the various congregations was the pastoral approach each adopted in Mozambique. Pastoral approaches differed in terms of the objectives that drove the work of the congregation and the methods it used. The objective of most early missionaries was to convert Africans to Christianity and civilization. They wanted Africans to convert to Catholicism as a European faith and culture. Accordingly, missionaries were often concerned about the danger of the Africanization ("cafrealization") of the faith. In terms of European culture, most missionaries agreed on the need to "civilize" Africans, although the content of that civilization varied. Portuguese congregations understood civilization along a (narrow) national line by which Africans needed to become Portuguese, while foreign missionaries had a more complex relation to Portuguese civilization and some even preferred other forms of colonization and civilization, as, for example, that practiced by the British Empire. The pastoral methods also differed between the congregations that imposed a uniform approach on their missionaries and those that did not. Unsurprisingly, this distinction overlapped with that of centralized/decentralized structures of the religious orders: Franciscans generally favored giving their missionaries leeway to decide for themselves how to proceed, while Jesuits and White Fathers preferred a centralized approach. Regarding pastoral strategy, Franciscans, Jesuits, and all foreign congregations except the Burgos fathers relied on financing from the colonial state, and this significantly shaped their work. They strove to use the state subsidies to build grand mission stations, schools, and hospitals, and some developed massive agricultural farms. For the evangelization work itself, they relied on African teachers and evangelists. The White Fathers, on the other hand, wanted to create an African Catholic Church, and thus educated their converts directly to become exemplary Catholics. One result was that they converted but few Africans. Although the White Fathers also engaged in construction and managing their mission stations, their focus was on evangelizing and inculcating the right ideas in their African converts. To this end, White Fathers adopted local customs, ate local foods, and conversed in the local languages, in contrast to the missionaries of the other congregations who strove to bring Africans to their own modes of living and believing.

The distinction between congregations in relation to their pastoral approach is starkest when looking at the question of the catechumenate, which is the instruction given in preparation for baptism. The White Fathers were unique in this respect. The White Fathers Society's rules stipulated that the catechumenate had to last *at least* four years and that baptism should not be automatic thereafter. It also stipulated that the catechumenate should be directed toward adults only and that special attention should be paid to chiefs or kings as they were expected to bring masses to conversion.[48] The founder of the White Fathers, Bishop Lavigerie, adopted such a strict approach because he was concerned about the depth of evangelization in Africa and the progress of Islam. To combat the latter, he believed the best strategy was in-depth evangelization, by which he meant an Africanized catechesis and a long catechumenate. The White Fathers applied this principle in central Mozambique—except that they soon dropped their focus on chiefs, who did not prove to be influential enough to convince their people to be baptized. The approach by the White Fathers stood in stark contrast to the method used by other congregations, in particular that of the Franciscans. First of all, the congregation of Saint Francis did not have strict rules regarding pastoral matters that all its members had to follow. In addition, none of its missionaries had received any particular training before coming to Mozambique. Third, each of its mission stations was largely autonomous. On the ground this meant that many Franciscans did not learn a local language—either because they felt it was not necessary, they had no time, or they were just not interested—even if their superior demanded it.[49] Regarding the catechumenate, most Franciscans considered one or two years of instruction that would automatically lead to baptism as sufficient. Many Franciscan missionaries baptized babies and some engaged in group baptism. In chapter 3 we will see the influence of such differences between the congregations on the development of Catholicism in Beira. For now, we turn to how the bishop saw and dealt with such diversity (see synopsis in table 2.3).

The Bishop and Internal Diversity

Chapter 1 demonstrated that Dom Sebastião Soares de Resende was a Portuguese nationalist as well as an ultramontane bishop. We saw that during his doctoral studies in Rome, he tried to reconcile these two apparently opposed elements—nationalism and ultramontanism. Once bishop of Beira, Dom Sebastião adopted a very ultramontane position when dealing with church affairs. In spite of the strong nationalism prevalent among his Portuguese clergy and the episcopacy in the colony, he fought hard to ensure that any missionary could come to Beira, including non-Portuguese. He did not hesitate to confront the government in Lisbon to ensure that German, Italian, and Dutch religious men could come to central

Table 2.3. Main differences among the Catholic clergy in Beira in the 1940s and 1950s.

	Bishop	Franciscans	Jesuits	Secular	White Fathers	Picpus	Burgos
Official category		Mendicant order	Order of clerical regular		Society of common life	Clerical religious congregation	Society of secular priests
National origin	Portuguese	Portuguese	Portuguese	Portuguese	Diverse	Dutch	Spanish
Arrival in Mozambique	1943	1898	Sixteenth century; 1881; 1941	Sixteenth century	1946	1956	1954
Missionary training	None	Low	Low	None	High	None	Low
Function in the diocese	Head	Parishes, missions, boarding schools, technical school	Parishes, missions, schools, boarding schools, teachers' school	Parishes, administration	Missions, schools, boarding schools, minor seminary	Parishes, missions, schools	Parishes, missions, schools

Mozambique even though they were at some point banned from Portuguese colonies; to him nationality did not prevail over Catholic identity. On this basis we can say that Dom Sebastião was generally speaking equidistant from all his clergy and from the different congregations working in Beira. In 1950 a comment on the competition between diocesan and religious clergy illustrates his general position, namely, his neutrality and his concern for the general good of the church. In a letter to a priest, he explained: "Here there is no religious question between diocesan and religious clergy. Here there is only the clergy of Christ and the Holy Church, all working for the major glory of God."[50]

Yet, even if he adopted a balanced attitude, Dom Sebastião saw the differences between the religious orders and, over time, even developed a preference for certain priests and congregations. These preferences coalesced into tendencies, and they are accentuated here to gain a better understanding of the dynamics of diversity within the Catholic institution. These inclinations do not contradict the idea that Dom Sebastião was ultramontane and that he worked hard at the unity of his clergy. In fact, we can even say that Dom Sebastião worked hard not to show any preferences and to ensure he held, and was perceived as having, a balanced approach. This comes up clearly on many occasions in his diary. On April 19, 1947, for example, the bishop wrote: "I want to be White with the White Fathers, Franciscan with the Franciscans, Jesuit with the Jesuits, Capuchin with the Capuchins, etc. etc."[51] Similarly, on September 5, 1947, he wrote: "I had lunch at the house of the Jesuits. What a great balance one needs to have in social life! Jesuits on the one hand, Franciscans on the other. And one must remain impartial, balanced in the middle, like the needle of a scale."

The bishop's preferences can be traced best in relation to the White Fathers. Dom Sebastião saw this congregation as the most efficient Catholic missionary organization or, as he wrote in a letter to the superior of a women's congregation in 1950, the "best specialists of missions in Africa."[52] Dom Sebastião recruited them for this very reason. As he told their superior in 1946, he wanted them to be a model for other congregations. Indeed, according to a White Fathers document, the bishop "hoped to find in us exemplary missionaries for his diocese."[53] In 1948 the bishop repeated this opinion to the White Fathers' regional superior on his visit to Beira. The superior reported: "[The bishop] wishes that the White Fathers serve as an example for the others!!"[54] And this was indeed the bishop's position for many years to follow. Dom Sebastião reckoned that the White Fathers' pastoral approach and technique were the best available, and he wanted these to be adopted by all other missionaries in the diocese. We shall see in the next section how he tried to do so. For now, we need to note that this approval did not place the White Fathers in an easy position. It placed an expectation on the society that the White Fathers struggled to meet. In 1948 the regional superior reported the following after discussing Dom Sebastião's enthusiasm for the society: "Yet the personnel [we have] is not first class except for 2 or 3! At least for now. They are very inexperienced and those who have been in Belgian territory 1 or 3 years say our Directory [internal rules] is just good for the principle, not in practice!!! Where are we heading for? You can imagine how much I reacted!! And how much I desire a serious PB [White Father] head of mission."[55]

Unsurprisingly, the bishop's admiration for the White Fathers did not prevent friction between him and the society. The bishop demanded ever more from the White Fathers and, at times, even against the rules of the society. In 1948, for example, Dom Sebastião requested the society to open a new mission station even though it did not have enough personnel. The society refused, saying the fathers had the obligation to have four religious clergy stationed at each post. The bishop did not accept this rule and threatened to withdraw payment of the travel costs of a missionary coming to Mozambique if the latter did not come to Beira straightaway. He did attempt to soften his stance by adding that this was the only exception he had ever asked the White Fathers to make, a demand he promised he would not make again.[56]

It is possible that Dom Sebastião developed a good relationship with the Jesuits in Beira because he had studied with this congregation in Rome. Over time, however, he faced what he called "deceptions," resulting from his own high expectations that the Jesuits struggled to fulfill and from diverging interests between the society and the diocese. First, the Portuguese Jesuits were unable to fulfill the many functions the bishop had envisaged they would take over. They did not have enough personnel, for example, to occupy the whole of Tete province or run the minor diocesan seminary of Zobuè.[57] The society's headquarters in Rome even proscribed its Portuguese province from running the secondary school in Beira as it feared that the fathers would become geographically too dispersed across central Mozambique, with Beira being at a significant distance from the society's core work in Tete. Dom Sebastião did not agree with this argument, since Beira was the seat of the diocese, and he considered the presence of the fathers there as more useful than elsewhere.[58] Second, the bishop and the Jesuits had divergent interests. Whereas the bishop wanted to train diocesan African clergy, the Jesuits wanted to recruit and train Africans to become Jesuits. Whereas the bishop thought in terms of the diocesan church, the Jesuits evaluated their resources and engagement according to their traditions and their own interests as a society. In 1952, for example, the society agreed to the bishop's request that they open a house in Beira city but, in return, attempted to exchange the Nossa Senhora de Fátima church, which they had served, for the church of Macuti. They preferred the latter as it was located in a bourgeois neighborhood and the congregation focused on the elite. Dom Sebastião commented bitterly in his diary: "This gentleman, as the good Jesuit he is, told me that they would do better work at the future church of Macuti than the church of Senhora de Fátima because there is more aristocracy there. That was it for my last illusions."[59]

The bishop's relationship with the Franciscans was his most difficult with a religious congregation. In 1940 the Franciscans hoped to take control over the territory of Manica and Sofala as a vicariate; because of this, they were reluctant to accept and deal with a diocesan bishop. The congregation repeatedly clashed with Dom Sebastião as it tried to retain and even expand its autonomy. They fought to reopen their own seminary and recruit Africans for their congregation, regardless of its occurring at the expense of the diocese. There are two underlying reasons for this tension. The first is historical: with the aim of establishing a vicariate, the Franciscans found it hard to accept being placed under the orders of a diocesan bishop. The second element is more ideological: the Franciscans saw the church in Mozambique as growing through the reproduction and expansion of their own congregation rather than through the planting of a local *diocesan* church. The Jesuits shared this approach, but seem to have been more reticent in expressing this opinion toward the prelate, and they were better able to manage the balance between their own interests and those of the diocese. When the bishop cited Pius XI's *Maximum Illud* encyclical (from 1919) to argue that the training of diocesan clergy should have preference above that of religious clergy, the Franciscans pointed out that the encyclical only spoke of an "indigenous clergy" without specifying whether this should be diocesan or religious.[60]

The disagreement between the Franciscans and Dom Sebastião became concentrated on two issues in particular. The first was the running of the seminary for African clergy at Amatongas, opened in 1931. When the prelacy of Mozambique was transformed into a diocese, the Franciscans wrote to the archbishop of Lourenço Marques (responsible for the Diocese of Beira until the arrival of Dom Sebastião) to ask whether they could continue to operate. The archbishop responded that as a temporary administrator of the diocese, he could not answer this query.[61] The issue was left to Dom Sebastião who, apparently, never showed any interest in the seminary.[62] In his diary, he commented on January 7, 1944: "I fear that such a seminary would give returns for the order of the Franciscan Fathers and nothing for the Diocese of Beira."[63] After closing down Amatongas, the Franciscans sent their students to a seminary in Nyasaland and, subsequently, new students to the seminary of Zobuè, in compliance with the bishop's orders, while retaining their dreams of having their own seminary. They tried to open one again in 1958 in the Archdiocese of Lourenço Marques, but failed when the cardinal of Lourenço Marques refused, fearing it would interfere with the interests of the archdiocese. He explained that if he allowed such a seminary in his diocese, he "would stay without any callings for his diocesan seminary, as almost all vocations spring from the area of the Franciscan missions."[64] With this, the Franciscans again shifted their interests back to Beira, where they finally managed to receive Dom Sebastião's permission to open a Franciscan seminary in 1960, when the diocesan seminary was already operating in full.[65]

The second issue of friction between the bishop and the Franciscans relates to the ownership of the society's mission stations. Traumatized by its anticlerical experience during the nineteenth century, the congregation of Saint Francis had been careful to buy land and buildings in its own name. When the 1910 anticlerical First Republic was established in Portugal, the Franciscans transferred the title deeds of their property in Mozambique to the prelate of Mozambique to avoid losing their property. When Dom Sebastião Soares de Resende arrived in Beira, the Franciscans demanded their deeds back, saying that the transfer had been but a temporary measure. The bishop refused, however, arguing that the 1911 transfer of deeds had been part of the normal transformation of the prelacy into dioceses. From 1944 to 1951, the Franciscans continued to demand "their" properties and the revenue collected there, or at least the negotiation of an intermediary solution. The situation was tense, and at times somewhat absurd. For example, the Franciscans claimed that the cathedral belonged to them, while the bishop could not imagine anything but that the cathedral belonged to the diocese. He wrote in his diary on January 30, 1947:

> I received the Father Provincial of the Franciscans. After talking a little, he proposed that I accept canonically to hand over the Beira missions to the Franciscans. That is, he wanted the Franciscan missions to run as their own religious houses from now on, though the diocese would [formally] retain ownership [of land and buildings]. He wanted me to canonically hand over the parish of Beira, which includes the cathedral! Pity the bishop who would have to govern them thereafter! He could [just as well] pack his bags and leave. [No,] The missions have to stay as they are. It leads to higher missionary successes, it helps them morally, it encourages discipline and it is more theological. It is the church constituted in its universal hierarchy.[66]

It is not clear how the situation evolved in relation to this question after 1947. In a letter to the former Franciscan prelate of Mozambique, Dom Rafael de Assunção, in 1950, Dom Sebastião stated: "The question of the property of the Franciscans will be resolved by the Holy See because it exceeds our jurisdiction."[67] When I conducted research in Mozambique in the 2000s, however, the issue still seemed to be current: the bishop of Beira and the head of the Franciscans both discussed this issue with me, and the Franciscan provincial superior asked me to provide the bishop of Beira with copies of the title deeds that I had found in his archive.

The Bishop's Management of Diversity

How did the bishop manage diversity within his church in Beira? Formally, there were laws and rules that regulated the relationship between religious orders and the bishop, in the form of canon law, missionary statutes, and the bilateral agreements the bishop had signed with each congregation.[68] Yet these rules clearly did not prevent differences and occasionally tensions, if not real conflict, from arising. In this situation, Dom Sebastião had to negotiate and work out compromises in a way quite similar to what Justin Willis describes for the British administration's "men on the spot" in colonial Kenya who operated through accommodation: "The making of local policy had to take account of the actual nature of the power of each party in this accommodation."[69] Dom Sebastião had a series of means to reach practical arrangements. As the head of the diocese, it was in his power to allocate (or deny) areas of work and influence to congregations; he had a say in the nominations of all missionaries and mission superiors; and he paid the salaries of missionaries and distributed the subsidies to the missions. In this capacity he was able to steer the diocese in a general direction and give it a certain dynamic. The documentation that is available does not allow a full analysis of the diocese's internal politics or finances—the archives consulted hold only few internal legal and financial documents. Still, this section traces the ways in which the bishop worked at satisfying the different and at times diverging demands of the missionaries, and how he worked with all of them—separately, together, and even playing them off against one another—to guide the diocese in the direction he wanted it to go.

A first strategic element in managing Catholic diversity was the geographical distribution of the congregations in the diocese. The allocation of an area to a certain congregation depended on the needs of the diocese, the congregation's aims, and the objective possibilities, notably in terms of the personnel that was available. Using geographical distribution strategically, Dom Sebastião allocated the areas already colonized by the Portuguese to Portuguese clergy and sent foreign orders to areas where the church had not had a (strong) previous presence. This generally placed Portuguese clergy in charge of urban parishes with many settlers while giving foreigners the responsibility of "missionizing Africans" in the rural countryside. This decision was based on the bishop's evaluation that foreigners were more expert at working with the African population whereas the Portuguese clergy would be more acceptable to the Portuguese settler population.[70] To make territory available to newer congregations, the bishop had to negotiate with older congregations to give up some of their areas. In this process, the Jesuits, for example, decided in the early 1950s to retain eastern Tete while passing the western parts of the province to the Burgos missionaries. While the bishop wanted the Franciscans in those same years to consolidate south of Beira and hand over their northern areas to the Picpus fathers, the Franciscans preferred to remain near the Zambezi River, influenced by the fact that Chupanga mission (in Marromeu district) was not only historic but also its most successful station. The bishop tried to counter that the Franciscans lacked sufficient personnel to keep this station, but the missionaries stood firm and Dom Sebastião had to allow them to retain Chupanga (where they stayed until the early 1960s).[71] Managing the geographical distribution of congregations and redistribution of areas was critically important in the 1950s when many new congregations arrived in Beira; it continued at a slower pace in the 1960s and beyond as yet more congregations moved to central Mozambique.

The second strategic element in managing Catholic diversity in Beira was the training of missionaries. In 1951, Dom Sebastião began to hold weeks of "collective study" in Beira, the seat of the diocese (where all congregations had a presence, if not a parish). At these meetings, dozens of missionaries met and discussed their religious work. Officially, such gatherings were about developing and updating missionary methods and approaches, particularly of older missionaries, many of whom (especially the old secular priests from Goa) had little missionary training.[72] Less directly, these gatherings also functioned as a way to discuss and bring together the positions and techniques of the younger clergy of Beira and to bring the congregations' divergent approaches closer together. The meeting of 1951, for example, was attended by representatives of forty-two missions. In preparation for the gathering, the diocese sent each mission a list of questions and topics to be addressed at the meeting, including population exodus, Protestantism, labor contracts, European settlers, the catechumenate, and the education of indigenous women.[73] It expected the religious staff to discuss these topics and expected each congregation to make a presentation on a specific topic at the meeting. At the 1953 meeting, one of the topics was politics and a common position was agreed on. The meeting even produced a list of demands addressed to António Salazar, the prime minister of Portugal, demanding that the government pass orders (a) to repress witchdoctors, prohibit traditional dances, and deport members of the Zionist, Adventist, and Watch Tower movements; (b) not to admit Protestants and Muslims into the state administration; (c) to exempt monogamous couples with four children from taxes; and (d) to allow indigenous people to choose their employer and to live with their families six months of the year.[74] According to the bishop, the aim of the meetings and the discussions was to find common responses to problems and to work out new directions for the future. Reporting on the meeting of 1953, the bishop wrote in his yearly report to the Portuguese administration: "The meetings give excellent results. The topics become better known; one person's experience inspires others; work methods are standardized; and a better conception of how missionary activity is organized in the diocese is transferred."[75]

A third element to mediate diversity was the diocesan regulation for missionaries. In 1940 the prelate of Mozambique published a set of rules (the "Directrizes missionarias") that applied to all clergy in the prelacy.[76] In 1944–45, Dom Sebastião wrote a new regulation that applied to his own diocese only,[77] which he rewrote and expanded on in 1956. This second version differs quite substantially from the prelate's 1940 rules, and possibly also from the bishop's first version of 1945. Whereas the 1940 regulations were thirteen pages in length, the 1956 version was ninety-five pages long. Half of the 1956 booklet explains the role, obligations, and rights of missionaries, sisters, catechists, and believers, and the rest contains templates of documents for use at the mission stations. The 1956 document thus represents a very clear attempt at systematizing and professionalizing the work of the church in the diocese.[78]

The manner in which the 1956 document was compiled also differed significantly from the earlier regulations. The prelate and the bishop had each written the regulations of 1940 and 1945 on their own, but the 1956 regulations were the result of a 1953 meeting of the bishop with the superiors of all male congregations, namely, the Franciscans, Jesuits, White Fathers, and Capuchins (the Capuchins were located in Zambezia, which was to split off from Beira as its own diocese in 1955).[79] The meeting took place during one of the "study weeks" discussed above. Significantly, the superior of the White Fathers called this meeting a "synod," implying that the church's personnel were being consulted before new rules were set up.[80] The holding of such a meeting was unprecedented in Mozambique as the Prelate Mozambique and the bishops had never held any synods or study weeks and ruled their clergy rather autocratically.

The 1953 "synod" took place in the city of Beira, between October 13 and 18. The stated objective of the meeting was to come to an agreement about a new regulation for the diocese. Numerous subjects were to be discussed, including the organization of schools, indigenous languages, boarding institutions, medicine, and indigenous weddings. The bishop had asked certain congregations to make a presentation on specific subjects. The White Fathers, for example, were asked to talk about the indigenous clergy and the catechumenate. The fathers thus wrote to their superiors in Rome to ask for guidance on the order's official position regarding the catechumenate as this was a particularly sensitive question in the Diocese of Beira and one of the most important objectives of the White Fathers. While the White Fathers demanded a minimum of four years of catechumenate before anyone could ask to be baptized, the diocese demanded only two years, and actual practice varied, even within a single congregation, between one and two years. The order's superior-general sent the following reply to his Beira missionaries:

> About the length of the catechumenate, the Ordinary [bishop] is allowed to regulate it [as he wishes]. You will have to respect his decision, which you will communicate to me along with all other decisions. I hope that he will maintain a reasonable period. If you look at it strictly, I mean if you consider the period as the one really useful in the preparation of baptism, and if this preparation is done seriously, then you will prevent the reduction of the traditional time of your catechumenate. Honestly, three years seems to me a minimum!

Cleary Dom Sebastião asked the White Fathers to report on the catechumenate because he wanted to increase the length of the catechumenate in the diocesan rule. The bishop could have imposed this by virtue of his authority but he did not want to act unilaterally. Instead he wished for the missionaries to reach a collective agreement, so he made it an object of discussion at the synod and asked the White Fathers to present their views on the subject. Tellingly, the bishop told the superior of the White Fathers that he expected everyone to make concessions so as to arrive at a solution acceptable to all.[81]

After the White Fathers made their presentation at the meeting, Dom Sebastião diplomatically declared his preference for a catechumenate of at least three years before putting to the vote the proposition for a four-year catechumenate (which he preferred). The first round of voting resulted in just less than half in favor of the proposition (with support from all White Fathers, some Jesuits and Franciscans, and one Capuchin). To salvage the proposition, the bishop then asked the prominent Franciscan Father Albano to decide on the issue in his capacity as the eldest father in Mozambique (with Dom Sebastião knowing that he favored the four-year rule). Reflecting on the fact that he himself used to teach the catechumenate for two years, having extended this to three years after the arrival of the White Fathers, Father Albano declared that he thought three years were sufficient. The bishop was disappointed and the local superior of the White Fathers subsequently (and privately) argued that Father Albano had lacked the courage to stand up to his congregation, which generally opposed the four-year catechumenate. In a final vote, the synod accepted the three-year rule, which became the new rule.[82]

The fourth and last element to mediate Catholic diversity in Beira, the bishop used his annual pastoral letters and his regular circular letters to the clergy. The pastoral letters were meant for all Catholics in the diocese and only one of their purposes, therefore, was to give orientation to the clergy. Dom Sebastião, however, considered these letters especially important. With few exceptions, he wrote one every year, and they were not only extensive but also well researched and carefully written (published in book form in 1994, they spanned no less than 1,100 pages).[83] While the letters often reflected the Vatican's view, the bishop also explicated his own views and leveled criticism at the social and political situation in the colony. Critical for the present discussion is the bishop's first pastoral letter titled "The Missionary Priest." The document spelled out what a good missionary was, what he should do and what he should avoid, what he should aim at, and what methods he ought to employ. The document also defined the relation between religious orders and the diocese and, more specifically, the relation between religious priests and their religious and diocesan superiors. It stated, for example: "As a religious, obey your religious superior, and as a priest or coadjutor, that is as a missionary, obey your bishop." Dom Sebastião cited the canons to prove that the views of the bishop should prevail in missionary matters if there were any differences between a religious superior and the bishop.[84] This addressed situations in the diocese such as when the Jesuit superior wrote a letter to Dom Sebastião in 1951 in which he posited that all questions of mission were questions of the religious order (by implication, thus, not of the diocese); he stipulated that all religious clergy had to ask for permission from their superiors before approaching the bishop on any subject.[85] So, while pastoral letters might have been contradicted in practice, the bishop used them to elucidate the guidelines for the clergy in his diocese.

One should not idealize Dom Sebastião's mediating measures. The bishop was particularly effective at mediating Catholic diversity and taking measures to move the diocese in the direction he wanted (for a comparison with subsequent bishops, see chapter 5). But at the same time, he only reached a form of "accommodation" with his measures. Religious orders and missionary individuals were quite effective at resisting any decisions and guidelines they did not like, as the example of the Jesuits' superior above illustrates. The issue of local languages serves as another example. Following the model of the White Fathers, which the bishop admired so much, all missionaries who arrived in Mozambique were required to spend their first six months learning a local language so they could work with Africans in their own languages. The 1956 regulation explicitly intended that missionaries had to make an effort to speak to Africans in their own local languages.[86] Yet, in practice, many missionaries did not do this and quite a few never learned any local language at all.[87] This had to do both with the personality and interests of each particular missionary as well as his or her ability to learn languages—most female missionaries did not learn any local language either. But it also had to do with the specific congregation in question and the way it ruled over its missionaries. Whereas the White Fathers tightly controlled this obligation among their men, this was not the case among the Franciscans, many of whom chose to ignore both the diocesan and their own congregation's rules without suffering any consequences.

To conclude, the Catholic Church in the Diocese of Beira was exceptionally diverse internally and the bishop of Beira was unusual—at least in the Portuguese colonial world—in the way he managed this diversity—that is, in the way he managed his diocese and his personnel. This uniqueness (both horizontal and hierarchical) of the church in central Mozambique permits us to see, in an exemplary fashion, how diversity plays out within the Roman Catholic institution (oscillating between congregations competing and collaborating) and how a certain type of episcopal leadership (inclusive and transformational) succeeded in managing internal diversity with few tensions or clashes (we will return to the issue of leadership styles in chapter 4). In turn, this internal diversity and the bishop's leadership style go a long way toward explaining what made the Diocese of Beira singular in Mozambique, if not beyond. The number and diversity of congregations active on its territory and the bishop's inclusive and transformational style contrasted with the usually less diverse and more autocratic dioceses in the rest of Mozambique. Thereafter we can say that the Diocese of Beira was in the minority in Mozambique, a kind of exception to the rule, something that on several occasions gave it a prophetic flavor or voice, as we will see in the coming chapters.

3

The Formation of an African Church

Up to the 1960s, most historical studies of Christianity in Africa focused on missions and missionaries.[1] In the 1960s and 1970s, a new generation of scholars critiqued this approach and demanded one that looks at religion from an African angle, by looking at African churches, African personnel, and African faith.[2] Missions came to be seen as external colonial institutions whereas African churches, personnel, and faith were considered genuine and more appropriate for understanding the development of Christianity in Africa. Today students of religion in Africa agree that the expansion and rooting of Christianity has two sides.[3] On the one hand is the missionary church and message, brought and "developed" by external powers and institutions—what I called the "imperial church" in chapter 2. On the other hand is the "local" (African) church and Christianity that was developed either by dissident churches or within the imperial church, thus by the people who converted to the church, reappropriated its message and structures, and went on to become the backbone and leaders of the new independent institution. These processes are not exclusive or even separate; the local Church developed historically at the juncture of the imperial and African processes—in a dialectical way.

Three dynamics are key to understanding the formation of the African Catholic institution in Mozambique. First, there is the conversion of men and women to Catholicism: who converted, where, how, and with what results? Since the present study covers a whole diocese, a macro approach is taken looking at statistics, analyzing them in detail, and trying to unpack trends across the region. Second, there is the issue of appropriation and reappropriation of the church and its message, which is also examined here at a macro level, to investigate whether the adoption of certain ideas and practices led to the formation of specific forms of Catholicism in Beira. Finally, there is the issue of the development of an African clergy, the education and formation of which took place in the local seminary. I look at these aspects in turn.

African Conversions

The statistics for the Diocese of Beira, which the bishop communicated to the state on an annual level and the latter reproduced in its official statistics until 1970, provide a clear picture of church growth after 1940. The number of baptisms grew slowly but steadily, from not quite 2,000 baptisms per year in 1943 to more than 4,000 in 1948, over 8,000 in 1960, to an eventual average of 10,000 baptisms per year after 1964—a fivefold increase in twenty years (see fig. 3.1). Conversion may have taken different forms and been variously invested in by Africans, but statistically the numbers increased steadily, so that Catholics constituted 9.7 percent of the total population by 1960 and 15.6 percent by 1974.[4]

Some may argue that official statistics are problematic because they may have been inflated or shaped by their authors to please the government or even to reinforce the bishop's yearly request for financial support from the state. It is therefore worth discussing how the Diocese of Beira collected its statistics. Annually, the bishop received figures from each mission station: according to diocesan regulations, each superior had to submit the numbers on his mission on a set form to the diocese three weeks after the end of the year.[5] Church officials at the diocese's secretariat in Beira

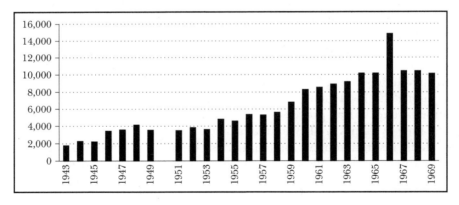

Figure 3.1. Baptisms in the provinces of Manica and Sofala and Tete, 1943–69. The year 1966 stands out, yet the reasons for this stark increase in baptisms are not clear. The only event I am able to identify that might have contributed to this is the introduction of the use of native languages in mass in May 1965, initially on an experimental basis. Source: *Anuário Estatístico da Província de Moçambique*, 1943–1969 (the yearbook for 1950 is missing).

compiled the lists and calculated the total overall figures for the diocese. The final figures were then sent to the Vatican, the nunciature, and the Portuguese administration for information. On his side the bishop used these figures to make decisions on the distribution of funds according to perceived necessities. Both the government and the Vatican received not only the condensed statistics but also the detailed figures for each mission station, including information on members, health posts, schools, baptisms, confessions, communions, weddings, and deaths. Based on these figures, the Catholic Church issued occasional statistical yearbooks—one was produced for the whole Portuguese Empire in 1960 and 1964, and one for Mozambique in 1974.[6]

Using these statistics and reading material about them from various archives (including diocesan and congregational archives and the bishop's papers), I have found no indication of an intentional distortion of the official figures. Figures are not always correct and elements do become lost, but the data seem to remain coherent over time (if shaped, of course, by the original questionnaire). I have therefore decided to accept the figures as they are, and examine them in detail and critically. The objective here is not to repeat the information already collected by the church, but to work with the figures to identify new elements, in this case variations between congregations and territorial units, and the social and religious dynamics at play. The aim of the analysis is to achieve a nuanced understanding of conversion in Beira and gain an idea of who converted, when, how, and maybe even why. This should help us to better understand the extent to which religious orders affected the matter of conversion and to uncover something of the social makeup of the African church in the Diocese of Beira.

Starting where we left off in chapter 2, I begin with a comparison of the conversion rates of the various religious congregations in Beira. The calculations are based on the year 1964, twenty years after Dom Sebastião Soares de Resende took control of the diocese and eight years after the last of the main congregations arrived in Beira.

The figures reveal a significant difference in the conversion rates between the congregations in Beira (see table 3.1). In 1964 the Jesuits and Franciscans had achieved two-digit rates of conversion, while the Picpus missionaries stood at half that rate, the Burgos missionaries only realized a third, and the White Fathers only one-tenth. While 12.9 percent of the population was converted in the Franciscan areas, only 1.9 percent of the population was converted in the areas under the control of the White Fathers. Such differences are substantial and may be surprising, because all missionaries worked under similar conditions, identical diocesan rules, and comparable financial

Table 3.1. Percentage of Catholics in the areas of operation of each congregation, 1964.

Congregation	Percentage of Catholics in area of operation
Franciscan	12.9
Jesuit	12.1
Picpus*	5.4
Burgos	3.0
White Fathers	1.4

*Marromeu passed from the Franciscans to the Picpus fathers in 1960, significantly raising the Picpus percentage. Their missions of Dondo and Cheringoma were at 2.4 percent and 4.7 percent in 1964 whereas Marromeu was at 8.4 percent.
Source: Figures calculated on the basis of data in Pedro, *Anuário católico do ultramar português 1964*.

means. Two factors can be cited to explain the differences. First, the bishop sent the Portuguese congregations to areas of old colonization and urban parishes, as he considered them to be more adequate at dealing with Portuguese settlers and the mestiço population. This explanation is relative, however, since the White Fathers and Picpus missionaries also worked in areas of old colonization, such as the Zambezi River basin, and urban parishes in the case of the Picpus. The second factor is each congregation's approach. Religious orders had different pastoral approaches and objectives, and this clearly shaped their rates of conversion. It is indeed no surprise that the highest rate of conversion is found in Franciscan areas since the latter baptized almost everyone. Conversely, the lowest rate of conversion is found in the areas under control of the White Fathers who had very exacting and challenging requirements for candidates wishing to convert.

Contrary to the hypothesis advanced by Pedro Ramos Brandão some years ago,[7] the figures reveal that there is no correlation between the political orientation of a religious congregation and the rate of conversion in the area in which it worked. "Progressive" congregations (pro-independence and/or adherers of liberation theology, like the White Fathers and the Burgos fathers) did not convert more Africans than conservative congregations (like the Franciscans or the Jesuits who were pro-Portugal and pro-empire on the colonial question). Indeed, the correlation is more strongly a negative one in that politically conservative missionaries converted many more people than the progressive ones. This strongly suggests that the conversion rates had little, if anything, to do with politics but were rather the result of the pastoral approach and aims adopted by each congregation: whereas the Franciscans tried to convert as many people as they could, the White Fathers strove to educate a small and committed Catholic elite.

If we further break down the conversion figures, by looking at rates within each district, a richer picture emerges, showing more complexity and revealing the role of Africans in their own conversion (see table 3.2). The figures show, first, larger differences between all districts, ranging from 0.4 percent Catholics among the Chemba population to 44.5 percent Catholics in Beira—more than a hundredfold difference between these two extreme cases. Second, while the figures confirm the distinctions between the congregations, they point to significant differences between

Table 3.2. Percentage of Catholics per congregation in each of the districts of the provinces of Manica and Sofala and Tete, 1964.

Congregation	District	Percentage of Catholics
Jesuits	Angonia	28.4
	Vila Coutinho	29.7
	Macanga	1.7
Franciscans	Manica	22.2
	Buzi	9.3
	Chimoio	20.4
	Mossurize	4.2
	Sofala	12.5
Picpus	Marromeu	8.4*
	Dondo	2.4
	Cheringoma	3.6
Burgos	Máguè	1.0
	Moatize	7.7
	Maravia	0.4
	Zumbo	2.2
White Fathers	Barué	2.2
	Gorongosa	1.1
	Chemba	0.4
	Sena	2.2
	Mutarara	1.1
Various	Tete	6.9
	Beira	44.5

*Marromeu passed from the Franciscans to the Picpus fathers in 1960.
Source: Figures calculated on the basis of Pedro, *Anuário católico do ultramar português 1964*.

the districts within the area worked by the same congregation. Such differences can be explained by demographics, number of missionary staff available, and the agency of Africans. I discuss each of these factors in turn.

The differences between the districts within the same congregation can be explained, first, by population density. Many high conversion rates are indeed found in areas with high population densities, such as in Angonia (28.4 percent Catholics in an area with a population density of 23.5 inhabitants per square kilometer) and Beira city (44.5 percent Catholics for an area with a population density of 273.4 inhabitants per square kilometer). The conventional explanation for this correlation between towns or cities and higher rates of conversion is that urbanization releases men and women from their traditional societies and obligations, leading to the development of new skills, new knowledge, and eventually individual choice.[8] While this argument works well for places like Beira, Moatize, and Angonia, it fails in relation to other cities. Tete had the second highest population density (63.5 inhabitants per square kilometer) at the time and yet boasted a low rate of Catholics (6.9 percent), though this may be a statistical mistake as it had 15.6 percent of Catholics in 1960, four years earlier); Dondo, with the fourth highest population density (at 12.3 inhabitants per square kilometer), had only 2.4 percent Catholics in its population. To be fair, in Beira the high proportion of white population (at 30 percent in 1964) probably contributed to the particularly high rate of Catholics in this district.[9] Nevertheless, the fact is that population density and urbanization seem to have played a role in the Diocese of Beira.

A second factor to explain rates of conversion is the number of missionaries and evangelists at work in a given area and population. Missionaries, evangelists, and teachers all had different roles in evangelization. Missionaries were the official face of the church, responsible for conducting all major ceremonies and baptisms; African evangelists and teachers, in turn, performed the actual dissemination of the Catholic faith to convince people to convert. In the Portuguese colonies evangelization occurred in particular at the schools, as the missionary accord had placed the majority of them into Catholic hands. Adding up all missionary staff (priests, sisters, brothers, evangelists, and teachers), I have calculated the numbers of Catholic actors involved in evangelization in relation to the population of each district. The ratios produced are not definitive, but do reveal some trends (see table 3.3). For example, the districts with the highest percentages of Catholics are usually the ones with the highest numbers of missionary staff. That is the case in Beira (with 502 individuals to be evangelized by each missionary staff), Chimoio (677), Manica (967), and Tete (709), all with rates of Catholics at or above 20 percent (except Tete, which is

Table 3.3. Percentage of Catholics to population density and to population per missionary, 1960–1964.

Congregation	District	Population density (inhabitants per km²), 1960	Population per missionary staff, 1960	Percentage of Catholics in 1964
Jesuits	Angonia	23.5	2.023	28.4
	Vila Coutinho	—*	—	29.7
	Macanga	2.6	2.766	1.7
Franciscans	Manica	3.5	967	22.2
	Buzi	11.6	1.594	9.3
	Chimoio	3.0	677	20.4
	Mossurize	6.3	2.850	4.2
	Sofala	3.1	1.518	12.5
Franciscans/ Picpus	Marromeu	5.8	1.037	8.4
Picpus	Dondo	12.3	3.833	2.4
	Cheringoma	2.4	2.751	3.6
Burgos	Máguè	**	1.711	1.0
	Moatize	3.7	1.592	7.7
	Maravia	1.2	1.492	0.4
	Zumbo	**	1.497	2.2
White Fathers	Barué	3.2	4.495	2.2
	Gorongosa	5.6	1.353	1.1
	Chemba	6.0	3.104	0.4
	Sena	**	1.864	2.2
	Mutarara	**	7.773	1.1
Various	Tete	63.5	709	6.9***
	Beira	273.5	502	44.5

*Vila Coutinho was excised from Angonia between 1960 and 1964.
**Information missing.
***The figure may be erroneous (because of a data error); in 1960 Tete had 15.6 percent Catholics, and it is doubtful that the percentage of Catholics went down (especially so significantly) in four years.
Source: Calculations made on the basis of Pedro, *Anuário católico do ultramar português 1960*; and Pedro, *Anuário católico do ultramar português 1964*.

probably a data error, as we noted). Conversely, the districts with the lowest percentage of Catholics tend to have the lowest number of missionary staff per inhabitant, for example, as in Baruè (4.495), Chemba (3.104), and Macanga (2.766), with rates of Catholics at 2.2 percent or below. Angonia stands as a counterexample with a low number of missionary staff, yet a high number of converts.

The last and probably most important factor to explain conversion is Africans agency. This factor is difficult to demonstrate statistically and in detail for a whole diocese. But two singular and particularly clear cases should convey the point for the whole diocese. In these cases an African society decided to convert (or refused to convert) *as a whole.* The first case is the district of Angonia, which had the second highest rate of Catholics in the population, at 28.4 percent. (The discussion of Angonia here includes Vila Coutinho insofar as the latter was separated from Angonia only just before 1964 and had a similar rate of Catholicism at 29.7 percent). The second case is Manica, with 22.2 percent Catholics in the population in 1964, the third highest in the diocese.

The Jesuits occupied Angonia in 1944, taking over the mission station of Lifidzi from a secular priest who had started it in 1900, and founding the mission station of Fonte Boa, which opened in 1945. No figures are available for the rate of Catholics for the area before 1940, but the records suggest that the conversion rate was high already. In 1941 the prelate of Mozambique noted that "the religious movement [activity] of this mission [Lifidzi] is extraordinary."[10] He added in 1942: "This is the mission with the highest religious movement in the whole colony."[11] And in 1943 he declared: "As I already said in my report last year, it is the best mission of the diocese and even of the colony. Some months ago, a French cleric, superior of the mission of Zana, told me it could be the best in Africa."[12] Interestingly, the overwhelming majority of the converts in Angonia were (and remain) Ngoni, about whom the prelate wrote the following in 1942: "There is in this race a religious mystic that brings the fast conversion of a region. Maybe this Angoni race is destined to a great future in the evangelization of the colony and the secret [of our success] would be to convert them and choose in their midst the apostles of their brothers."[13] In 1945 the new bishop of Beira, Dom Sebastião, wrote that he believed that *all* Ngoni would eventually be converted in Angonia.[14]

Success with the Ngoni contrasted with an almost total failure among the Chewa, who lived both in Angonia and in the neighboring district of Macanga where the proportion of Catholics was a mere 1.7 percent of the total population. Much has been made of the *nyau* secret society and the *chinamwali* female initiation rite as obstacles to evangelization among the Chewa.[15] But these "traditions" seem to have been more a means of resistance than cultural blockages, more a means of resistance against Ngoni domination than against Catholicism or colonialism. The cause of Chewa opposition to Catholicism seems indeed to have been based on the fact that the Ngoni had converted en masse. The Ngoni invaded this northwestern area of Mozambique in the late nineteenth century and came to dominate the Chewa politically as well as socially. Ngoni owned Chewa slaves right up to 1940 and occupied all posts of "traditional" chiefs that the Portuguese set up in the early twentieth century as part of their colonial administration.[16] The more the Ngoni converted, therefore, the more the Chewa rejected Catholicism. Ian Linden describes the same situation at a Catholic mission station in Malawi just across the border.[17] Ngoni alliances with the Catholic missionaries and the colonial state allowed them to perpetuate and consolidate their domination over the Chewa, substantially undermining Chewa institutions. The Ngoni called on the colonial state to help convert the Chewa, and when the administration was worried about the possible spread of the Kenyan Mau Mau movement into Mozambique in the 1950s, the Ngoni swiftly denounced Chewa institutions for being "subversive."[18] Unsurprisingly then, the successful adoption and appropriation of Christianity by the Ngoni led to a reciprocal rejection of the same by the Chewa.

The other example of mass conversion in the Diocese of Beira is in the district of Manica where the rate of Catholics in the population reached 22.2 percent in 1964. The presence of the church in the area went back to the sixteenth century and had seen the development of significant Christianities in the sixteenth and seventeenth centuries. The institution collapsed in the nineteenth century, however, as a result of the anticlerical policies of the Portuguese state and the invasion of the Ngoni during the Mfecane. The parish of Manica was reopened in the late nineteenth century thanks to the chartered Companhia de Moçambique, but the rate of conversion remained low for decades. It only began to pick up in the 1920s after the Franciscans took over the parish and the mission of Macequece (Manica), as a result of improving relations between church and state and after modern colonialism was firmly established in the area. The last anticolonial/precolonial revolt in the region, the Baruè rebellion, was crushed in 1917, and migration to the mines and plantations abroad increased markedly.[19] In 1924, the parish of Macequece was transformed into the mission of Jécua and the parish was transferred to the Manica town center. In 1934 the Jécua's superior noted that the Franciscans had visited the population intensively and had opened various schools: "At the beginning, schools were opened where it seemed we would have the best return; nowadays it is the natives themselves who ask us for schools."[20] The prelate of Mozambique, in turn, described the situation in Jécua mission in his report to the government in 1943 in the following terms: "Of all missions of this district [province of Manica and Sofala], the one that has the highest return is that of Macequece. Its old tradition, the disposition of its people and the unity of the missionaries working there are all reasons for such a flourishing."[21]

In 1955 Dombe mission was opened as the second mission in the Manica area. It fared modestly both before and after 1964. While Jécua mission had 9,440 Catholics by 1964 (73.2 percent of all the Catholics in the district), Dombe had a mere 1,500 (11.6 percent). While Dombe's late founding date might partially explain its low rate of conversion, it was also located in a Ndau area, and statistics show that all Ndau areas had low rates of Catholicism in spite of being evangelized by the same Franciscan congregation. Conversely, areas in the neighboring district of Chimoio, populated by Manica people, had high rates of conversion: the mission of Marera, for example, had 4,945 Catholics (no less than 38.7 percent of all Catholics in the district), more than the urban parish of Chimoio. At this point, it is not possible to offer any detailed explanation as to why this is the case, and I am wary about advancing a simple ethnic explanation. People did not convert because they were Manica or refused to convert because they were Ndau or Chiteve. But it seems probable that some social issue or historical event led one society to convert en masse and the other to be much less interested—possibly for reasons similar to those we saw in the Ngoni-Chewa conflict. Nevertheless, the general point is that Africans, and even whole African societies, had an important role in shaping the rate of conversion to Catholicism in Beira.

Statistics for 1974 confirm these dynamics. First and foremost, they show a consolidation of the areas with high conversion rates as opposed to those low rates. Several districts grew by only a few percentage points (Mossurize and Buzi, for example). Three areas, however, show signs of a significant increase between 1964 and 1974: Marromeu, Songo, and Tete city. All have to do primarily with a reorganization of Catholic administrative units however. The church divided, first, the area of the district of Tete into three units after 1964. Chioco and Marara, which were more rural in nature, became mission stations in their own right and saw lower conversion rates, while Tete city was reduced in size to contain only urban areas, which had higher rates of Catholicism. Second, the Songo mission was created in 1970 out of the district of Maravia, and its area was designed around the new town of Songo, which was experiencing massive investment and in-migration after the building of the Cahora Bassa dam started in 1969. Last, the Marromeu district of 1964 was reduced in size with the creation of the more rural mission of Chupanga out of Marromeu, making it smaller and more urban, hence more Catholic too. There, as in many other areas of the diocese, people also began in the early 1970s to migrate toward urban areas in search of places of safety as the liberation war expanded into their area. This consolidated Catholicism further in urban areas.

Comparing the maps of the conversion rates for 1964 and 1974 (see figs. 3.2 and 3.3), a final factor stands out. The visual representation of the figures reveals that the areas with the highest numbers of Catholics are zones of modern colonialism and transport corridors (such as the Beira corridor and the Tete corridor), and do not include areas of old colonization (such as the Zambezi Valley). This suggests that the urban argument could apply here too, with the development of a capitalist economy favoring individuation and the conversion to Christianity. While it would require extensive additional research to confirm this hypothesis, here we can simply recap the findings so far. First, we can note that the rate of conversion in the Diocese of Beira varied significantly across space and time. Several factors influenced this: a religious congregation's approach to evangelization and the missionary staff available, the population density and level of urbanization in the area, the incursion of modern capitalism into the area, and African choice. Second, the analysis of the statistics allows a first characterization of the makeup of the church of Beira before independence. Catholicism took root in areas of modern capitalist development, particularly strongly among the Ngoni of eastern Tete and the Manicas of Manica and Sofala province, and in the multiethnic cradles of the cities. Conversely, Catholicism remained numerically weak in the rural areas of western and southern Tete (particularly among the Chewa), in the north of Manica and Sofala province (in the territory of the White Fathers) as well as south of the Beira–Rhodesia corridor (among the Ndau).

African Christianities

In this section I push the subject further by examining which social groups the Catholic Church converted and what results the conversion of certain people *by certain congregations* might have had. While we saw demography and a social/ethnic dimension feature in the previous section, here I want to discuss the social makeup of Catholicism in the different areas of the diocese, how it was articulated by the various congregations, and whether this could have resulted in different forms of Catholicism. As stated in the previous section, it is difficult to be precise on such questions at the level of the whole diocese; yet focusing on the level of the congregation provides some insight and might allow an examination of the hypothesis that the faith articulated by the various congregations to different people led

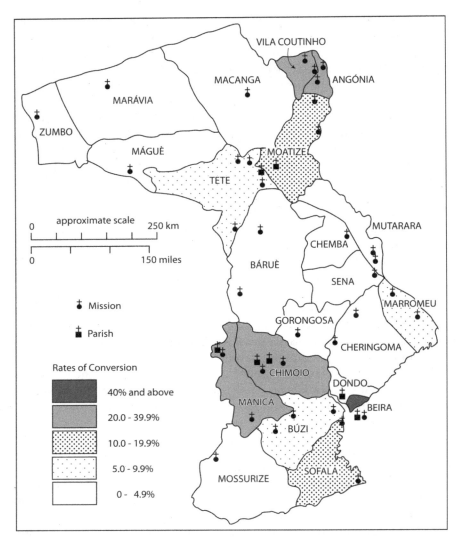

Figure 3.2. Rate of conversion in the Dioceses of Beira and Tete in 1964. Map by Maura Pringle. The divisions are the administrative units of the state (districts). At that stage, the diocese's territorial divisions followed strictly those of the state. The map is designed on the basis of data from Pedro, *Anuário católico do ultramar português 1964*.

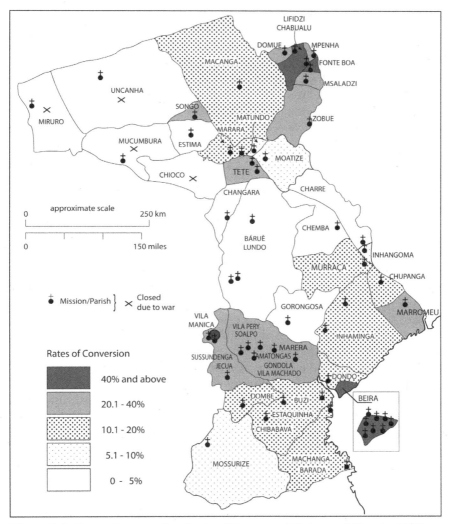

Figure 3.3. Rate of conversion in the Dioceses of Beira and Tete in 1974.
Map by Maura Pringle and Valérie Alfaurt. The divisions are the church's
units (parishes and missions), with a few exceptions where population
data were available only for a whole district (containing several parishes
or missions). The map is designed on the basis of data from Pinheiro, *Na
Entrega do Testemunho 1975.*

to different forms of Catholicism, thus allowing us to advance our understanding of the African church in central Mozambique.

Regarding social class, chapter 2 showed that the White Fathers and the
Jesuits aimed at training, if not creating, a new African elite. This was done
at the local level by fostering the creation of well-educated Catholic families and training the elite of the church at the Teachers' Training School
(Jesuits) and at the minor seminary (White Fathers).[22] Whether or not
these congregations converted many people is not relevant here. Rather,
what is significant is that both congregations shaped a small but influential
class of people, namely, a new African bourgeoisie. In contrast to the Jesuits and White Fathers, the Franciscans chose to convert polities en masse,
which indicates that they converted and shaped African peasants and farm-
ers rather than (or separately from) an elite (the Franciscans reopened
their minor seminary in 1960). The Burgos fathers were not interested
in elites as they worked in the remote countryside and among miners in
Moatize, Tete province, and among factory workers in Chomoio district, in
Manica and Sofala province. And lastly, the Picpus fathers worked mostly in
parishes and in urban settings, thus by implication mainly with an African
working or middle class. Such connections and influences are not straight-
forward since many congregations catered to different social classes at the
same time, in the same place or in different areas, and many Africans were
mobile, easily switching between the services of different religious congregations.[23] Still, the White Fathers and Jesuits invested much of their energy
in creating an elite while the Burgos fathers did not, nor did the Picpus
fathers until 1960. This cannot but have created connections; while they
may not have been fully thought through by the actors, they must have had
objective consequences.

I discuss the shaping of a particular elite in the next section and in
chapter 4. For now I want to explore whether particular Catholic "styles"
or forms of African Christianity developed in Beira. To understand this,
we need to return to the issue of the pastoral approaches of the Catholic
congregations. In chapter 2, I noted that the Franciscans had unexacting
criteria for baptism and required only a short catechumenate. They were
concerned in particular with people attending church services and practicing the rituals correctly. In contrast, the White Fathers were very demanding, requiring candidates to undergo a minimum of four years of teaching
before being considered for baptism. The reason for the White Fathers'
approach was the conception that the church needed "quality" rather than
"quantity": to them it was better to have a few well-educated Christians
rather than a mass of "nominal" Christians. Needless to say, "quality" is a
normative and relative term. In reality, what was at play were two different

understandings of what was expected from catechumens and from baptized Christians thereafter. From a sociotheological position, we can say that the White Fathers were concerned with *orthodoxy* (believing correctly) while the Franciscans focused on *orthopraxis* (correct practice).[24] The White Fathers were thus concerned primarily with how Catholics thought while the Franciscans emphasized Catholic behavior (baptism, the attendance of mass, and receiving of the sacraments).

This difference in approach—in addition to the distinction between converting few and converting many—suggests that different styles of Catholicism might have developed in Beira. With the baptism of large numbers of people and the promotion of orthopraxis, it is possible that the Franciscans fostered a form of folk Catholicism, an open, lived, and inclusive type of faith, flexible in terms of principles and focused on rituals.[25] In contrast, it is likely that the White Fathers promoted an elite and intellectual style of faith (a form of elite Catholicism), selective, demanding, and focused on orthodoxy, with the result that few people became and remained Catholic in their area.

The difference in approach between the White Fathers and the Franciscans is captured in writing of the missionaries at the time, with all its biased language. To start with, Father Charles Pollet of the White Fathers described his order's strict approach to the catechumenate to his superior general in Rome eight years after his arrival in Mozambique in the following terms: "We are becoming ever stricter regarding the entry to the catechumenate. There is more than one individual who has not been admitted despite 4 or 5 years of catechism."[26] Similarly, in 1950 the superior general of the White Fathers emphasized orthodoxy when he offered advice to a missionary in Vila Gouveia:

I hope you will slowly be able to make progress. Do it with prudence, and since they [candidates to baptism] are so superstitious, as you say, start well and insist at length on this. Yes, start by giving them an exact idea of the good God, of the commandments and the big Truths that relate to their life. I think you should insist on this in particular, so that they arrive almost by themselves at the conclusion that the dances of the spirits and fetish activities are condemned by our good God. It should be a conclusion and it seems to me that it would be better if they drew it by themselves, or rather that you helped them draw it, but that you did not start by telling them that these dances and fetish activities should be rejected.[27]

When the White Fathers took over the post of Magagade (the future mission station of Murraça) from the Franciscans in 1946, they commented as follows on the Franciscan emphasis of orthopraxis:

The catechism of the Franciscan fathers is found to be incomplete in various aspects: commandments, grace, perfect and imperfect contrition, baptism of desire. . . . We shall try to complete it as soon as possible, and establish the procedure to teach it. The [Franciscan] fathers of Chupanga had adopted the following method: when a schoolchild knew enough of the catechism off by heart, he went to the mission for one or two weeks to be prepared for baptism.[28]

In the same year, the White Fathers described the work by the Franciscans in the nearby Gorongosa district as severely lacking: "Little organization in the evangelizing work. The father superior confided humbly that mission work was not their domain and that they expected some lessons [help] from us!? There are no catechists, the teachers are few and of little quality. They have no other work but to make the catechumens learn the catechism off by heart. Apart from that, they have few evangelical preoccupations."[29]

Finally, the superior of the White Fathers in Mozambique described the inclusivity and flexibility of the Franciscan approach and focus on rituals in a general report dated to 1949:

The fathers could not always assist and instruct adults as they wished since their time was taken by the more or less centralized schools, the distance between schools was too great, and the territory to be missionized is immense. Hence, as the society was not prepared, many of those who came out of school easily fell back into ancestral habits or, coming of age, entered into marriage with pagan women as they could not find educated Christian women. . . . Catholics just baptize their children and sometime send them to learn the doctrine, lightly, just enough to get their first communion. Baptized Blacks and those who live near the mission generally all practice; those baptized who live farther away almost always come for the sacraments when the fathers visit the schools of their region.[30]

As illustrative as these passages may be, the question is whether the differences between orthodoxy and orthopraxis translated into different forms of Catholicism among believers. To find an answer, I conducted dozens of interviews with missionaries and believers in the Diocese of Beira and attended masses in Beira, Chimoio, Manica, and other places.[31] Yet the results of my investigation proved inconclusive. Most of the people I interviewed did not see much difference between congregations and reported that they easily switched from one to another when they traveled in the country or moved to live in a new area before independence. I was thus unable to find evidence that different religious orders led to different forms of Catholicism. The only difference between orders that the interviewees raised was about politics, specifically in relation to the liberation struggle. This aspect is not only vividly remembered but also of great significance in contemporary Mozambican politics. Often, it informs the ways in which people view the past and overrides other considerations.

Does this invalidate my hypothesis? For one, the distinctions I suspected are not easy to see or remember and it is possible that Catholics may not be eager to acknowledge differences between congregations. For another, a few people *did* see the differences I talked about. In an interview in 2009, the bishop of Beira stated, for example, that it was possible to recognize a difference between areas where the catechumenate had been long and areas where it had been short and relatively superficial, and that the former presented stronger Catholic communities today.[32] While the data and information collected are too inconclusive to positively validate my hypothesis, they still allow for a further characterization of Catholicism in central Mozambique. We can indeed say that there were low numbers of Catholics in the areas run by the White Fathers but that they developed small groups of believers who stood for a form of elite Catholicism. The Jesuits had areas of both high and of low conversion rates, and they trained an elite, particularly among the Ngoni, focused on orthodoxy. The Franciscans had areas of high and low conversion too, in which they developed a more folk type of Catholicism. The Picpus, in turn, achieved only a low rate of conversion and possibly started with a type of folk Catholicism but shifted to a more orthodox form in the 1960s. Finally, the areas of western Tete under the control of the Burgos fathers had a low number of believers with the possible presence of folk Catholicism.

African Clergy

By definition, the clergy in the Catholic Church is constituted by ordained men who belong to the ecclesiastical hierarchy and can administer the sacraments. Mozambique had numerous clerics after 1940, but they were all part of the imperial church since there were no African priests at first. This was against the teachings of various popes who called for the training of local clergies, notably in the 1919 *Maximum Illud* and the 1926 *Rerum Ecclesiae* encyclicals. The bishop of Beira saw the lack of African clergy as a serious problem from the start and understood the training of African men as the most important task of the church in Mozambique. In his second report to the Portuguese administration in 1944, Dom Sebastião called for the creation of a diocesan minor seminary, explaining: "The life of the church in Africa will only become normal when the priests are Africans."[33]

He passed this urgency on to his missionaries, notably in his diocesan regulations of 1956:

81   There is a grave obligation that falls, first, upon the bishops and, second, on the missionaries, the faithful and even the unfaithful: to educate a native diocesan clergy.

82   Missionaries should lose no opportunity to talk of the priestly vocation, whether in public preaching or in private colloquia, and to push in that direction any school learners and boarders who show an intellectual and moral capacity for priestly life from a young age. No missionary should regard himself released from this duty until a few students from his parish or mission are enrolled at the seminary.[34]

Not a man to wait, in 1946 the bishop asked the state for land to build a diocesan seminary. He received a piece of land in Zobuè, in northern Tete province bordering Nyassaland, and began the construction. Upon completion of the first phase in 1949, the White Fathers took over the seminary with a first batch of thirty-two students as well as responsibility for the final phase of construction. The bishop officially opened the Zobuè Seminary on September 15, 1950, a minor seminary at secondary school level (see fig. 3.4).[35]

Figure 3.4. Seminary of Zobuè, n.d. Courtesy of Father Mollina Mollina.

As we saw earlier, a minor seminary for local clergy existed in central Mozambique when Dom Sebastião took power in 1943. Yet this seminary was not diocesan in nature but Franciscan. Founded in 1935, it was located in Amatongas (on the road going from Beira to Rhodesia), and by 1944, it had about twenty students. Dom Sebastião was quite critical of the seminary after his first visit in 1944, because it was not isolated enough (as seminaries should be, he argued) and because it risked benefiting the Franciscan congregation rather than the diocese:

> The house is not good for a seminary because the road [that passes by] has undone everything. Nowadays it is not an isolated mission anymore as it should be for a seminary. . . . There are approximately 20 seminarians. Two are in the fifth year, and none in the fourth and second years. I interviewed one about vocation and was satisfied with his answers as well as those from the younger one. It is to be feared that such a seminary will benefit the Franciscan fathers and not the Diocese of Beira.[36]

Based on the argument that Amatongas was not delivering sufficient graduates (it had not yet produced any graduate) and had inadequate conditions, the bishop refused his support, leading to its closure by the Franciscans in 1944.[37] The closure of Amatongas left the bishop of Beira with a clean slate to run his diocesan seminary, especially since the archbishop of Lourenço Marques also refused to give permission for a Franciscan seminary in his diocese. From then on, the Franciscans sent their candidates to Zobuè, as all other congregations did.

A group of thirty-two students began classes at Zobuè in the 1950–51 academic year. The bishop had asked all mission stations to send two students each, but this proved difficult. So mission stations did not send only younger students, but also older ones who had worked as catechists for several years already. Most students were Africans, with a few mestiços. Only twenty-eight students remained by the end of the first year, of which 41 percent failed their exams (see table 3.4). The course at the seminary lasted five years (soon increased to six), starting with a propaedeutic (preparatory) year. The syllabus corresponded to the first two years of the *liceu* (a secondary school such as the one for white children in Beira run by the Marist brothers), with a stronger focus on Latin and Portuguese.[38] After they finished their degree, the graduates were sent to the Major Seminary of Namaacha in southern Mozambique (opened in 1949 and run by the Dutch Blessed Sacrament fathers), where they studied philosophy and theology for another six years before they could be ordained.[39]

The White Fathers ran the diocesan seminary of Zobuè and this gave it a particular orientation. In-line with the society's principles and culture, it

Table 3.4. List of the first seminarians at Zobuè, 1950–1951.

Name	Sending mission post	Failed?
First grade, preseminary (4 students)		
Franco Azita	Mugeba	F
João Boror	Mualama	
Manueli Osman	Barué	
Valierano Sabonete	Mugeba	F
Second grade, preseminary (12 students)		
Eduardo Baixo	Namacurra	
Simão Benjamin	Macequece	
Antonio Chapo	Chemba	F
Vincente Damasc.	Coalane	F
António Disse	Lifidzi	
Tarcisio João	Alto Molocué	
José Malua	Mugeba	F
Pedro Mário	Alto Molocué	
António Mouzinho	Boroma	
Nuno Nhampanga	Marara	
Vincente Paulo	Boroma	F
António Santos	Ilé	F
Alberto Thonja	Lifidzi	
Tome Viagem	Mutarara	F
Third class (first-year Latin) (10 students)		
Gabriel António	Mossurize	F
José Costa	Alto Molocué	
João Domingos	Vila Pery	
Almeida Haussen	Vila Pery	
Agostinho José	Coalane	F
Manuel Makaulo [Mucauro]	Sofala	
Ciro Malunga	Boroma	
Alfred Morais	Namacurra	F
Mateus Pinho [Gwenjere]	Murraça	
Luis Ruben	Nauela	F

Source: Father Th. Prein, "Seminário Episcopal de Zobuè, Ano Lectivo 1950–51," July 2, 1951, Folder "Missões de Tete, 1949–51," Arquivo da Diocese de Beira, Beira, Mozambique.

operated as a "total institution," where every aspect of life was organized and controlled. The students not only lived at the seminary but also spent most of their holidays there; they went home only once every three years.[40] The seminary operated as a closed society, with its own rules and ritualism, and much discipline. The aim was to educate and discipline students so that they developed and fully internalized the Catholic faith and culture.

An annual students' retreat in 1952 discussed two themes that are relevant in this respect: "to stimulate in the spirit and heart of students the love of a life heightened and made larger by the ideals of priesthood; and to push students to feel the beauty of the highest virtues in life: sincerity, straightforwardness, open-heartedness, simplicity, and love of the work done for the devotion of God only."[41]

The students' daily life was tightly regulated. Each day started at 5:30 a.m. with a swim at a small dam close to the seminary, running and gymnastics. Mass took place at 7:00 a.m., followed by breakfast, and classes started at 8:00 a.m. They broke for lunch at noon and a rest period. A second set of classes from 2:00 p.m. to 4:00 p.m. focused on music, gardening, or other similar activities. At 6:00 p.m. the bell rang for the orations (prayers at mass), followed by dinner, evening studies, and bedtime at 8:00 p.m.[42] The timetable was infused with religious practice. Apart from morning and evening mass, students attended a daily spiritual reading of thirty minutes and there was another fifteen minutes of meditation in the morning. Four times a week students attended catechism classes and went to confession. They also attended a yearly retreat.[43]

Control was important at the Zobuè Seminary. The priests limited and closely supervised all contacts with the exterior. Postal correspondence was under strict censorship. The bishop asked the superior to intercept "all correspondence, wherever it comes from, which tends to divert seminarians from their diocesan priestly life toward secular careers or toward other congregations or religious orders. Absolutely no manuscript of this type should reach the hands of the seminarians."[44] Just as interestingly, the White Fathers created a system of age groups, with a leader for each group, and they established a "traditional tribunal" run by the seminarians themselves, headed by a student-magistrate and two assistants. Every Wednesday, the tribunal sat to judge those who had broken the seminary's regulations. Priests did not attend the tribunals, but the superior kept a close watch to make sure things ran fairly and smoothly.[45] In his annual report of 1952, the superior explained that the aim of this initiative was to have students "take responsibility, and in this way foster a spirit of initiative and of self-government."[46] Another aim was to promote good relations between students who belonged to groups "differentiated by language and even by certain customs." This organization, grounded in values of self-reliance, autonomy, and tradition, was typical of and possibly unique to the White Fathers and contrasted with the approach of Portuguese missionaries and administration who aimed to assimilate Africans into Portuguese culture.

The way in which the White Fathers ran the Zobuè Seminary and educated seminarians produced a particular outlook among their students, and eventually shaped a particular African Catholic elite in central Mozambique—by 1968, 826 students had already passed through the seminary.[47] For one, Zobuè's seminarians held a deep Catholic faith, with a strong focus on orthodoxy. For another, their faith was deemed compatible with African traditions. The White Fathers appreciated the importance of the African heritage, some elements of which they thought should be kept to better convert and Christianize Africans. The seminary not only recognized and celebrated the students' traditions and differences but also used them for the "good" of the students and their faith. A consequence was that students often developed a deep appreciation of their own culture and were proud Africans. This stood in stark contrast to other seminaries and the majority of other congregations, which demanded that Africans reject their own traditions when converting to the Catholic faith and Portuguese culture, the two being seen as one and the same. For these missionaries, assimilation was vital. A consequence of this was that when African nationalists rejected colonial Portuguese culture, they tended to reject the Catholic faith with it. In contrast, Zobuè seminarians accepted and celebrated African traditions and recognized Catholicism as compatible with African nationalism. They could become nationalist and remain strongly Catholic. On the other hand, they tended not to support socialism or communism, which the Vatican and the White Fathers opposed strongly and officially. These three elements—Catholic faith, African pride, and anticommunism—can be summarized as part of a liberal or conservative nationalist outlook. They were to become a major bone of contention between nationalists in the 1960s, as we will see in chapter 4.

In comparison with neighboring countries, the opening of the minor seminary of Zobuè (and the Major Seminary of Namaacha) came very late (in 1950 and 1949, respectively); in contrast, in South Africa the first minor seminary opened in 1924 and the first major one in 1929.[48] The ordination of African priests in Mozambique thus came even later. With one single exception, the first ordinations only took place in the late 1950s.[49] In comparison, by 1957 Uganda already had 184 African priests while Tanzania had 186, Malawi 34, Zambia 27, and Kenya 26.[50] The reason for late ordinations in Mozambique has much to do with the history of the Catholic Church in Portugal and Mozambique and its conflictual relationship with the state in the preceding one hundred years. The first students from Zobuè proceeded to the Major Seminary in Namaacha in 1955 and the first African priests from central Mozambique professed their final vows from 1962. It is necessary to note here that the dropout rate at Mozambican seminaries was not a factor in the late ordination of Africans. The rate was certainly high, but this was the case across all seminaries in

Africa. At the time, the White Fathers calculated that their diocesan seminaries in Africa produced on average only 1.5 priests per hundred students.[51] Novices died of accidents or disease (this was the case in 1953 with a seminarian who should have become the first African priest of Beira);[52] they left the seminary because they did not like it; they discovered they did not have a vocation after all; they failed their exams; or they were expelled for being deemed inadequate, undisciplined, or because they had committed a "sin."

Eventually, seven African priests were ordained in Beira and Tete before independence—Tete became an independent diocese in 1962 only, hence I consider it here for consistency. The priests in Manica and Sofala were the Franciscan Francisco Pinho Pereira, ordained in 1962 (in Portugal), and the diocesan priests Mateus Pinho Gwenjere and Samuel Abudo Mucauro, ordained in 1964, and Jaime Pedro Gonçalves, ordained in 1967. In Tete, both religious and secular priests were ordained: the Jesuits João de Deus Kamtedza in 1964 and Domingos Isaac Mlauzi in 1966, and the diocesan priest Domingos Ferrão in 1966. After their ordination, these priests were assigned to a mission or parish in central Mozambique. Pereira went to work at Amatongas, Mucauro in Gorongosa, Gwenjere in Murraça, Mlauzi in Lifidzi, Gonçalves in Beira, and Ferrão in the city of Tete while João de Deus was sent to Portugal for further studies—he returned before independence to become the superior of the mission of Fonte Boa.

Life as an African priest in a colonial society was complicated, and the war of liberation, which began in 1964, made it even more difficult. Priests were monitored both by the state and their own congregations or bishop. Most African priests had some connection, if only through old friendships, with African nationalists. Some developed more substantial ties, such as Father Ferrão who went on to help some parishioners join the Frente de Libertação de Moçambique (Mozambique Liberation Front, Frelimo), the main nationalist movement, in exile.[53] He was jailed for this in April 1968. According to documents in the archive of the colonial state's security police, the Polícia Internacional e de Defesa do Estado (PIDE), he was imprisoned only because his bishop distrusted him and refused to send him to Portugal in order to avoid jail; the bishop of Tete was politically very conservative, as we will see in chapters 4 and 5.[54] When Ferrão returned to his mission work in Tete after serving five months in prison, he was placed under increased surveillance by both PIDE and the bishop. He remained in Tete until independence and continued with some clandestine nationalist activities, most importantly secretly documenting the Wiryiamu Massacre in the Tete countryside in 1973. The revelation of this massacre in British newspapers in July 1973 (based on Ferrão's evidence) created an international scandal that shook the traditional alliance between the United Kingdom and Portugal.[55]

More serious yet was the case of Father Mateus Gwenjere. He was very pro-Portuguese when he studied at the Zobuè and Namaacha seminaries. Once appointed as deacon in Murraça, however, he came under the influence of Father Charles Pollet and witnessed the daily humiliation of Africans by settlers, and became passionately nationalist. He began to write to his bishop asking for his intervention in favor of grieving Africans; confronted the local administration (for which he received a suspended jail sentence); and helped youngsters flee to join Frelimo in exile. PIDE closely followed the activities of Father Pollet and increasingly worried about his influence on Father Gwenjere. In a confidential note in 1965, Sub-Inspector Lontrão remarked: "The African priest Mateus Pinho Guengere of the mission of Murraça, who was wholly on our side when I arrived here, has changed significantly in recent times, even making public statements that clearly show his transformation and the fact that he is being skillfully worked by the superior of the mission, Father Pollet."[56]

In contrast to the bishop of Tete, however, Dom Sebastião protected Father Pollet and Father Gwenjere from the security police, going as far as writing to the governor-general and to President Salazar in Portugal to prevent the former's expulsion in 1965.[57] Both priests remained under close surveillance, but the security police took no further action against them thereafter. After Dom Sebastião passed away in January 1967, PIDE seized the opportunity and closed in on the two priests. It expelled Pollet from Mozambique in June 1967, and opened a formal case against Gwenjere. When the vicar-general of the diocese informed Gwenjere in July that he would be transferred to a parish in Beira city, the priest saw the writing on the wall and decided to flee across the border and join the liberation movement in exile.[58]

Africans training to be priests became embroiled in politics too. As we will see in chapter 4, the Major Seminary of Namaacha faced a significant crisis in relation to politics between 1961 and 1964, leading to the loss of many students. In 1963, the state and the archbishop of Lourenço Marques agreed to withdraw the Dutch Blessed Sacrament fathers from the seminary and to hand it over to a more trustworthy Portuguese congregation.[59] A similar crisis took place at the seminary of Zobuè three years later. After Dom Sebastião's death, the bishop of Tete and the state agreed to take the seminary away from the non-Portuguese White Fathers and hand it over to the Portuguese Jesuits. While only a few students had left the seminary due to nationalist considerations before then, in the second half of 1967 the new Jesuit rules, Portuguese nationalism, and the church's decision to "root out" politics from the seminary led a majority of students to leave the seminary, most fleeing into exile to join Frelimo.[60] The crisis eventually settled, but student numbers at Zobuè never recovered: the seminary was still only half-full by the time of independence. Facing the loss of actual and potential African priests, the Diocese of Beira went on the defensive and decided to send its two remaining African priests abroad. In 1968 Father Mucauro was sent to Rome to study theology and pedagogy, and the following year Father Jaime Gonçalves was sent to Canada for a short course in social leadership followed by studies in theology and social sciences in Italy. After concluding his courses in 1970, Father Mucauro went on to study medicine, something that kept him in Italy until 1979 (four years after independence). Father Gonçalves finished his studies in Italy in 1975 and returned to Beira a month after independence to become the vicar-general of the Diocese of Beira. Soon thereafter he was appointed coadjutor bishop in the diocese, with a right to succession.

Whereas only seven priests were ordained before independence, a few more were ordained during the transition and immediately after independence. The Franciscans contributed two priests whom they trained at their new seminary, opened in 1960. As we noted earlier, after the seminary of Zobuè started to run at full capacity, Dom Sebastião acceded to the Franciscans' request to reopen a religious seminary in central Mozambique. The Franciscan seminary opened in September 1960 in Amatongas, on the site of the old seminary, with twenty students. In 1967 it had ninety-two students and the congregation decided to move it to Vila Pery where they built new facilities. In 1973 the seminary was run by the first African priest of Mozambique, Frei Alexandre José Maria dos Santos (future cardinal of Maputo, after independence) who became the first African running a seminary in Mozambique. Out of this seminary were ordained Frei Guilherme da Costa, in 1975, and Frei José Macieira Wassiquete Muconde, in 1976.[61]

Finally, while not legally part of the Catholic clergy, religious sisters are a major element of the Roman Catholic institution nonetheless. The training of African Catholic sisters is, therefore, very important when looking at the formation of an African church. In Mozambique, the training of African sisters began late, as did the training of African priests. Some congregations in Beira, such as the Franciscan Missionaries of the Mother of the Divine Shepherd, did not even train African sisters before independence.[62] This said, the opening of novitiates for African sisters began in the 1950s. The first novitiate seems to have been that of the Franciscan Missionaries of Mary, which opened in 1949 in Namaacha (southern Mozambique) and received its first African postulants in 1951.[63] The Franciscan Sisters of Calais opened a novitiate in Vila Pery in 1967 with four trainees. The first African sister to take her vows was in 1968; by 1974 the congregation had ordained fifteen African sisters.[64] The Cluny sisters, in turn, had eight Mozambican sisters at independence.[65]

4

Gathering Storm

Vatican II Meets African Nationalism

The year 1958 is a turning point, in Mozambique, in Portugal, and internationally. The Non-Aligned Movement, formed in 1956 as an association of countries attempting to stand outside the power fields of the Cold War, brought the case of the Portuguese colonies to the attention of the General Assembly of the United Nations for the first time in 1957. In the following years, various African countries (some of them neighbors of Mozambique) were granted independence while, for a short while, the US government dropped its policy of supporting Portugal's colonial rule. Within Portugal, profound changes were taking place too. When an opposition candidate gained unprecedented support in the 1958 presidential elections, Salazar manipulated the polls to stay in power, strongly undermining his legitimacy. The regime was shaken and felt under pressure to introduce social, political, and religious reforms to respond to both these internal and external challenges. In Mozambique's neighboring territories, African nationalist movements began emerging in the late 1950s; by the mid-1960s they had entered into armed struggles. Finally, in the religious sphere, major changes came when the College of Cardinals in the Vatican elected John XXIII to succeed the late Pope Pius XII in 1958. Within a year, Pope John announced the holding of the Second Ecumenical Council of the Vatican (Vatican II) to examine the position of the Catholic Church in the modern world. The council opened in 1962 and lasted until late 1965, unleashing a new dynamic in the Catholic world.

This chapter and chapter 5 examine in detail how these significant changes affected the politics of the Catholic Church and its constituent parts in Mozambique, this chapter focusing on the years from 1958 to 1969 and chapter 5 looking at the period 1967–74. This chapter examines in detail how the religious orders in Mozambique and the bishop of Beira related to the developments of Vatican II, how African nationalism developed in central Mozambique, and how the church in the Diocese of Beira and in Mozambique more generally reacted to the rise of African nationalism. The aim is to understand how nationalism and Vatican II affected the church, and how, in turn, the religious orders and the bishop of Beira positioned themselves in relation to the tectonic changes unfolding in their territory and in the church. The coming pages do not try to find a top-down or bottom-up explanation, but look at change through the prism of religious orders on the assumption that an understanding of the orientation of each part and its relation to the hierarchy allows a more efficient grasp of the position of the church as a whole.

Note that while the Diocese of Tete was created out of the Diocese of Beira in 1962 (upon which Beira became an archdiocese), this and chapter 5 include Tete diocese in their considerations for reasons of coherence and comparability.

Vatican II Comes to Beira

After a period of strong antimodernism and neo-Thomism, the Second World War unleashed new ideas and debates in Catholic theology. Until then, the dominant missiological model had aimed at changing people's faith and culture—Christianization and civilization through colonization. After 1945, new ideas asserted that "paganism" and "idolatry" contained elements of truth that should not only be respected but valued and promoted. The idea was that one needed to preserve the customs that ensured the cohesion of (African) families and societies: one thus needed to "Christianize tradition" rather than substitute African traditions with a foreign culture. The most famous proponents of this view were Father Pierre Charles, in writings between the 1930s and the 1950s, and Father Placide Tempels, whose thoughts led to heated debates into the 1950s.[1] The Vatican adopted a position in favor of local cultures as early as 1939, not least with the Encyclical *Summi Pontificatus*, but according to Claude Prudhomme the Vatican's position was rather vague at the beginning and left much leeway to missionaries on the ground.[2] Portugal was not immune to the influences of these new missiological currents. Some of Charles Pierre's writings were made available in Portuguese early on. His 1923 work *The Prayer for All Things* was translated into Portuguese in 1934 and, interestingly, Dom Sebastião Soares de Resende, the bishop of Beira, wrote a preface for the fourth Portuguese version of the volume in 1957.[3]

These new theological currents were resisted by many in Portugal and its colonies. But some tried to find a compromise. For example, in the early 1960s, the leading Portuguese missiologist António da Silva Rego developed an approach that aimed at being intermediate between what he called the missionary method of "assimilation" and that of "adaptation" (i.e., assimilation into Portuguese culture vs. adaptation to local cultures). In a treatise dated 1962, he explained:

> As we only have to deal with Portuguese overseas territory, there is no difficulty in unifying the two concepts—missionary adaptation and integrating assimilation—into a single one: assimilation-adaptation. In the first place it is assimilation, true to the traditional Portuguese policy. In the second place it is adaptation, forming a new culture that fits the human and physical environment. And the concept of integration, within which everything, absolutely everything, takes roots, also fits in this concept of assimilation-adaptation.[4]

While sectors of the Portuguese church might have been sensitive to such compromise (if they were open to a new missiology at all), most foreign missionaries were influenced directly by the new theology.

The Second Ecumenical Council of the Vatican, called for in January 1959, unfolded in four sessions in Rome between October 1962 and December 1965. The gathering brought together thousands of cardinals, bishops, and theologians as well as some laymen and laywomen to discuss and decide on the future of the church. The overall process has been described using the term "aggiornamento" (update) to capture the council's aim of bringing the church's doctrine, practice, and identity up to date. It brought about three general changes in particular: a strategic option for ecumenism; an increased role for the laity and episcopal collegiality; and a reform of the liturgy.[5] Of note here is that the council also discussed and legislated on religious men and women. The key element here was the relation between religious orders and the Catholic hierarchy. Several bishops wanted to reduce the existing duality of power and called for a reduction in power of the religious congregations.[6] Some of the changes approved by the council had been in the making since the 1950s, such as the increased role of the laity in the church, for which a congress had been held in 1958 and participated in by the bishop of Beira. Similarly, the reform of the liturgy (which included the abandonment of Latin as the language for mass) built on earlier changes in theology, not least in relation to local cultures (such as that called for by Father Charles). Whether they were wholly new changes or the officialization of new currents already under way before the council, the fact is that transformation came with

Vatican II and that new theological currents were able to emerge and blossom on that basis. This was most remarkably the case with liberation theology, a synthesis of Christian theology and Marxism, which would reach Mozambique and the Diocese of Beira in the late 1960s.

The reforms of Vatican II first began to manifest themselves in Mozambique in 1963 with the start of yearly Missionary Weeks, to train missionaries, launched under the authority of a few bishops (later under the authority of the whole episcopal conference).[7] The first week was held in Quelimane and took a classical approach by focusing on "missionary spirituality" and "the catechumenate." While the content was classical, however, the attempt to train missionaries at the national level was very new. A second step was taken in 1966 when a small group of Portuguese secular priests arrived in Mozambique to spread the Movement for a Better World, an international movement launched in Rome in 1952 in response to Pope Pius XII's appeal for renewal. The group offered training called "Exercises for a Better World" that dealt with change, dialogue, and secularization. It toured the territory under the direction of Manuel Vieira Pinto, the future bishop of Nampula and Apostolic administrator of Beira.[8] A third step came in 1968 when priests launched annual Pastoral Weeks for the clergy. In contrast to the missionary weeks, the pastoral weeks moved around the country, with a delegation (composed of men from different congregations) offering training in each diocese. The aim was to update and train both male and female missionaries. The only diocese in which the courses were not allowed was Lourenço Marques, where the conservative archbishop would not permit them.[9] Finally, from 1968 onward a series of catechetic centers were set up across Mozambique to train laymen and laywomen.[10] The first center (called Nazaré) was opened at Inhamuiza near Beira and included a Center for Pastoral Investigation, where research was conducted and published on African cultures so as to better "inculturate" the church.[11]

Religious orders in central Mozambique responded in various ways to Vatican II and its developments. Officially the church was united behind the new central directions and instructions emanating from the Vatican and being pushed by most local bishops. On the ground, however, things were more complicated and not all congregations engaged with the renewals to the same degree and in the same way. While the White Fathers were most active in taking up and integrating Vatican II, the Franciscans do not seem to have been very interested, if they did not actually resist the changes. The White Fathers were most active in the missionary and pastoral weeks and one of their members was the first director of the catechetic center at Inhamuiza. In contrast, only two Franciscans seem to have been sensitive to the winds of change coming from Rome—both from the younger generation of missionaries. While these two men were not supported by their congregations, they were still given permission to get involved, and they became very active, taking part in the traveling delegation of the pastoral weeks.[12] Among Jesuits, Vatican II divided the society, with younger members more inclined to follow the new teachings. For a while they faced internal opposition, but this changed in 1967 when a new, open-minded superior was nominated and gave them support.[13] Nationality played a significant role in determining whether a missionary supported or doubted the *aggiornamento*, with Portuguese religious staff generally being less interested and foreigners generally supporting Vatican II. Only a few Portuguese members of the clergy actively supported Vatican II, with one of them leading the Movement for a Better World in Mozambique.

Dom Sebastião himself was strongly in favor of Vatican II. He was a "modernist" who liked change and who, tellingly, appreciated modern architecture and had a very modern palace built for the diocese (see fig. 4.1). He had been in favor of reform for many years, attending the Laity Congress in 1958 and favoring "adaptation" (what would come to be known as "inculturation" after independence). A citation from his diary for 1963 illustrates his position in relation to culture:

Figure 4.1. New bishop's palace, Diocese of Beira, 1961. Reproduced by permission from Arquivo Histórico de Moçambique (Historical Archive of Mozambique), Maputo.

I said mass, I preached and I confirmed during a service that basically took up all the morning. The church was packed. There was a new note, an African drum instead of the harmonium. It is noisy and shocking, but for them it is attractive. One has to adopt what is theirs, since it is for God through them. It has always been like this in everything. Since using the drum, the people sing with more enthusiasm and even pagans want to come and listen to everything.[14]

The bishop's attitude led him not just to support Vatican II, but to attend all sessions in Rome in person and to actively contribute to the event. Dom Sebastião was the Portuguese bishop who contributed most to the council, raising almost 30 percent of all Portuguese interventions. His contributions were from Africa and fed back into Africa. Throughout the council, Dom Sebastião wrote several chronicles for each session that he published in his newspaper, the *Diário de Moçambique*.[15]

The Vatican II reforms had two significant effects in central Mozambique. First, they introduced a new dynamic in the institution, which affected the bishop, the congregations, the missionaries, the laity, and the believers. Among Portuguese congregations, the council influenced young priests, creating new lines of tension and fractures within the Jesuit and Franciscan congregations and leading to some new alignments between congregations, as we will see later. Second, the council made the church more sensitive and favorable to African cultures. This began as an issue of Catholic adaptation, but some priests drew additional conclusions in religious, social, and political matters. In its most radical development, Vatican II allowed the blossoming of liberation theology, which developed in Beira among the Burgos fathers. Less dramatically, the bishop and an ever-larger number of religious men and women began to appreciate African cultures and to approve of the Africanization of the church—just as the first African priests were ordained and African nationalism began to arise. This fostered a new sense of ownership of the church among Catholic believers as well as a new sense of cultural pride. Articulated toward a Catholicism organized "nationally" (the Episcopal Conference of Mozambique was created in 1967), this new cultural pride fed into the imagination of a particular national community in central Mozambique.

The Rise of African Nationalism

After the Second World War (during which Portugal remained neutral), authoritarian regimes and colonialism lost much legitimacy as liberalism and anticolonialism became the dominant political ideologies internationally. The regime of the Estado Novo therefore had to adapt and reform. It changed the constitutional makeup of the colonies, transforming them into overseas territories (1951), and launched major developmental plans (1953). Lisbon legislated the free circulation of people and capital between the metropole and the colonies, and strengthened the union of colonial and metropolitan markets, which stimulated industrialization. New white settlements were created and the number of whites in Mozambique increased rapidly, eventually reaching 205,000 individuals in 1970 (of a total population of 9.5 million).[16] Internationally, these colonial reforms met with the approval of Portugal's Western allies. Although Portugal's policies increasingly diverged from those of the other colonial powers, in particular in relation to forced labor and decolonization, the Salazar regime maintained solid alliances in the United Nations and in Europe—indeed, Portugal was a founding member of the North Atlantic Treaty Organization (NATO) in 1949.[17]

In Mozambique, these reforms to modernize colonialism had contradictory effects. On the one hand, the opening of the colonies to the free movement of capital from the metropole led to industrialization and economic growth. In Beira, a number of factories were built while mining developed, in particular in the province of Tete. Similarly, the free movement of people led to a rise in immigration from Portugal and made a significant labor contribution to the development of new industries. On the other hand, while the African population was growing rapidly during this period (see table 4.1), the benefits of this economic development were primarily channeled toward the white settler population, while forced labor and forced cultivation of cotton and rice continued.[18] The assimilation process (to achieve the status of *assimilado*, which granted exemption from forced labor and cultivation, among others) was so taxing that only an infinitesimal minority of Africans managed to gain that status. Education for Africans was limited to an "adaptation" level and three years of primary school. The "fourth grade," which anyone wishing to achieve assimilado

Table 4.1. Population growth, 1940–1960.

Year	Manica and Sofala	Tete	Total Mozambique
1940	462,944	412,582	5,085,630
1950	610,562	438,678	5,738,911
1960	781,070	470,100	6,578,604

Source: *Anuário Estatístico 1964*, 30.

status was required to attend, was limited to settlers and mestiço children before the 1960s, so that in the 1950s, religious seminaries and teacher's training were the only channel for Africans to gain that level of education and assimilado status.[19]

Portugal reformed its colonial policy further when the wars of liberation began in the region. In 1956, it ratified the international Forced Labor Convention and thus put an official end to forced work and cultivation.[20] In 1961, it scrapped the *indigenato* (native) legal status and a year later replaced it with a rural labor code that aligned Portugal with United Nations labor policies. While this meant that forced labor no longer had a legal basis, the practice of racial discrimination continued, not least in the persistence of the distinction between the "traditional" legal system and officially recorded Portuguese legislation.[21] In relation to education, new laws had the unintended effect of ending the monopoly of the Catholic Church on the education of Africans, so that both the colonial state and non-Catholic religious organizations were able to step in. Education for Africans expanded greatly as a result, including at the secondary level, but as Michel Cahen says, it was too little too late.[22] A large number of the middle-class African youth joined the liberation struggle all the same in the early 1960s, to use political and military means to fight for independence.

Mozambicans started to launch nationalist organizations in 1960. They created them in exile in countries where they were allowed to do so and often under the influence of the nationalist structures there. The first Mozambican nationalist parties appeared in Southern Rhodesia and Tanganyika. In 1960 migrants from south and central Mozambique launched the União Democrática Nacional Moçambique (National Democratic Union of Mozambique, UDENAMO) in Bulawayo, Southern Rhodesia.[23] The same year migrants from northern Mozambique launched the Mozambique African National Union (MANU) in Dar es Salaam.[24] The following year, migrants from central Mozambique founded the União Nacional Africana de Moçambique (African National Union of Mozambique, UNAMI) in Malawi and, in 1962, individuals from the same area founded the Kilimane Freedom Party in Salisbury (Southern Rhodesia), soon thereafter renamed the Mozambique African National Congress (MANC).[25] Following the independence of Tanganyika in 1961, many nationalists moved to Dar es Salaam where parties from the whole subregion were encouraged to open offices. There they enjoyed open and active support from the new party in power, the Tanganyika African National Union (TANU), the Organization of African Unity's Liberation Committee, and some foreign countries. With its interest in supporting African nationalism in Mozambique (and in competition with Ghana), TANU soon put pressure on the

Mozambican parties to merge into a single structure. A fractious process of fusion ensued, resulting in the launch of Frelimo in 1962. After some of its men received military training in Algeria, Frelimo launched a war of liberation in September 1964—both MANU and UDENAMO had already staged attacks on colonial targets in July and August 1964.[26]

What the official historiography calls the "merging" of early nationalist parties into Frelimo in 1962 was, in reality, a partial, difficult, and conflictual process. It involved only UNAMI, UDENAMO, and MANU; MANC emerged just after Frelimo was created. UDENAMO was the dominant element in the Frelimo "fusion," many of its leaders filling key positions in the new party and writing Frelimo's constitution and political program. Members of the other parties felt marginalized—UNAMI's president, for example, was at first given no position at all. As a result, several elements left Frelimo while others refused to conform, conspired, and eventually either left or were expelled from the party. A few months after the merger, Frelimo decreed the official extinction of all other parties and also that all their property should pass to itself, which TANU enforced. While most rank and file in Tanzania (in particular MANU men) joined Frelimo, many MANU, UNAMI, and UDENAMO leaders left both Frelimo and Tanzania to try to resurrect their parties abroad. Thus, as the new Frelimo party established itself, the older parties resuscitated their existence in countries such as Southern Rhodesia, Zambia, Malawi, and Sudan. Yet they had few members left and operated in countries that were either far from Mozambique or could only halfheartedly support the parties' struggle against Portugal in view of their economic dependence on the white regimes of southern Africa (for example, Malawi).

In 1963, several parties, including MANC, MANU, and two reestablished versions of UDENAMO, merged into the Frente Unida Anti-imperialista de Moçambique (United Anti-Imperialist Front of Mozambique), but this new structure did not last.[27] In 1964 contacts were made between UDENAMO and Frelimo in Cairo, and in 1965, a few months after it had become independent, Zambia promoted a conference to unite all Mozambican nationalist parties, including Frelimo. The negotiations were difficult, not least because Eduardo Mondlane, Frelimo's president, was threatened internally and could not afford many concessions. Blaming Frelimo, Zambia declared the talks to have failed in the second half of February 1965 and the other parties united into a new nationalist organization called Comité Revolucionário de Moçambique (Revolutionary Committee of Mozambique, COREMO).[28]

Considering the constraints of being in Zambia, COREMO managed to work reasonably well until the early 1970s.[29] As white regimes applied extra pressure on Zambia and the organization fell afoul of its own factional fights, COREMO lost its impetus, leaving the space for Frelimo to dominate the liberation struggle at once.[30]

Analysts have examined the differences between Frelimo and its predecessors and competitors, and an important debate needs discussion here. Many analysts see MANU, UDENAMO, and UNAMI (they usually ignore MANC) as traditionalist ethnonationalist movements, and place them in contrast to Frelimo, which they see as modern and supra-ethnic, and therefore as truly nationalist.[31] According to the literature, UDENAMO was launched in Rhodesia and brought together mainly southern Mozambicans; UNAMI was founded in Malawi and brought together nationalists from the center of Mozambique; and MANU began in Tanzania and united Mozambican nationalists from the north of the colony.[32] Against this argumentation, Michel Cahen proposes that the founding of Frelimo did not lead to a qualitative jump in nationalist politics: the "unification process . . . was not the expression of either the unification of Mozambican anti-colonialism or of the massive emergence of nationalism."[33] It was a rather problematic and difficult merger of different political parties and, instead of resulting in a unified and dominant front, the new Frelimo party faced several crises right from the beginning. The biggest crisis took place between 1966 and 1969 and led to the crystallization of its leadership around people of similar social background (urban, from southern Mozambique, and the professional bourgeoisie) and with a similar social and political project (modernist, internationalist, and socialist).[34]

In order to understand the 1966–69 crisis in more detail, we need to investigate the role of the central Mozambican elite in nationalist politics. Indeed Catholicism had much to do with this elite, which constituted an important group in Frelimo's internal factional fights.[35] People from Manica and Sofala and Tete were involved in the formation of three nationalist organizations: UNAMI, MANC, and UDENAMO. UNAMI was created by Balthazar Chagonga in Nyasaland (Malawi) in 1961. It developed out of the Club Africano de Tete that (contrary to what is usually said) had members from diverse regional origins—many from central Mozambique, but some from the south too. In Malawi, the party enjoyed the support of the ruling Malawi Congress Party. In 1962, UNAMI took part in the founding of Frelimo, but found Chagonga excluded from leadership in the new political structure at first. When he was subsequently given only a minor position as head of the party's social services, Chagonga abandoned Frelimo in 1963 and returned to Malawi to relaunch his party. Unsurprisingly, UNAMI lost several cadres in the process and the relaunch was not successful. After various difficulties, some failures, and much underhanded manipulation by the Portuguese security police, the UNAMI leader passed to the Portuguese in April 1965; whether he handed himself over voluntarily or was captured is unclear. Subsequently, the Portuguese administration instrumentalized Chagonga and UNAMI against Frelimo's armed liberation struggle.[36]

MANC was formed in Salisbury, Southern Rhodesia, in October 1962 as the Kilimane Freedom Party.[37] It had the support of the Zimbabwean African People's Union and the Malawi Congress Party. Many Mozambican nationalists in Rhodesia had been involved in the founding of UDENAMO and had left for Tanganyika when MANC was founded. Thereafter, MANC seemed to have recruited supporters from a different milieu of Mozambican migrants. The first name of the party came as a result of the fact that the majority of its initial members were from Quelimane; the others were mostly Sena and would have liked to call the party the Sena Freedom Party.[38] In the face of divisions that emerged over the name, the party rapidly adopted the more neutral name, Mozambique African National Congress. On the occasion, the party president declared that with this new name the party was choosing to be less exclusive and more nationalist, and that it aimed to "unite Portuguese Africans from Mozambique and to prevent them from forming their own parties confined to various districts [provinces], as in the past."[39] The party grew rapidly and integrated elements from the biggest welfare societies in Rhodesia—the Tete East Africa National Globe Society, the Portuguese East Africa Society, and the Zumbo Beira Society. The Portuguese were concerned with the emergence of this organization. What worried them most was the radicalization of the party president's discourse and his attempt to recruit Mozambicans serving in the Rhodesian Reserve Police: not only did these men work on the border with Mozambique but they included many men of Chikunda origin, an ethnic group constituted of former military slaves.[40] In his speeches, party president Peter Balamanja drew on a fairly radical socialist and pan-Africanist ideology. In early 1963, he declared that he was setting up a secret army to expel Europeans from Mozambique.[41] This strategy and the sudden prospect of international support—Joshua Nkomo in Rhodesia promised to enable Balamanja to travel to London—led the Portuguese security police to step in. Upon a Portuguese request for assistance to the Rhodesian Special Branch, the latter arrested and deported MANC's two main leaders to Mozambique in June 1963.[42] This was a major blow to the organization, which lost much of its dynamic as a result and never really recovered from it. In 1965 the party merged into COREMO.

UDENAMO is the third and most important party that drew in people from Manica and Sofala and Tete. The party was created in Bulawayo by Mozambicans from the southern and central parts of the country. It included individuals from the elite of Lourenço Marques, Gaza, and Inhambane, and from the Protestant elite of Manica and Sofala. This Protestant elite belonged mainly to the Congregationalist church, with some members being the sons of the fighters of a famous 1954 anticolonial uprising in Machanga district.[43] Most important among these individuals was Pastor Uria Simango, whose father was deported to northern Mozambique as a result of his involvement in the 1954 uprising. Simango trained as a Congregationalist pastor in Mozambique and Zimbabwe. After studying at the Protestant Ecumenical Seminary in Ricatla, near Lourenço Marques, Simango should have gone to study in the United States (the Mozambican Congregational Church having its roots in the United States),[44] but was prohibited from doing so by the Portuguese administration. Simango then moved to Southern Rhodesia where he worked as pastor for the Presbyterian Church from 1959 onward. This is where he became involved in the establishment of UDENAMO. As the most prominent nationalist leader in Rhodesia, the Portuguese state security police (PIDE) tried to arrest him in 1960. He managed to escape and fled to Tanganyika where he contributed to the formation of Frelimo, of which he became the vice president.[45] With him, many UDENAMO members joined Frelimo—as a result of which UDENAMO became the organization best represented within the new nationalist party launched in Dar es Salaam in 1962.

Members of the Catholic elite of Manica and Sofala and Tete were actively involved in these early nationalist politics. Some of its members in UNAMI and UDENAMO, including future leaders such as Inácio António Nunes (UNAMI) and Feliciano Gundana (UDENAMO), joined Frelimo in 1962 and reinforced the central Mozambique presence in the front.[46] In 1965 those who had remained in UNAMI or UDENAMO joined the new COREMO organization into which their parties merged. Parallel to this, a stream of Catholic nationalists from central Mozambique joined Frelimo directly after 1962. This stream contained two groups. The first was constituted of Catholics from Manica and Sofala and Tete who fled the country with the help of a network operated by the White Fathers. Priests helped these individuals reach the border, offered them overnight accommodation at their missions, assisted them with finding their way, and provided them with food and money. Father André de Bels at the Zobuè Seminary seems to have been the first missionary to get involved. Using contacts with UNAMI and indirectly with the American, Israeli, and Soviet Russian embassies in Malawi, he sent dozens of young men across the border over a period of three years (before he was caught and expelled from Mozambique in 1965).[47] Several of these men made their way to study in America,

Russia, and Eastern Europe.[48] Many of them returned to Dar es Salaam to serve Frelimo after completing their studies, though some disliked Frelimo and remained in these foreign countries from which they supported other movements such as the relaunched UDENAMO and COREMO.

The second group of Catholic elites who joined Frelimo was made up of young Catholic seminarians, with a first wave in 1963 coming from Namaacha Seminary and a second wave in 1967 coming from Zobuè Seminary. This was the result of the repression of African nationalism by the Portuguese colonial state and, connected to this, the church's replacement of the foreign congregations in charge of these seminaries with Portuguese leadership. Seminarians in Namaacha started to flee abroad after a crisis between students and the church leadership in 1963 (of which more in the next section) while seminarians in Zobuè abandoned the seminary halfway through their studies in 1967 after the bishop removed the White Fathers from the leadership of Zobuè. Some of these students continued their education at the Frelimo secondary school in Dar es Salaam (or at universities abroad for students from the Major Seminary) while others joined the armed struggle.

The Catholic contribution to Frelimo's liberation struggle took a qualitative turn when Father Mateus Gwenjere joined Frelimo in July 1967 (see fig. 4.2). Within days of his arrival in Malawi, Gwenjere was transferred to Dar es Salaam where Frelimo celebrated his arrival as a major gain. Frelimo's president, Eduardo Mondlane, and the president of Tanzania both received him personally—Gwenjere was seen as a rare nationalist priest and a hero, insofar as he had enabled dozens of men to join Frelimo in exile.[49] The enthusiasm was such that, by the end of October, Frelimo's president asked Gwenjere to accompany the party's vice president, Reverend Uria Simango, to address the General Assembly of the United Nations in New York. They did so on November 6, 1967, speaking for two and a half hours about the social, economic, and political situation in Mozambique. The speech was well received and the Sierra Leonean representative at the UN is reported to have stated in his concluding remarks that: "It was unusual for ministers of the Gospel to be in the forefront of an armed conflict and speak in its defense, but the situation in the Territories under Portuguese administration was unusual and he congratulated the petitioners on having recognized that, since human freedom was God-given, it was their duty to risk their lives in its defense."[50] Gwenjere and Simango's mission to the United Nations was a success. On their return to Dar es Salaam, Father Gwenjere went to work at a nursing school in town and he visited the Frelimo headquarters regularly to see former seminarians and other Catholics from central Mozambique. As an influential priest, he was soon perceived

Figure 4.2. Father Mateus Gwenjere, ca. 1970. Courtesy of Father André de Bels.

as their natural representative and became embroiled in Frelimo's politics in their name.

At the time of Gwenjere's arrival, Frelimo was in crisis. Filipe Magaia, its secretary of defense, had been killed in October 1966. Many Frelimo members from central and northern Mozambique suspected that he had been assassinated (rather than killed in combat), and saw the choice of Samora Machel, a military commander from the south of the country, as his replacement not only as unconstitutional but as part of an ethnic conspiracy. They suspected Magaia to have been assassinated and his deputy to have been sidelined to substitute for Magaia because he was a northerner (a Makonde).[51] In addition, in the same period, the party's Central Committee decided to "reform" the rules of the Mozambique Institute, its educational facility in Dar es Salaam. Students who completed the secondary school degree at the Mozambique Institute were no longer able to proceed to the Kurasini African American Institute, a secondary school established by the Africa-American Institute. They had to stay at Frelimo's school where the intermediate curriculum was shorter and taught in Portuguese. The committee also decided that those who failed in their studies could not repeat their year, but now should be sent to fight in Mozambique, that all students needed to undergo politico-military training, and that they had to teach in the liberated areas of Mozambique during their school holidays. The students, overwhelmingly from central and northern Mozambique, strongly contested these decisions: they questioned why they should study less or follow a Portuguese curriculum only. They saw these decisions as part of a wider conspiracy by southeners to marginalize individuals from the center and the north of the country. As a result, a majority of students rejected the Central Committee decision. When the leadership insisted on its rulings, tensions worsened and an open conflict erupted.[52]

The conflict began at the Mozambique Institute in 1968. On March 3 or 5, the students beat up one of their colleagues whom they suspected of being an informer for the Frelimo leadership. To restore discipline, some Frelimo leaders stormed the student dormitory with arms and beat up the young men. The students called the police, who arrested two of the Frelimo leaders and beat them in front of the students.[53] At a meeting a few days later, the Frelimo leadership decided to close the school and to move all students to the Frelimo Nachingwea military base in southern Tanzania. When the leadership presented this decision to the students, the latter beat up the Frelimo delegation. On May 11, 1968, the crisis intensified when the Frelimo Council of Elders, Baraza la Wazee (dominated by Makonde, with significant influence over Frelimo's military leadership and the liberated areas in Mozambique) tried to oust the Frelimo leadership by force. Seizing an opportunity to resolve a long-standing regional conflict within Frelimo, the Council of Elders mobilized men to march on the Frelimo headquarters. The attempt was unsuccessful as Mondlane was abroad and the other top leaders managed to flee in time. Some of the leaders, however, were badly beaten and one was killed. This led the Tanzanian government to intervene further in the Frelimo crisis: it decided to deport the striking students of the Mozambican Institute to the Lindi refugee camp on the Tanzanian coast.[54]

Now openly in alliance with each other, Gwenjere and the Makonde elders worked together to change the liberation movement's leadership, focusing in particular on convening a long overdue Congress. Aside from the date, a major issue was where to hold Frelimo's second congress. There were three possible locations: Niassa, Cabo Delgado, or Tanzania; Gwenjere and the Makonde elders preferred either of the last two while the "southerners" preferred Niassa where they had a firmer control of the movement. The congress was eventually held in Niassa in July 1968. Several Makonde leaders and Gwenjere boycotted the event. At the congress Mondlane still only narrowly won his reelection as Frelimo president against Uria Simango.[55] During the next six months, factional fighting focused on the possibility of an extraordinary congress being called for February 1969. But before this could take place, Gwenjere was arrested by the Tanzanian authorities and placed under house arrest (December 28, 1968), and Frelimo demoted Lazaro Kavandame, the leader of the Bazara la Wazee, from his position as Frelimo provincial secretary (i.e., head of Frelimo in Cabo Delgado province). After a bomb sent by the Portuguese secret services killed President Mondlane on February 3, 1969, Kavandame surrendered to the Portuguese while Gwenjere abandoned Frelimo at once. Many of Gwenjere's students followed suit and went into exile in Kenya. Thus, by 1969 most of the Catholic elite from Manica and Sofala and Tete either had abandoned Frelimo or had been expelled from it.[56]

The 1966–69 conflict within Frelimo was multifaceted. There was an element of international politics with the Chinese, Russians, and the West competing for influence in the organization. There were issues of regionalism and ethnicity as well as differences in social trajectories and ideology. For some in Frelimo today, Gwenjere was simply an agent of the Portuguese state security police and/or a reactionary plotter who exploited divisions (and students) to undermine a progressive (Socialist) cause.[57] The archives that are available on the matter do not contain any evidence that Father Mateus Gwenjere ever worked as a PIDE agent.[58] It is therefore important to place him socially and historically to understand his politics within Frelimo, taking into consideration his origins, his Catholic education, and the influence of the White Fathers who were so important to him. Former Burgos priest Miguel Buendia wrote some very insightful lines about this issue. He stated:

> [Gwenjere] lived with the fathers of the missionary organization of the White Fathers who strongly influenced his way of thinking about the world. This missionary organization had fathers spread all over Africa and it was thus able closely to follow the process toward independence in many African countries in the 1960s. As a result, the White Fathers who lived in Mozambique clearly favored the independence of the Portuguese colony. . . . Being in favor of the right to independence does not mean that they were indifferent to the form the future independent state would take. Most of them had a negative vision of socialism. Their

philosophical-theological education did not permit them to disregard the official position of the Catholic Church in relation to socialism, and particularly toward Marxist socialism. I believe that, apart from the quite traditional theological education he gained at the seminary, Father Gwenjere's life with the White Fathers reinforced Father Gwenjere's anti-Marxist position. I think this is one possible explanation for the origin of his problems with Frelimo's "socialist" faction. He was also accused of having a racist attitude in relation to white members of the Front. There existed a mentality within the church that held that socialism or, better, Marxism was an ideology foreign to African realities. It is possible that this conviction underlay [Gwenjere's] "racist" position, accusing Frelimo's non-black elements of having brought a non-African ideology to the Front.[59]

Former students at the Mozambican Institute who later became Frelimo dissidents reject the suggestion that Gwenjere was a racist or an anti-Marxist. They claim that race and Marxism were not the issue—that the conflict was about ethnicity, regionalism, and factions. They point out that Gwenjere disliked Mondlane who was not Marxist and liked others who were Marxists. They also highlight that he tried to get rid of *some* white Portuguese individuals in Frelimo's leadership, but not others, in other words not *all* whites. Indeed, while he was wary of former settlers in particular, he did not dislike all foreigners, and actually befriended several non-Africans, even sharing a flat with a German national at some point.[60] A more recent argument holds that the conflict within Frelimo pitched "cosmopolitan internationalists" against "provincials." In this scenario, the likes of Gwenjere were "provincials," patrimonialists, and ethnic operators, unfit for the construction of a modern "bureaucratic pattern of governance."[61] This argument is ironic, in that the Catholic Church was the least ethnic religious organization in Mozambique while the famous Swiss Mission, said to have been central to Mozambican nationalism and its national hero Eduardo Mondlane, was an explicitly ethnic church.[62]

Based on the preceding analysis, I suggest that Gwenjere was not a provincial and possibly not a racist, but rather a rural liberal or conservative nationalist with a particular outlook. Like many of Zobuè's students who joined Frelimo, he was the product of the Catholic Church of Beira in the 1950s and 1960s. He was a strong and orthodox Catholic, proud of his African culture (which he wanted to assert); he came from the countryside and worked there most of his life. He joined Frelimo in the middle of a factional fight and was rapidly convinced by his students (possibly by Simango too) that a regional or ethnic conspiracy was unfolding within the liberation front. Thus, what was fundamentally different with Gwenjere was his social trajectory and his weltanschauung, which clashed with those of the faction that won Frelimo's leadership with its predominantly southern, urban and bureaucratic background. The latter's vision was militantly anti-racist, critical if not opposed to African traditions and religion, and ever more in favor of socialism, if not communism; Gwenjere and his supporters' vision was Africanist, protradition, proreligion, and anti-Communist.

The Church and African Nationalism

The first case of African nationalism to rock the Diocese of Beira, if not the whole Catholic Church in Mozambique, took place in 1960. It began when missionary staff intercepted a letter by a student at the Major Seminary of Namaacha. In his letter to a friend, André Saene, a graduate of Zobuè, made strong statements against the Portuguese, and the seminary's superior thought it necessary to send it to the cardinal of Lourenço Marques, Dom Teodósio de Gouveia. The cardinal was upset and wrote to the bishop of Beira demanding action. In a letter dated December 9, 1960, he stated:

> There are two subjects that need an urgent solution. The first is the seminarian A. Saene, from [?]. This youngster cannot continue as a seminarian in Namaacha in view of his anti-Lusitanian [anti-Portuguese] ideas, a matter that you can confirm yourself in the attached letter that he wrote to a friend. I did not expel him immediately because I awaited your visit to L. M. [Lourenço Marques] on your way back from [?]. In any case, we planned that he would [return?] to Beira during the Christmas holidays. His Excellency D. Sebastião will do what he wants. These ideas are penetrating from all sides, in particular through the youngsters who come from Zobuè seminary. The rector of our seminary even stated the following to Father Cristiano about a seminarian who arrived in October: "He would be an excellent minister of Mr. Banda." I understand we need to react against such a [situation?].[63]

I have not found Dom Sebastião's response to the cardinal's missive (if there was any) in the archive or any indication of what specific action Dom Sebastião took in relation to André Saene. From the record, it is clear that Dom Sebastião appreciated André Saene and that Saene was considered one of the brightest seminarians in Namaacha.[64] He was, nonetheless, expelled from Namaacha, after which he fled Mozambique with the help of the White Fathers. He traveled to Dar es Salaam where he joined Frelimo. When the latter refused to give him a scholarship to study abroad, he joined UNAMI, which, despite Frelimo's opposition, found him a place at the University of Rochester in the United States. By 1965 Saene identified himself as a member of UDENAMO.[65]

As a result of the Saene affair and concerns resulting from the 1961 bloody uprising in northern Angola, Dom Custódio Alvim Perreira, the auxiliary archbishop of Lourenço Marques (after Cardinal Teodósio passed away on February 6, 1962), felt it necessary to issue a number of instructions regarding politics for his seminarians:

- Independence is irrelevant to the welfare of man. It can be good if the right conditions are present (the cultural conditions do not yet exist in Mozambique).
- Until these conditions are established, it would be acting against nature to take part in independence movements.
- Even if the right conditions were to exist, the Metropole has the right to oppose independence if the freedoms and rights of man are respected, and if [the Metropole] provides for the well-being of all and for civil and religious progress.
- All movements that use force are against natural law because independence, if it is to be assumed that it is good, must be obtained by peaceful means.
- The clergy has the obligation, in good conscience, not only to refrain from taking part in a terrorist movement but also to oppose it. This [obligation] derives from the nature of his mission [as a religious leader].
- Even when a movement is peaceful, the clergy must not join it in order to retain their spiritual influence over all people. The superior of the church may impose the prohibition from joining and hereby imposes it for Lourenço Marques.
- The native people of Africa have the obligation of thanking the colonialists for all the benefits that they receive from them.
- The educated have the duty to lead the less educated from the illusion of independence.
- Almost all of the existing independence movements show signs of revolt and communism; they have no reason; therefore they must not be supported. The doctrine of the Holy See is quite clear concerning atheistic and revolutionary communism. The great revolution is that of the Gospel.
- The slogan "Africa for the Africans" is a philosophical monstrosity and a challenge to Christian civilization, because today's events tell us that it is communism and Islam that wish to impose their civilization upon Africans.[66]

Rather than calming the situation, these instructions added fuel to the fire. Many seminarians were outraged and dismayed, with some abandoning the seminary and fleeing abroad to join Frelimo—upon which Frelimo used the instructions for propaganda purposes.[67] The situation among the remaining students remained tense and a spirit of rebellion prevailed. Seminarians challenged the new rules, citing theologians to back up their arguments, so that the auxiliary bishop eventually found no alternative but to resort to an argument of authority in order to enforce them. By 1963, the situation was so tense that the archbishop of Lourenço Marques called on Dom Sebastião to visit Namaacha. As the bishop of Beira described in his diary for February 25, 1963:

> D. Custodio and I left for the seminary of Namaacha to resolve grave problems that exist there. The youngsters, or at least a group of them, are so consumed by political concerns that they go as far as justifying the worst and bloodiest terrorism. Worse, there is a group that proclaimed that terrorism here [in Mozambique] would be worse, crueler and bloodier and of bigger [?]. I started by listening to the youngsters, one by one, and examined the case. They are terrible and masters at escaping. . . . I liked Tomé a lot, but in this he made a very negative impression. I hope I am mistaken. He is the Dean.[68]

The following day, Dom Sebastião noted further:

> I held a meditation for the seminarians on three points: priests and politics; priests and racism; and priests and the independence of Mozambique! I spoke strongly, reflecting only on the doctrine of the church, without missing a single element. I celebrated mass and continued to receive youngsters until almost 10h30. I received the vice-rector and told him that he was partly responsible [for the situation]. This state of affairs has gone too far. Some of them are losing their vocation. We returned to L. Marques and there we solved the question in the hope that until the end of the year the students calm down.[69]

It is not clear what solution the two archbishops developed. But in 1964 the Blessed Sacrament priests who ran the Namaacha seminary were replaced by the Congregation of the Mission from Portugal (also called Vincentians or Lazarists) and the seminary itself was moved from the Namaacha mountain town to Lourenço Marques, the capital city of the territory, so that the archbishop could visit it more regularly.[70] According to a source among the White Fathers, the result was negative as the Vincentians had no training or experience in managing a major seminary, only having run the minor seminary of Magude until then. It was so bad, in fact, that seminarians continued to abandon their religious vocation and the bishop of Beira considered opening his own Major Seminary in his Diocese of

Beira.[71] Many of the students who finished the Zobuè minor seminary now refused to transfer to the Namaacha Major Seminary; some asked instead to be accepted into the White Fathers society while others gave up on their religious vocation altogether.[72]

This episode reveals tensions between African seminarians on the one hand and the white clergy and Catholic hierarchy on the other. It also reveals differences between the two archbishops. While Dom Custódio was wholly opposed to African nationalism, Dom Sebastião was much more nuanced. Before we further explore Dom Sebastião's views, we need to consider how much the bishop of Beira knew about the activities of his priests supporting African nationalism at the time. He obviously knew something was happening, but it is unclear how much and when he knew.

A first reference indicating that the bishop of Beira knew that his missionaries supported African nationalism can be found in his diary in December 1963:

> This morning I received Father Cross [superior of the White Fathers] with whom I talked at length about many subjects. Among these matters, I spoke about youngsters going into exile outside of the country, with the help of the White Fathers. This is how André Saene and others left the country. He told me that there was some truth in the rumors, though not all of it was true. In addition, he said that he did not know whether the college [of Zobuè?] would remain there [in Zobuè?]: "If it does not, it would show that I do not trust them."[73]

This diary entry shows that the bishop did not know all that was happening in the parishes and missions in relation to African nationalism and the church, and that the White Fathers' superior might have not been totally open with him. The tone of the entry is indeed one of partial disbelief by the bishop. Yet, little ambiguity was left thereafter: the bishop knew what was going on. Even clearer was the case of a letter from Father Pollet, which the bishop received in February 1966. In it, Pollet explained that he had finally taken a firm and public stand in favor of independence for Mozambique. This had radically altered his work with Africans for the better, he explained. He asked the bishop whether he would give his support when problems with the colonial administration arose.[74] While I was unable to find the bishop's answer in the archive, there is evidence not only that the bishop did stand by Father Pollet but that he went quite far to protect him; we know, for example, that the Portuguese colonial state only expelled Pollet after the bishop had passed away. On the other hand, Pollet was moved to the Gorongosa mission in mid-1966, though it is not clear on whose order (see fig. 4.3).

Figure 4.3. Father Charles Pollet, Gorongosa, n.d. Courtesy of Josef Pampalk.

Pollet's letter sheds light on two areas. First, while Pollet had been assisting people to go into exile for several years, he did so secretly and only informed the bishop in 1966. Second, the bishop knew about some of the White Fathers' activities, but probably only got a full and definitive confirmation from Father Pollet in 1966 (otherwise the White Fathers would not have published this letter from him but an earlier one or an earlier document). In sum, it is clear that the bishop knew from at least 1963 onward that some fathers supported African nationalism, but he probably did not know the full extent of their activities before 1966. This suggests that the bishop's change of heart in regard to colonialism had no direct relation to this discovery. Indeed, after a period during which he showed high interest in Lusotropicalism, the bishop had already discarded the idea of Portuguese colonialism in 1962, concluding that to save the church, he and his institution had to think beyond colonialism. The bishop's diary for 1962 is missing, so we cannot date precisely when he changed his mind, but an entry for 1963 confirmed the change. In January that year, after listening to a speech by Salazar who declared that Portugal needed to hold on to its colonies, Dom Sebastião wrote: "To hold on is not a definitive solution. Mozambique has its rights and, when possible, it needs to become independent with blacks and whites governing. That is the Christian thesis."[75]

The bishop's change of heart was and remained a private one. He did not reveal it to anyone, not even to the White Fathers with whom he seems to have shared many views. To understand this, as well as his way of leading his diocese, it is worth reflecting on some statements he made on politics to his clergy in 1964. His thoughts are interesting for their perspective and tone, and for the way they contrast with the instructions Dom Custódio had given the Namaacha seminarians two years earlier. In his address, the bishop stated:

> I would like to say to all missionaries, and in particular to those who are not Portuguese of origin, that they should not get involved in political questions. Priests are not ordained to do politics, but "ut offerat dona et sacrificia pro peccatis."[76] Priests are priests for everyone in their parishes, or missions, or dioceses, regardless of which party they are from, or whether they are democrats, socialists or communists. If they [the priests] ostensibly support one side, they will become incompatible for those who support other parties, a situation that will frustrate their universal mission. God has taught us to "Give God what belongs to God and to Caesar what belongs to Caesar."[77]

This quote illustrates the contrast between Dom Sebastião's private beliefs and his position as bishop, and it furthers our understanding of how he ran his diocese (in contrast to other bishops). As an ultramontane and neo-Thomist bishop, Dom Sebastião withheld his personal views and adopted a position that would avoid division among his clergy and flock, so as to better promote the interests of the church, and he asked his missionaries to do the same.

Turning to Catholic congregations in central Mozambique, we saw above that various White Fathers supported African nationalism, that some actively helped seminarians and others to join the liberation struggle in exile, and that their superiors and the heads of the congregations in Mozambique were supportive of such actions. As noted by Miguel Buendia (discussed above), this support was specific. The White Fathers were in favor of Christian nationalism and rejected communism. Hence various fathers supported Gwenjere not only when he joined Frelimo but also after he left it again because, like him, they thought that the party had been taken over by a communist clique. Not all White Fathers were in favor of African nationalism, of course. Some missionaries did not care about it, and a few were opposed to it. The nonsupportive missionaries were mostly of the older generations, many of whom German. They had come to Mozambique after having been expelled from Tanganyika after the Second

World War and were grateful to Portugal for having taken them in. The dominant tone in the order from the mid-1960s, however, was in favor of African nationalism as the older priests and brothers retired from the field and new, young missionaries took over.[78]

The Spanish Burgos fathers showed little active support for African nationalism before the mid-1960s. The changes that took place within the order in the 1960s, however, led to a change of position. For one, they began to recruit significantly in those years, meaning that soon the majority of its staff was young. The congregation's seminary in Spain tripled its intake between 1958 and 1964, and the number of its missionaries more than doubled, from 185 to 553, between 1963 and 1969.[79] The new missionaries were open to new ideas and were more critical of Spanish society; in addition, the church in Spain was more open than that of Portugal. Some Burgos missionaries came from the Spanish Basque region where the nationalist armed group Euskadi Ta Askatasuna began to fight for independence in 1959. For another, many Burgos fathers began to move toward liberation theology in the wake of Vatican II and Catholic developments in Latin America (where the order did most of its missionary work). As a Burgos sociologist-priest put it in 1976, a majority of the institute's priests identified themselves with "the new [Catholic] currents that had a strong humanist tendency."[80] As a result, the order changed profoundly and underwent something of an internal revolution. To participate in its second general assembly in 1969, it invited representatives from its mission areas (rather than having only the leadership decide on its own). After four months of work, the assembly made decisions that were not only in line with Vatican II but allowed liberation theology to blossom in its midst. In Mozambique, this meant that many priests aligned themselves with the interests of the poor in society (following the "preferential option for the poor") and reorganized their work toward the working class (they already had a presence among working class communities in Beira, Moatize, and Soalpo) as well as in favor of base communities, the autonomous religious groups typical of liberation theology.[81]

The Burgos fathers worked mostly in the new Diocese of Tete, specifically in several areas where Frelimo began military operations in 1967. The fathers thus soon came into contact with the Frelimo liberation fighters—the first contact took place in 1968—which forced them to make choices in relation to colonialism and liberation.[82] They discussed the political situation at their yearly regional meeting in 1970 and, for the first time, talked openly about supporting Frelimo.[83] Father Fontes, who had first been in touch with Frelimo, wished for the fathers to work in the "liberated areas." Several fathers agreed (often those who originated from the autonomist

Basque region), but the majority feared the consequences that such action could have on missionaries from other congregations. The assembly thus decided to opt for "clandestine methods" to support Frelimo.[84] More generally, the 1970 meeting produced a report that was telling for its language. The report referred to the need to confront "macro-structures," the necessity to reveal "the abuses of bosses, capitalist trusts, businesses, etc. committed at the margin of positive law," and the desire to deploy a "prophetic testimony in the face of the situation of injustice."[85] A year later, in mid-1971, after the residents of Mukumbura village in Tete province were massacred by Rhodesian troops in a cross-border operation in an area where the priests worked (see chapter 5 for a detailed account), the Burgos fathers decided to abandon their restraint and to actively support Frelimo and the independence of Mozambique.[86]

There is relatively little information about the Picpus fathers and African nationalism. In Portugal, some priests were very sympathetic to the Estado Novo regime (one priest was very close to Salazar himself) while others were adepts of liberal Catholicism (pre– and post–Vatican II). In Mozambique, Picpus fathers were similarly divided. Father João Maria, the priest at Dondo parish, was denounced in 1961 and eventually had to leave Mozambique because he had criticized the regime in front of catechists and expressed his support for the liberation movement.[87] While this case was considered to be singular and possibly even exceptional, the situation changed in the subsequent decade. For one, Vatican II influenced the way missionaries thought. In 1969 a Picpus father disapprovingly noted (at a meeting of all priests from the order's Portuguese region, which included Mozambique) that nowadays they spoke of the development of the Third World whereas in the past they had spoken of "conversion and evangelization."[88] For another, the context in the Netherlands—the missionaries' home country—had changed significantly. In 1970, the Portuguese government expelled three Picpus fathers from Portugal, not because they would have done anything subversive there, but because 742 priests and pastors had signed a petition in the Netherlands against NATO involvement in the Portuguese colonial wars.[89] Between Vatican II reforms and a radicalization of the religious and political context, the Picpus fathers soon followed in the steps of the White Fathers to support the independence of Mozambique. Nothing much actually happened as a result; this was underpinned by the fact that the missionaries tended mostly to settler parishes, worked far away from the conflict zones, and had few opportunities to be in contact with Mozambican nationalists. However, events in the early 1970s eventually led the priests to take a radical stand against colonialism in early 1974, in the last weeks of the regime, as we will see chapter 5.

The majority of religious women had no association with anticolonialism and African nationalism. Most sisters were Portuguese—there were only a few Spanish and Italians sisters, mostly in the congregation of the Franciscan Missionaries of the Mother of the Divine Shepherd. While some of the sisters were well educated, as were the Sisters of Cluny, most were primarily trained in practical skills, and had few opportunities to travel, engage with African societies, and engage in political discussions with others. Just as important, sisters had a subordinate position in the church, something that was institutionalized by the "charism" of their original founder and the function they were assigned to in the church. As a result, a majority of female missionaries were politically quietist. Only a few sisters made political statements or took a political stand in relation to the independence of Mozambique in the early 1970s. Two factors seem to have played into such politicization: their nationality and the male order their own congregation worked with. Thus the sisters of the Franciscan Missionaries of the Mother of the Divine Shepherd were not all Portuguese and they worked with White Fathers and Burgos fathers who were engaged politically. By the 1970s they became involved in supporting, or at least understanding the involvement of, priests who acted in favor of the national independence of Mozambique. In Tete, some sisters went further and actively helped Frelimo on their own account—the Daughters of Saint Paul seem to have done the same in Beira city.[90] At the mission of Murraça and after some initial hesitation, the sisters began in 1971 to collaborate with the Burgos fathers after they took over the mission from the White Fathers who had departed.[91] Conversely, some Portuguese sisters, even within the female congregations already mentioned, were (or openly became) pro-Portuguese in the 1970s. In 1969 at the mission of Baruè, for example, several sisters of the Repairing Missionaries of the Sacred Heart of Jesus denounced a White Father for being too critical of the regime, as a result of which his residence permit was not renewed and he had to leave the country.[92] Overall, the majority of sisters were quietist; a few, especially from the Franciscan Missionaries of the Mother of the Divine Shepherd and the Daughters of Saint Paul, became involved in supporting African nationalism while some actively defended the colonial regime and status quo.

An overwhelming majority of male Portuguese missionaries were in favor of Portuguese colonialism. A significant exception can be found in the secular clergy around the bishop of Beira and the younger priests who arrived in the early 1970s. This does not mean that all Portuguese missionaries held the same position. While most fathers and brothers were quietist and passive in their support of the regime, some were proactive in defending Salazarism and colonialism. Similarly, while some were pro-Portuguese and ultramontane (which could lead to contradictions), others were pro-Portuguese and anti-Roman (and thus supported Portuguese colonialism particularly strongly). Several Franciscan missionaries fell into the latter category: regalist in approach, their gratitude that the Salazar regime had supported the church after many decades of anticlericalism in the nineteenth and twentieth centuries meant they supported the Portuguese regime at all costs. Most Franciscans raised the Portuguese flag at the end of every mass until at least 1965, and possibly even after.[93] After Vatican II, some younger Franciscans became more critical, but they dared not think aloud or act in-line with their political beliefs.[94] Conversely, when the situation in the Diocese of Beira became tense because of the liberation war in the late 1960s and 1970s, some Franciscan missionaries got involved on the side of the government, which led missionaries from other congregations to accuse the Franciscans of offering a "countertestimony" (about which more later).[95] A few Franciscans went as far as supporting the army and the state police in their work, not just by acting as chaplains but by denouncing African nationalists and missionaries. Frei Manuel de Oliveira Vieira, for example, is said to have assisted the special Portuguese military forces and helped the security police in its spying activities and repression.[96] A White Father accused another Portuguese priest (possibly Franciscan) of taking part in PIDE's torture and assassinations.[97] In parallel, PIDE noted in its documentation that not a single Franciscans had ever "entered into politics" on the anticolonial side. More specifically, it stated:

> Among the Franciscans of Manica and Sofala, we even count elements who collaborate with us whenever possible, sometimes spontaneously and at other times when we ask them—a situation that we acknowledge with satisfaction. . . . It seems to us, indeed, that there is no need to be alarmed by the ideological position of the Franciscans in this Diocese. On the contrary: we can congratulate ourselves to still have priests in this corner of Mozambique who work for the interests of the church and respect the rights of the state, led by the maxim "Give to God what is God's and to Caesar what is Caesar's."[98]

The Jesuits also supported colonialism, but they were not as regalist as the Franciscans. This had much to do with the congregation's history and dynamics. The Portuguese province of the Jesuits was not anti-ultramontane like the Franciscans and it allowed "modernist currents" (as they were called) to develop among its members. After 1959, the rather modernist (if politically conservative) Father Joaquim Ferreira Leão was elected provincial for Mozambique, while in Rome the liberal Father Arrupe was chosen

as general of the congregation in 1965.[99] The Jesuits thus officially promoted and disseminated Vatican II (this was enabled by the congregation's
centralized and hierarchical structure) and encouraged their missionaries
in Mozambique to participate in the pastoral and missionary weeks organized after 1963 to update the methods of the clergy. Though fearful of
African nationalism,[100] the Jesuits worked actively to promote an Africanized church in Mozambique.[101] Politically, Father Leão and some of his
men hoped for a "multiracial integration" in Mozambique in which everyone would have the same rights and duties, irrespective of color or social
origins.[102] While this placed him and his congregation on the side of the
government and its Lusotropical discourse, this position was quite different from that of the Franciscans or the archbishop of Lourenço Marques
who did not want any change at all.[103] This positioning also meant that
the Jesuit superior could appreciate the religious work of foreign fathers
while disagreeing with their politics. In 1971 he wrote, for example, that
the only problem with foreign missionaries was that they could not accept
the Portuguese solution of "multiracial integration."[104] While not all Jesuit
fathers shared the views of their superior (including the Jesuit bishop of
Tete who was very progovernment), one priest tried to bring multiracialism to its logical conclusion by establishing a multicultural (white and
black) mission station. This was too much for the congregation and for
the bishop of Tete, upon which the priest in question, Father Albano da
Silva Perreira, left the order and went to conduct his experiment in the
Diocese of Quelimane.[105] The point is that there was diversity within the
Jesuit society in Mozambique, with the superior and a number of missionaries being in favor of multiracialism. The diversity turned into division in
the 1970s when the start of the war in Tete led some priests to take a more
critical view of the regime. While the Jesuits remained united in Beira and
Tete, farther south, younger Jesuit priests ran into serious conflict with the
archbishop of Lourenço Marques.[106]

Overall, the position of the Catholic Church in relation to African
nationalism was internally diverse. While the bishop of Beira officially
opposed priestly involvement in politics, some missionaries did get
involved and did so on both sides of the political divide—in support of
African nationalism and in support of Portuguese colonialism. The literature has already noted that there was a major distinction in this respect
between foreign and Portuguese missionaries, but examining this question
in terms of each individual congregation has revealed that this division was
relative and much more complex and nuanced than has been acknowledged so far. The situation in central Mozambique was critically altered
by the unfolding of Vatican II. First, it reinforced the group of modernist

priests in the diocese and allowed the development of liberation theology. The postconciliar church also shaped the emergence of a group of African nationalists who were to have an important, if contested, role in the liberation struggle. Second, Vatican II and the development of African nationalism exacerbated differences and divisions between missionary groups. Dom Sebastião managed to maintain control of his diverse clergy thanks to his unique "neutral" (ultramontane and neo-Thomist) stance. His death would soon lead the diocese to implode.

5

Decolonization?

War, Implosion, and the Vatican

The years 1967 and 1968 constituted another turning point in central Mozambique. First, after a long illness the bishop of Beira, Dom Sebastião Soares de Resende, passed away in January 1967, which significantly destabilized the church. His successor, nominated the same year, struggled to impose his rule on the diocese. Because the clergy disagreed over the way in which the diocese should be run, "mistakes" on the part of the bishop led to more conflict among the priests and a situation that subsequent bishops struggled to surmount. Second, in 1967 Frelimo successfully relaunched its liberation war in the province of Tete, leading to armed conflict in the region. It directly affected the Catholic Church in central Mozambique and added to the sense of crisis among Catholics in the area. Third, in August 1968 Salazar suffered a heart attack, and Marcelo Caetano took over the position as ruler of the Estado Novo. In the ensuing "Marcellist spring" the new prime minister introduced some reforms, but they were neither as extensive as expected nor sufficient to change the course of the regime and the liberation struggle. The war continued and expanded, increasing the sense of crisis in the state, society, and church of central Mozambique—until the Estado Novo regime fell in 1974.

The crisis that the Diocese of Beira (and the new Diocese of Tete, after it was founded in 1962) faced after 1967 was unprecedented. During it missionaries fought each other, the bishop of Beira fled his diocese and stepped down, and some clergy engaged directly in politics on both sides of the divide. It is important to analyze this historical moment for itself as well as for what it reveals about the inner workings and evolution of the Catholic Church, including the relationship between the church hierarchy and the religious orders. Through these crises, various internal documents from this period were made public or ended up in the hands of outsiders.

These materials enable a detailed examination of the dynamics of the church under different bishops, hence a comparison of the different styles of episcopal leadership enacted by the various bishops. Moreover, in terms of scope, the documentation also allows an exploration of the relationship between the Vatican and the Diocese of Beira: the final section analyzes how religious orders *in the Vatican* influenced the policies of the Holy See in relation to the dioceses of Beira and Tete.

War, "Multiracial Independence," and the Church

The war of liberation in Mozambique began in 1964. It started in the provinces of Cabo Delgado and Niassa, where it remained confined for many years. In 1964 and 1965, Frelimo tried to open military fronts in Tete, Zambezia, and Manica and Sofala, but these attempts failed. Subsequently, political events in Malawi played into the hands of the Portuguese and prevented Frelimo from waging war from this country. It was thus only in 1967 that Frelimo managed to launch its armed struggle in central Mozambique—starting with the province of Tete. The guerrilla movement's objective was twofold: first, it aimed to threaten the Cabora Bassa dam that was being built by the Portuguese to strategically tie their colony more closely to the interests of the Rhodesian and South African regimes; and second, it wanted to disperse the Portuguese armed forces and supplies to interrupt their increasing success in northern Mozambique.[1] As it entered the province of Tete, Frelimo gained a solid foothold among the Chewa people in the hilly and forested northwest of the diocese, along the borders with Malawi and Zambia, thus among the very people who had refused to convert to Catholicism because the Ngoni had done so en masse and had allied themselves with the colonial authorities against the Chewa. From here Frelimo expanded toward both the east and the south. In 1970 the liberation movement passed a strategic and psychological threshold when it crossed the Zambezi River. In 1972 it managed to enter the province of Manica and Sofala, and in 1973, to shell military targets near Cabora Bassa. In January 1974, the movement attacked the fortified Portuguese garrison of Inhaminga, close to the provincial capital of Beira. In this manner Frelimo managed to shift the center of the anticolonial war from the north of the country to the center, and thus toward the dioceses of Beira and Tete.[2]

The start of the anticolonial war in Mozambique in 1964 surprised neither the Portuguese army nor the colonial state. Both had anticipated these developments and had prepared themselves for it. Since the late 1950s, the

Portuguese army had developed a military strategy and capacity based on counterinsurgency; after the Angolan uprising of 1961, it had restructured itself and moved additional troops to Africa to fight any African nationalist "insurgency" that might arise.[3] This state of preparation permitted the Portuguese to counter and successfully stop Frelimo's offensives in Tete, Zambezia, and Manica and Sofala in 1964 and 1965. In anticipation of further attempts, the Portuguese expanded state and private militias and engaged in psychosocial activities; some of these involved religion, for example by co-opting (some) Muslims, Protestants, or Jehovah Witnesses. Following the French example, the Portuguese developed *aldeamentos* (protected hamlets)—by the end of the war in 1975, there would be 953 such villages, comprising about 10 percent of the total Mozambican population.[4] It began to build these aldeamentos in the province of Tete in 1968.[5] Similar hamlets were built in Manica and Sofala province in the 1970s, reaching the town of Sena in 1973. Finally, PIDE, the infamous security police, arrived in Mozambique in 1958 and quickly expanded its influence and power. Informants were recruited, and spying, arrests, and torture became a central feature within (and a pervasive fear for) Mozambican society, and for Africans in particular.

Frelimo's opening of a military front in Tete after 1967 marked a deepening of the war as well as its regionalization. The white Rhodesian and South African regimes were preoccupied with the movement's advances as these had opened up a corridor for Zimbabwean and South African fighters to travel from Tanzania to Rhodesia and South Africa. To curtail this movement, in 1970 the Portuguese, Rhodesian, and South African regimes established an alliance, codenamed "Exercise ALCORA," to enable intelligence and military cooperation between the regimes.[6] On this basis, Rhodesians were allowed to intervene militarily in Mozambique. As a result, from April to November 1971, Rhodesian troops and Portuguese commandos committed a series of four massacres in the area of Mukumbura, west of the city of Tete. Two Burgos fathers and the sister at Mukumbura mission investigated these events and wrote several versions of a report that they sent to their bishop and to the civil and military authorities. Soon the report made it into the press too. The two Burgos missionaries were arrested and put in jail, where they remained in solitary confinement for twenty-three months until the Portuguese government passed an amnesty in late 1973 in order to avoid having to bring them to court. As soon as they were released, the two missionaries were expelled from Mozambique.[7] While the subsequent massacre by the Portuguese army in December 1972 at Wiriyamu, Mozambique became an international cause célèbre and is often interpreted today as having given direction to the war, it is the Mukumbura massacre that had the greatest effect on the church in Mozambique. Among other effects, it led the Burgos fathers to actively support Frelimo and the cause of independence.[8] After this massacre, the war became very violent and directly affected the Catholic Church.

The war led to another (unanticipated) development after 1967—the rise of a white-led "multiracial" independence project. This came in the person of Jorge Jardim who was the deputy for the province of Manica and Sofala in the Portuguese Assembly in Lisbon. He represented some of the biggest capitalist interests in Mozambique (such as Champalimaud, Boullosa, and Abecassis) and had been a secret and special agent for Salazar, with whom he had corresponded intensively.[9] Officially the director of the Lusalite firm in Dondo, near Beira, Jardim had been involved in secret negotiations with the Indian government over the invasion of Goa in 1962, had worked at securing the power of President Hastings Banda in Malawi after 1963, and had carried out negotiations with the new white regime of Rhodesia after 1965. In local politics, Jardim at first allied himself to the bishop of Beira; over time, however, their views diverged and Jardim ended up opposing the bishop and most of the Beira clergy. In the 1960s, he bought Beira's second newspaper, *Notícias de Beira*, to undermine the hegemony of the diocese's *Diário de Moçambique*, and opened his own radio station to undermine Radio Pax, launched by the Franciscans in 1954.[10] In a letter to Salazar in 1968, Jardim explained:

> Regarding the latest incident involving the *Diário de Moçambique*,[11] I believe that we have all reason to be satisfied with our decision to have a trusted newspaper at our disposal in Beira, as is the case with the *Notícias da Beira* that is under my direct command. Thanks to the coordinated and disciplined action of the *Notícias da Beira* and the *Areroclube da Beira* radio station (which I also control), it has been possible to minimize the impact that the justified suspension of the *Diário de Moçambique* could have caused among the Beira listeners. In effect, our adversaries in Beira no longer have the possibility of shaping public opinion as they did a while back.[12]

Jardim's actions against the church increased in the course of the early 1970s as missionaries began to protest openly against the war. In 1970, Jardim managed to buy the diocesan newspaper *Diário de Moçambique* and its African sister publication, *Voz Africana* (more below). On January 1, 1972, he orchestrated a scandal against two secular priests of Macuti parish after they denounced injustice and war in their homily on the International Day of Peace and used the Mukumbura massacre to illustrate the excesses. The scandal grew more acute a week later when the same two fathers tried to prevent the Portuguese flag from being brought into the church. Jardim grabbed the occasion to attack the fathers in several scathing articles over the subsequent days and to organize a mass protest in the streets of Beira. On January 14, the two fathers, Joaquim Teles Sampaio and Fernando Marques Mendes, and their house employee, João Chabuca, were arrested and transferred to PIDE's central prison of Machava in southern Mozambique. A year later the two fathers were brought to court (as they were Portuguese, they could not be expelled) in what constituted the first case ever in the Portuguese Empire of priests on trial in a military court.[13] They were accused of glorifying the separation of Mozambique from Portugal, disrespecting the national flag, committing crime against the security of the state, promoting disobedience of the laws, and disturbing public peace.[14] After thirteen months in jail (and extensive negative publicity for the regime), the clergymen stood trial in January 1973. The trial was short and the men were only charged with minor offenses in what many believed was a way for the state to avoid embarrassing revelations in court about the massacre of Mukumbura.[15] The fathers returned to Beira, but when Jardim's daughters organized more demonstrations and even some violence, the fathers decided to leave the city.[16] In a letter to Prime Minister Caetano, Jardim explained his actions in the following terms: "The "lefties" think that they hold the exclusive rights to activism (or even to use violence) by controlling young people in particular. I believe that Beira was a surprise and a lesson for them."[17]

Jardim's collaboration with Salazar's successor Marcello Caetano was smooth at first, both due to a close affiliation between them in earlier years and because Jardim had the "unbeatable vocation of a chameleon," as his biographer put it.[18] Caetano's plan for the colonies differed from Salazar's in that he wished for a policy of decentralization of the empire: "participative and progressive autonomy" as part of a strategy of "renovation in continuity." In his eyes, the colonies were to achieve a multiracial independence within some sort of a Portuguese commonwealth in the medium term, a plan that put him in the "modernist" camp within the Estado Novo regime.[19] Jardim contributed to the realization of Caetano's vision by recruiting African individuals for medium-level positions within the colonial system so as to start its Africanization. Based in Beira, Jardim chose men and women from the Catholic elite of central Mozambique, some of whom were Frelimo dissidents. Miguel Murrupa, both a former seminarian and a former Frelimo leader, was the central figure in charge of recruiting others.[20] Jardim recruited him to work at the *Voz Africana* after he had bought it from the Diocese of Beira.[21] Together with General Kaúlza de Arriaga and drawing on the experience in Angola, Jardim also founded two special African regiments to fight Frelimo and the Revolutionary Committee of Mozambique (COREMO) in central Mozambique: the Grupo Especiais (GE) in 1970, and the Grupos Especiais Paradequistas (GEP) in 1971. They were partly financed and controlled by Jardim, and by 1974 reached between 6,000 and 8,500 men.[22]

While working with Caetano in the 1970s, Jardim was tempted to follow his own political path. By then, there were numerous ideas about what should happen to the colonies: Caetano wanted decentralization and an eventual granting of independence to the colonies; white liberal democrats in Mozambique proposed the immediate establishment of a "Federal Portuguese Republic," with independence to be granted in the medium-term; while another set of colonialists considered the Rhodesian option of a unilateral white declaration of independence.[23] When it became clear around 1973 that Caetano's plan was mostly cosmetic, Jardim invested in his own, aiming at a multiracial unilateral declaration of independence. Seeing that Frelimo had officially adopted Marxism in 1968, Jardim argued that Mozambique needed an alternative to both colonization and Frelimo; he wanted to prevent power from being handed over to Frelimo. Salazar's former "secret agent" built his strategy on the prospect that his suggestion for multiracial independence would develop "naturally," though he also considered staging a coup d'état. While Jardim hid most of his new political activities from the Portuguese government in Lisbon, he reorganized his military forces and support structures and negotiated with neighboring countries, particularly Malawi and Zambia, to offer Frelimo joint multiracial independence. In September 1973, Jardim signed a so-called Lusaka Program with the Zambian government, according to which the latter expressed its openness to negotiations with Frelimo. Caetano was eventually informed of these maneuvers and was not pleased. Before he could do anything about it, he was ousted by a military coup d'état in Lisbon and the Portuguese regime collapsed.[24]

Jardim's plans do not seem to have gathered much (if any) support from the Catholic Church in the dioceses of Beira and Tete. The project was conducted in secret, though rumors circulated and made it into the foreign press. I have not gained access to the archives of the Portuguese Jesuits or Franciscans in Lisbon, which might reveal some so far unknown connections. Yet many of my interviewees and the extensive documentation I have worked with suggest that while a few religious individuals were close to Jardim, no congregation supported his political project in any significant way. According to a priest who subsequently became close to his family, Jardim's plan did not gain traction in central Mozambique or in the church at large.[25] The clergy was either quietist or showed complete support for one of the two sides, the regime or the liberation struggle. We will see in the next section how these divisions played out politically and religiously. For now, we should note that the eruption of the war in the provinces of Tete and Manica and Sofala both radicalized and entrenched the political positions of the missionaries, leaving no interest in a third way. In Tete, the war led the Jesuits to develop more empathy with the regime and more support for the army,[26] while the Mukumbura Massacre radicalized the Burgos fathers in the opposite direction to give direct support to the liberation struggle.[27] In Manica and Sofala, the Franciscans became more closely tied to the regime and the army, while the White Fathers were pushed into leaving Mozambique, a development I examine in the next section.

Episcopal Death, Succession, and Crisis

Dom Sebastião Soares de Resende passed away of cancer of the esophagus on January 26, 1967. When the disease was discovered in February 1966, it was already too advanced to be treated. During the last months of his life, even the available medication was not able to alleviate his pain. By the end of November 1966, Dom Sebastião was forced to stay in bed. He kept running the diocese from his room, however, where he received his advisers, the heads of congregations, missionaries, and people who wished to say goodbye.[28] In a last attempt to find a cure, the bishop traveled to Stockholm, Sweden, in December 1966. But this was in vain and he decided to return to Mozambique so that he could die in his diocese. He was buried in Beira's cemetery, on January 28, 1967, one day after his passing, in the presence of 25,000 people.[29] The bishop of Quelimane, Francisco Nunes Texeira, read the eulogy at the funeral. Dom Francisco had worked under Dom Sebastião until the formation of the Diocese of Quelimane in 1956, and had remained close to him. PIDE, illustrating a sign of the times, prohibited the publication of his eulogy because it contained a passage criticizing the civil authorities. As PIDE explained its position: "The words of the bishop of Quelimane, D. Francisco Nunes Teixeira, hurt our sensitivities in that, as a whole, they challenged our nationalist fiber, our principles of political adequacy and possibly even our own principles of political sanity, that kind of sanity and moderation that is the prerogative of those who bend under the weight of the responsibility of the position that they occupy."[30] As a result, the clergy of Beira wrote a letter to Salazar in which they argued that the censors had intentionally insulted a dead man and not respected the "peace of the dead."[31]

While the church searched for a new prelate for Beira, the bishop of Tete and the Mozambican Episcopal Conference took advantage of the situation to change the missionaries in charge of the Zobuè Seminary. This had been a long-standing desire of the cardinal of Lourenço Marques, and discussions about it had been taking place since 1964. With the formation of the Diocese of Tete in 1962, the seminary—which was being run by the White Fathers—had been placed under the control of the bishop of Tete. He supported the change, but as Zobuè was an interdiocesan structure, any change of that nature needed the approval of Dom Sebastião; yet he had opposed the change. In addition, the Jesuits—who were envisaged to take over the seminary—had refused the offer in view of their lack of personnel and because they did not want to disrupt their good relations with the White Fathers.[32] The Jesuit position did not change after Dom Sebastião's death, so that the Mozambican Episcopal Conference asked the Vatican to put pressure on the Jesuit leadership in Rome. Under this pressure, the Jesuits accepted and the takeover took place in August 1967, in time for the new academic year of 1967–68. Even according to Jesuit sources, the transition was difficult. Many students rejected the authority of the new fathers and half of them left the seminary in the following three months— many fleeing abroad, joining Frelimo, and getting involved in the factional fight in Frelimo.[33] In a report in early 1968, the Jesuit superior blamed the White Fathers for the difficulties, arguing that they had trained very few priests, that many seminarians had left Zobuè to engage in exile politics, and some had even gone to study in Moscow. He further reckoned the seminary should be moved to an urban center and away from the border with Malawi.[34]

A New Bishop: Dom Manuel Ferreira Cabral

After the death of Dom Sebastião Soares de Resende in 1967, the Vatican proposed Father António Ribeiro as successor. Father Ribeiro had the typical profile for a Portuguese bishop. He came from a rural district, had studied at the Gregorian University in Rome, and was a teacher at the seminary of the Diocese of Braga. He was also a teacher at the Instituto Superior de Ciências Sociais e Políticas Ultramarinas (Higher Institute of Social Sciences and Overseas Policies, colloquially called the Colonial School) and a speaker for the religious programs of the Portuguese national radio. It was during one of these programs that Ribeiro had expressed support for a papal visit to India shortly after this country had invaded (Portuguese) Goa. The Portuguese government strongly opposed the visit, believing that it enshrined India's annexation of Goa.[35] Due to Ribeiro's comments on this occasion, Salazar refused his nomination, as the Concordat allowed him to.[36] This was the first and only time that Salazar used the state's veto to block the nomination of a bishop. The Vatican then proposed Dom Manuel Ferreira Cabral. Born on the Portuguese island of Madeira, Dom Manuel was fifty-nine years old at the time. He too had trained at the Gregorian University and had been a rector of a diocesan seminary. At the time of his nomination, he was the auxiliary bishop of the Diocese of Braga, in northern Portugal. Salazar's government accepted the proposal and in August 1967 Dom Manuel took up his position in the Diocese of Beira.

Dom Manuel was conservative, nationalist, and in favor of the regime (see fig. 5.1). On his arrival in Mozambique, the PIDE chief in Beira commented to his superior in a secret report:

> From a quick skim of the newspaper reports on what D. Manuel Ferreira Cabral has stated in the past, a new idea emerges clearly. It is an idea that we have not been used to, about the personality of the new bishop

Figure 5.1. Dom Manuel Ferreira Cabral second bishop of Beira, visiting Nazaré. In the foreground, left, is Father José Augusto Sousa, SJ, Sister Maria José (Pauline Sisters), Sister Joaquina Neves (Sisters of the Mother of the Divine Shepherd), Sister Teresa Ramos (Pauline Sisters), and unidentified sister on the right. Courtesy of Josef Pampalk.

of Beira: he has always focused on the idea of the motherland, on our heroes, on our presence here. He has tried to link the ecumenical concept of the church with the eternity of our motherland. This is something that, compared to his predecessor, can be seen as a good omen in terms of its potential social and political implications, considering the importance of the present moment.[37]

According to PIDE, Dom Manuel came to Beira with the intention of "modify[ing] certain things that were not well and even correct[ing] certain attitudes of some religious individuals who for a long time have mixed religious activities with the political scene."[38] While the state was pleased, the bishop's views, actions, and difficulty in relating with missionaries rapidly alienated a large section of his clergy.[39] Fifteen months after his arrival, twenty-five priests (half of the total) had already written a letter asking him to resign. Their argumentation is most interesting for its exposition of how the bishop ran his diocese (in contrast to his predecessor). They raised three complaints: first, the bishop lacked any interest in pastoral work; second, he did not guide the pastoral and other Catholic works in the diocese; and third, he refused to engage in dialogue with his clergy and ignored his presbyterium.[40] The fathers argued that not only had the previous bishop worked closely with the presbyterium, but the Second Vatican Council highly recommended that all bishops engage their local priests through this office. In their view, Dom Manuel's actions (or lack thereof) were not just unpleasant but directly opposed to Roman guidelines, and divided the clergy. Indeed, the priests argued that the bishop's approach led to significant division among them: "Our sober and level-headed reflection on these serious problems has led us to discover that the main causes of this situation [these divisions] are a total lack of pastoral sentiment and absence of dialogue with the clergy that have emerged since your arrival in the diocese."[41]

In addition, the bishop had failed to defend his missionaries in the face of the secular authorities, and PIDE had therefore easily expelled a number of White Fathers.[42] This was not a new problem for the White Fathers. In fact, the leadership of the Society of the Missionaries of Africa had sent an envoy to Mozambique in April and May 1968 to consult with its missionaries there about withdrawing from the territory—something the fathers at this point unanimously refused.[43] As we will see below, however, these new expulsions and Dom Manuel's lack of support would soon tip the scale in the other direction for this congregation. Another bone of contention was the *Diário de Moçambique* newspaper that the bishop decided to sell soon after his arrival due to what he called serious financial constraints. Many priests argued that the publication had always been

Table 5.1. Missionaries who actively took a progressive stance, Beira, 1971.

Jesuits	2
Burgos	3
Secular	3
White Fathers	14
Comboni	1
Unknown	1

Source: PIDE-Moçambique, *Informação* n°726/71/DI/2/SC, April 8, 1971, vol. 6, "Missionarios no Ultramar," Processo SC-CI(2) 1734, PIDE/DGS, Instituto Nacional dos Arquivos Nacionais/Torre de Tombo, Lisbon.
Note: This list is drawn from a letter of protest that twenty-four missionaries in Beira wrote to the archbishop of Lourenço Marques in 1971. They protested against his agreement to the expulsion of Father Regoli, an Italian, on the suspicion that he had been involved in anti-Portuguese activities. There was no proof of this involvement. The signatories formed 28 percent of the male clergy of Beira. Their distribution by affiliation (captured in the table) is specific to the "Regoli case"; the number and distribution of activist missionaries was to change very quickly thereafter.

in financial difficulty and that Dom Sebastião had always managed to keep it running since he saw it as crucial to push Beira toward a form of Christian democracy. Despite the opposition, the new bishop sold the newspaper in 1970 and, to make matters worse, accepted its sale to none other than Jorge Jardim.[44] This scandalized not just many religious men and women in Beira but also many lay Catholics. Several secular priests who held key positions in the diocese decided to leave Beira at once, including Monsignor Soares Martins, the newspaper's administrator, Alberto da Assunção Tavares, the diocese's secretary, and Monsignor Seraphim Brum do Amaral, in charge of the Chinese Catholic community. Dom Manuel took advantage of these vacancies to bring in his own men from Portugal (priests who were quickly accused of being too young and inexperienced), deepening the internal conflict and playing a significant role in convincing missionaries that quietism was no longer the correct position to take.

In the face of opposition, the new bishop of Beira began to lean increasingly on the Franciscan missionaries. Like him, this congregation was religiously and politically conservative as well as favorable to the regime. The Franciscans were numerically significant in Beira, constituting 42 percent of the male missionary body and almost all of the female missionaries (see table 5.1). To cement the alliance, in 1970 Dom Manuel demoted Beira's vicar-general, Monsignor Duarte de Almeida (a modernist secular priest close to Dom Sebastião), and replaced him with the Franciscan superior of Mozambique, Frei Manuel dos Reis Miranda. This alliance with one congregation against the rest was to prove detrimental to the bishop. The excluded congregations (including the Jesuits and the secular priests) reacted vigorously against Duarte de Almeida's demotion and his marginalization within the diocese—he was given no new post.[45] During the third pastoral week, held in October 1970 (bringing together fifty priests, twenty-five sisters, and twenty catechists), the participants demanded that the bishop assign a new post to Monsignor Duarte de Almeida and that he adopt a more open pastoral stance, a clearer position on pastoral work and financial matters, and include the presbyterium in his decision making.

Instead of answering these demands, Dom Manuel left the meeting and departed for Lisbon. On his return two months later, the bishop had a meeting with his clergy on Christmas Eve. When the bishop still did not respond to the October demands, a group of male and female missionaries went to the bishop's palace to call for a response. Under pressure, the bishop appointed Monsignor Duarte de Almeida to the parish of Macuti.[46] But it was too little, too late. The clergy took matters into their own hands and decided to work without the bishop. In early 1971 they held several meetings to set a pastoral line for the diocese. The bishop did not attend and the Franciscans had a very low-key role. Reporting on this affair to their superior in the Netherlands, the Picpus fathers noted that "'the Brothers of St. Francis' remain[ed] shyly neutral. Conscientiousness is rising among some of the young [Franciscans], but they do not have the slightest support, nor the slightest chance [to express themselves], for they could be forced to leave the diocese."[47]

Accused of having divided the clergy with their lack of support to other congregations, the Franciscans explained to the nuncio in Portugal that they had refused "to collaborate with an open war against Monsignor Dom Manuel Ferreira Cabral, who was our bishop and—as such—deserved our respect and obedience as any other bishop deserves our respect and obedience, even when we do not agree with some of his ideas."[48] By the beginning of the 1970s, the situation of the White Fathers became tenuous. Various fathers had been expelled and more were under threat of expulsion. In early 1970 a missionary was refused a visa after he was denounced by religious sisters for a joke about elections that they thought was portentous (though the superior of the society thought the joke was "futile").[49] As a result of his removal, the mission of Baruè had to close and the society's superior, Father Bertulli, was very upset. This was the last straw for the society in Mozambique. Bertulli asked the new bishop to intervene with the authorities and asked the Episcopal Conference and the newly created Federação dos Institutos Religiosos de Moçambique (Federation of Religious Institutes in Mozambique, FIRM, see more below) to take a stand. But both of these bodies were unwilling and the bishop of Beira seems to have tried unsuccessfully to challenge the father's removal. The White Fathers thought that the situation had gone too far. The society's General Council met in Rome in January 1971 and considered whether the society should withdraw from its work in Mozambique. The council decided that before it could make any final decision, its superior general needed to travel to Mozambique and Portugal for discussions with the missionaries, the Mozambican Episcopal Conference, the nuncio (the Vatican's ambassador), and both the Ministry of Foreign Affairs and the Ministry of Overseas Territories.[50] In Mozambique, a majority of the fathers and brothers now supported the society's abandoning of Mozambique. Upon his return, the superior general briefed the General Council on his findings. On April 30, 1971, the council voted unanimously to withdraw the society from Mozambique. A total forty-five priests and brothers, of eight different nationalities, were to leave within two months. Before the White Fathers could even begin to organize their departure, however, the Portuguese authorities expelled them *manu militari* (see fig. 5.2).

The departure of the White Fathers was a first in the Catholic world. It sent shock waves through the church in Mozambique and Portugal and had a huge echo worldwide. It is important to understand the exact reasons for which the White Fathers decided to leave Mozambique. The letter of the superior general to the bishops of Beira and Tete explained the decision in the following terms:

> It is above all the ambiguity that hangs over the mission today that informed the decision for us to leave, in spite of the grave impediment it poses to Christianity and the significant suffering it imposes on the missionaries. Sent to preach the Gospel and make the church present in the heart of the people of this part of Africa, the missionaries notice that the constant confusion between state and church gravely prejudices the revelation of the true face of the church.[51]

Thus, it was not so much a political decision about independence or the war in Mozambique that motivated the society's departure. Rather, it was

Figure 5.2. The White Fathers who were expelled from Mozambique, in Rome, June 1, 1971. Reproduced by permission from the Société des Missionnaires d'Afrique (White Fathers), Rome.

the fact that the church's work was under peril, in their view, because the Catholic institution in Mozambique had overly "compromised" itself with the colonial state. The White Fathers perceived that there was a "confusion" between the state and the church and that the neo-Thomist principle of the church being separate and above politics so that it could provide moral direction was being compromised. The issue was, ultimately, not about state politics (what is right or wrong for the state in Mozambique and Portugal) but about church politics (what is right for the church).

Now, if Bishop Ferreira might have considered leaving Beira in 1969 because of the troubles then,[52] the conflict of 1970 seems to have convinced him completely. In January 1971, as the White Fathers considered leaving and many other priests opposed him and set up an independent plan for the future of the church in Beira, the bishop secretly slipped out of town and flew to Lisbon where, two months later, he handed in his resignation to the nuncio.[53] For some reason, the nuncio in Lisbon did not accept his resignation until May, and the pope only accepted the resignation in July, after the expulsion of the White Fathers from Mozambique. In the absence of the bishop (though he was still officially in charge), the

Franciscan vicar-general, Manuel dos Reis Miranda, formally ran the diocese. Apparently, he was even more proactive than the prelate in his conservative, progovernment stance. PIDE noted:

> Dr. Miranda is known as a righteous and tough man, capable of taking
> drastic measures irrespective of their consequences. We know that he
> himself called the attention of the bishop to the necessity to "clean" the
> [episcopal] palace from its pernicious elements, simply and purely by
> firing them, as the diocese should not be prepared to enter a compro-
> mise with them. This suggestion was not considered acceptable because
> it "would harm sensibilities." Dr. Miranda responded that this was the
> easiest position, but that it was not prudent or shrewd to sacrifice the
> common good for the whim of a few.[54]

The vicar-general's sense of the need to clean up does not seem to have
been acted on during his short reign either. It is possible that the balance
of forces did not lean sufficiently in his favor to succeed or that he already
had too much on his plate. Nevertheless, six months later the Vatican nominated the progressive Dom Manuel Vieira Pinto, the bishop of Nampula, as
(transitional) apostolic administrator of the Diocese of Beira. The vicar-general understood this choice as a vote against his own mandate (and proof
that the Vatican did not approve of his work). Hurt, he left Mozambique,
following Dom Manuel Ferreira Cabral back to Portugal.[55]

The Administration of Manuel Vieira Pinto

After the expulsion of the White Fathers, the Vatican sent an envoy to
Mozambique to evaluate the situation in the territory and find solutions
for the Diocese of Beira. The Vatican needed to nominate a new bishop,
or at least an apostolic administrator, to succeed Dom Manuel Ferreira
Cabral. It seems that the Vatican initially considered appointing the bishop
of Quelimane as apostolic administrator of Beira (as he had been Dom
Sebastião Soares de Resende's secretary), but the missionaries of Beira
convinced its envoy to nominate Dom Manuel Vieira Pinto instead.[56] Pinto
was the bishop of Nampula and well-known because he had been active as
a leader and speaker for the Portuguese branch of the Catholic Movement
for a Better World before his appointment as bishop.[57] Dom Manuel took
up the position in Beira in July 1971. Tellingly, the pope's appointment
letter made reference to the trust Dom Manuel enjoyed in the Diocese of
Beira. The cardinal's secretary of state, in turn, asked the bishop to make
"diocesan communion" his first pastoral objective.[58]

While Dom Manuel Vieira Pinto was Portuguese like the preceding bishop of Beira, theologically he was strongly aligned with the Vatican II reforms. His approach toward his new diocese is reflected in the first sermon he gave at the Beira cathedral on July 11, 1971—reflected here through the eyes of the state security police:

- Assertion of his presence at the head of the Diocese "only to SERVE."
- Referring to the exit of the White Fathers and of Dr. Duarte de Almeida, he made it felt that these events had opened a gap very difficult to fill, and that all that happened in Mozambique constitutes a very painful experience. "We need to reflect on what God tried to tell us . . . ," he emphasized. Continuing, he said: "Beira already has very beautiful traditions and therefore we—the laity, the presbyterium, and the clergy— we need to feel responsible. It is a difficult moment. We have to pardon each other, just as God pardoned, so that this diocese continues to be a light, because the problems of this diocese are many and large." To conclude: "Trust in me as I trust in you. Continue to struggle and to pray so that the church continues to be built in brotherly love."[59]

From this excerpt, one gains the impression that the bishop aimed to accept all social, theological, and political sensibilities and to work along lines closer to those of Dom Sebastião than Dom Manuel Ferreira Cabral. Tellingly, immediately on his arrival Dom Manuel Vieira Pinto met with the clergy at Manga mission to choose a new presbyterium and elect a new vicar-general. For the presbyterium, Dom Manuel appointed a representative from each congregation. For the position of vicar-general, he held a secret vote—the first time this had ever happened.[60] Interestingly, after the result was compiled, he managed to convince those voting to appoint the person who came in second—José Augusto Alves de Sousa, the young Portuguese Jesuit who worked at the Catechetic center of Inhamuiza, on the grounds that he had better a relationship with the colonial state, which, he argued, was needed at that juncture.[61]

Dom Manuel's balanced approach was not to last or have a significant influence, however. Already at the Manga meeting, he asked the presbyterium to establish a permanent commission to draft a message to all members of the diocese, to be approved by the presbyterium and the bishop, and then read in all churches. Though the message was mostly a matter of the diocese only, it had a national dimension: Dom Manuel wanted the diocese to take a stand in relation to the situation of the church, not least in regard to the departure of the White Fathers about which the episcopal conference had up to then remained silent.[62] The text was rapidly drafted and adopted on August 13, 1971. It was quite radical in its theological approach as well as in the language it used to describe the situation in Mozambique. Among other things, it stated that "we prefer a church persecuted but lively to one privileged but gravely compromised by the temporal powers."[63]

As was to be expected, the "Message from the Presbyterium Council of Beira" (as the document was called) was not well received by the authorities. Mozambique's military commander in chief demanded that the governor-general expel all those who signed the document, including the bishop. PIDE suggested that only two of the signatories should be expelled, namely, those who had a history of "compromising" with the enemy. Finally, the governor-general took one and a half years to send PIDE's information to the minister with a note saying that Dom Manuel Vieira Pinto should be removed from Mozambique and a "good Bishop" be found for Beira instead.[64] If the state reacted slowly, this probably had to do with the fact that removing a bishop was complicated and would draw more bad publicity for the regime. It was probably also related to the fact that the document had been signed by the whole presbyterium of the diocese, including the Franciscan representative, though the new head of the Franciscan congregation subsequently denounced this "affair" to the nuncio as a "conspiracy" and said that he had neither signed the document nor ever heard about it.[65]

Conspiracy or not, the publication of this document led to a rapid degeneration of the relationship between the Franciscans and the bishop. A PIDE report noted in November that Dom Manuel had complained during a meeting with his clergy about the Franciscans' lack of collaboration.[66] Then, in December, the bishop sent the Franciscans a one-page document called "Points of Study for the Plenary Council," in which he asked the congregation to introduce the following changes:

- to make a missionary available to the diocese;
- to pay more attention to the ways in which the population was changing;
- to nurture elite and true Christian families;
- to evangelize not only through schools but in people's whole lives;
- to pay more attention to the poor;
- to invest in more modest physical structures;
- to be more inclusive in relation to the laity;
- to create councils at their parishes;
- to create peasant cooperatives for community development;
- to transform [their] Radio Pax into an organ of fostering justice, peace, and development; and
- to transform their newspaper [*O Domingo*] from a parish publication to a diocesan one and possibly even an interdiocesan one.[67]

The document was neither diplomatic nor balanced. The bishop showed no empathy for his Franciscan colleagues and made demands from a position of authority, without leaving much space for negotiation. Unsurprisingly, the Franciscan congregation reacted strongly to the bishop's document. In a letter dated January 21, 1972, it approached the matter diplomatically, to start with, by saying that the bishop's text had enriched Franciscan reflection. Then it proceeded to refute every one of the bishop's points. The missionaries legitimately contested some points (e.g., the Franciscans had nurtured a local elite and followed the principle of poverty) and challenged others that did not make sense to them (e.g., they might not have cooperatives but had developed excellent agricultural schemes and worked for peace, justice, and development in their own way). What the two documents show is a significant divide and lack of understanding between the two sides: a mutually exclusive weltanschauung. Unsurprisingly, the Franciscans perceived the bishop's letter as an attack against their work, or even against their charisma. We can infer from this event that within a few months, by late 1971, Dom Manuel was no longer supportive of all missionaries and congregations under his watch and had decided to openly side with one group. PIDE pronounced that the bishop was being partial, with several of its reports giving different explanations for this: mostly that Dom Manuel was allowing himself to be manipulated by progressive missionaries, or had chosen to ally himself with the progressive clergy.[68] Whichever explanation is the correct one, and contrary to his discourse, Dom Manuel had chosen not to proceed in the tradition set by Dom Sebastião Soares de Resende—being balanced and above his clergy's differences.

The Short Reign of Dom Altino Ribeiro Santana

While Dom Manuel Vieira Pinto acted in a transitional capacity in Beira, retaining his position as bishop of Nampula, the Vatican looked for a new bishop for Beira. After the departure of the White Fathers, the Vatican's secretary of state sent an envoy, Monsignor Gaspari, to Beira in June 1971 to evaluate the situation of the diocese and of Mozambique as a whole. According to the regional superior of the White Fathers, Monsignor Gaspari wrote a secret report for the Vatican on his visit in which he recommended that all bishops in Mozambique who had compromised their position by working with the colonial state should be removed.[69] In February 1972, it was the turn of the nuncio in Lisbon to travel to Mozambique and he informed the episcopal conference that a number of bishops would soon be appointed in an act "which will exceed all your expectations."[70] And, indeed, a number of assignments were made a few days later: two bishops were moved out of Mozambique, one was placed in a different diocese, and two new bishops were appointed.[71] In Tete, Dom Félix Niza Ribeiro was moved to the southern Diocese of João Belo (today Xai Xai). He was replaced by Dom Augusto César Alves Ferreira da Silva, a Lazarist (also known as Vincentian) who had previously been the superior of his congregation's Portuguese province and the director of the Major Seminary of Namaacha/Pio X in Lourenço Marques.[72] For Beira, the Vatican chose Dom Altino Ribeiro de Santana, a secular priest who had been bishop of Sá da Bandeira in Angola from 1955 onward. While he was trained at the Gregorian University as were all other bishops, Dom Altino was different in that he was of Goan origin (a high-caste Indian) and the first nonwhite bishop in Mozambique.

Dom Altino entered the Diocese of Beira in April 1972. Soft-spoken and kind, a bit like Dom Sebastião, if simpler in nature,[73] Dom Altino's personality and balanced approach seem to have rapidly soothed relations among the clergy and brought back peace to the diocese. The political situation in central Mozambique soured in January 1973, however, and what retrospectively looks like a truce soon ended. In January 1973, Jardim was instrumental in the eruption of a scandal involving two priests from Macuti parish and organized a demonstration to increase "public pressure" on the church (see discussion in the previous section). As part of that campaign, on February 11 a military grenade was thrown at the bishop's palace. As more demonstrations against the church were announced, the bishop needed police protection.[74] When Dom Altino was informed on February 27, 1973, that three Burgos fathers (involved in the public exposé of the Mukumbura Massacre) were to be expelled from Mozambique, he suffered a fatal heart attack.[75] His death halted a short period of internal calm for the Diocese of Beira that seems significantly related to the bishop's approach, balanced and inclusive of all congregations and of all religious and political stances.

Dom Altino's successor in Beira, as transitional apostolic administrator, was Dom Francisco Teixeira. Although he had been Beira's first vicar-general until 1956 and he retained the consensual vicar-general, José Augusto Alves de Sousa, he was contested and eventually did not manage to rule the diocese smoothly.[76] A report by a Picpus father to his superior-general explains why and with what consequences:

> The diocese is passing through a moment in which there is nothing that grants comfort. The departure of D. Altino, who was beginning to raise high hopes, brought disappointment. Especially with the imposition of

D. Francisco. . . . On March 2, on the induction of D. Francisco, they told him to his face what they felt. And Father José, supported by brother Manuel and some sisters (Pauline and Heart of Mary), [asked] D. Francisco whether he had forgotten what he had done when the White Fathers left. He stated that he hoped past errors would be forgotten. They answered that it would be difficult to forget the famous meeting, here in Beira, where he had made a number of problematic assertions in front of the whole clergy. [Upon this] he only answered: "I have no responsibility if the Holy Father nominated me." . . . He left the room, in a spirit of fighting. . . . These problems, added to the old ones, have reduced this diocese to a dismantled community. In the meetings I attend, one hears only words of discouragement. A sensation of death reigns.[77]

Thus, while Dom Altino had brought some respite to the church in 1972, his death and the nomination of Dom Francisco reignited both the conflict among the congregations and that between the congregations and the bishop. Thereafter the Diocese of Beira continued on its course of implosion—until the coup d'état in Lisbon in April 1974.

The Diocese of Tete (created in 1962) experienced a dynamic similar to Beira's in those years. Tete's first bishop, Dom Félix Niza Ribeiro, was a secular priest while his diocese was made up of diverse congregations—Jesuits, White Fathers, Burgos, Comboni, Sisters of Cluny, Franciscan Missionaries of the Mother of the Divine Shepherd, Missionary Daughters of Calvary, Mercedarian Missionary Sisters, Daughters of Mary Help of Christians, Sisters of Saint Dorothy, and Daughters of the Charity of Saint Vincent de Paul. While the bishop seems to have had a good relationship with the Jesuits and most sisters, his association with the White Fathers, the Burgos fathers, the Comboni fathers, and some female congregations was tense. Part of the problem was their divergent theology and weltanschauung. In 1969 the Burgos fathers contrasted the "narrow mentality and vision that the bishop manifested in relation to the pastoral ministry, totally influenced by the stench of colonialism" to their own "line, markedly open, based on the authentic principles of catholicity, at the margins of any colonialism."[78] What made matters worse was that Dom Félix did not stand up for his missionaries when the latter had problems with the civil or military authorities.[79] PIDE liked and trusted the bishop, considering him "wholly ours."[80] As noted in chapter 3, in 1968 Dom Félix refused to send Father Domingos Ferrão abroad to help him avoid being jailed by PIDE, on the grounds that he did not "trust" Ferrão; he also did nothing to help his ex-seminarists in jail. The bishop had difficult relations with his presbyterium as well. In September 1971, the latter rebelled against Dom Félix after he tried to appoint the Jesuit Luís Gonzaga Ferreira as vicar-general of the diocese.[81] Gonzaga Ferreira was an ultranationalist who embarrassed even his own Society of Jesus—the Jesuit superior deemed some of his interventions "bad publicity" for the society.[82] Finally, in February 1972, forty fathers, brothers, and sisters of the Diocese of Tete (about 30 percent of the Tete clergy) wrote a letter to the nuncio in Lisbon to complain about what they perceived as collusion between church and state.[83] A few days later, the Vatican announced the nomination of Dom Félix to another diocese; in his place, it appointed Dom Augusto César Alves Ferreira, a Vincentian who arrived in the diocese on July 9, 1972 and had a pro-Portuguese but less controversial reign until independence.

The Vatican and the Diocese of Beira

Little has been written on the Vatican and the position it took toward the decolonization of the Portuguese colonies in general and in relation to Mozambique specifically. What has been written usually reduces the topic to what the pope (or the Vatican) did or failed to do, declared or failed to declare. The discussion often switches from an analysis of the Portuguese Concordat and Missionary Accord of 1940 to a discussion of the various events at which the pope and/or the Vatican took a position in favor of or against Portugal, such as the pope's visit to the Sanctuary of Fátima in Portugal in 1967, the audience at which he received three Angolan, Mozambican, and Bissau Guinean nationalist leaders in 1970, or the departure of the White Fathers from Mozambique in 1971.[84] This results in a picture in which the Vatican was tied to Portugal structurally, did not wish to undo these ties until independence, and only gave a nod toward African nationalism by referring to the pope's audience with representatives of the African nationalist liberation movements.[85] Alternatively, the papal audience is presented as a turning point signaling that the papacy was beginning to recognize African nationalism and its move to power. Bruno Cardoso Reis writes, for example: "The papal audience of July 1970 with the leaders of the MPLA, the FLNA and UNITA [*sic*][86] . . . marked a new phase in which the Vatican was distancing itself from the Estado Novo. The papacy was now prepared to enter a phase of increased tension with Portuguese authoritarianism and colonialism that it considered obsolete."[87]

The problem with such an approach is that we get a teleological history, going from a unified concordarian church to increasing dissidence and internal dissent. It goes from strong ties between Portugal and the Vatican to weaker ones, as if these were predestined and inevitable—Amelia Souto talks of an "awakening" of the church (*uma tomada de consciencia*) to the existing injustices and to the rightfulness of the liberation struggle.[88] Further, this approach also presents actors as united or unified on each side of the relation—the Vatican versus Portugal or Frelimo. Last but not least, it advances a hierarchical understanding of the church and ignores the horizontal structuring of the institution. Moving to examine what happened in the Vatican, this section investigates the position taken by religious congregations in Rome in relation to Mozambique and the role they had in shaping Vatican policies.

Before we proceed, it is important to understand how religious orders function within the central administration of the Catholic Church in Rome. Religious congregations are independent from the Catholic hierarchy and their superiors are only answerable to the Vatican or the pope. In Mozambique, as we have seen, religious men and women were answerable to both their bishop and their religious superior—which a Jesuit superior in Mozambique called a "double jurisdiction."[89] In view of this situation, how do religious congregations relate to the Vatican in Rome? The answer is that the Catholic Church operates like a moderate monarchist state. Supreme authority lies with the pope and the College of Cardinals (the body that elects the pope), but the day-to-day affairs of the church are left to the Curia, the central body through which the pope conducts the affairs of the universal Church. Like most state administrations, the Curia is organized into "ministries," called "congregations" or "councils" before Vatican II and "dicasteries" from the 1960s onward.[90] The Congregation for Religious and Secular Institutes is dedicated specifically to the affairs of religious men and women (today it is called the Congregation for Institutes of Consecrated Life and Societies of Apostolic Life). The congregation supervises the affairs of religious congregations, deals with their requests, and helps them solve problems with diocesan bishops. When it comes to their activities abroad, religious orders have to deal with the Propaganda Fide congregation. Due to the Padroado, religious orders in Mozambique did not report and respond to Propaganda Fide, but to the Secretariat of State which had a representative in Portugal in the person of the nuncio (ambassador) in Lisbon who covered both Portugal and its colonies/overseas territories. Occasionally, a religious organization or individual can engage directly with the pope who, as any monarch, has the power to receive whomever he wants and give guidelines and rulings. Otherwise, national bishops are in direct contact with the pope only at their five-year "ad limina" audience in the Vatican.

The administration of religious congregations by the Vatican has greatly increased in the twentieth century. In the early years of the century, the Vatican asked the religious orders to move their headquarters to Rome. Most

Catholic organizations moved their central offices close to the Vatican, especially with the Second World War. While this has meant an increased centralization of the Catholic Church, it has also increased the opportunity for religious superiors general to meet, organize, defend their interests, and increase their power within the Catholic Church. In 1951, Pope Pius XII encouraged religious congregations to organize themselves nationally and internationally into unions or federations. In Portugal, such a union was set up in 1953,[91] whereas in Mozambique FIRM was established for the male congregations in 1965. A federation for the female congregations in Mozambique was founded only after independence.[92] FIRM was created with the authorization of the Mozambican bishops, in parallel to the new national conference that they founded for themselves, the Conferência Episcopal de Moçambique (Episcopal Conference of Mozambique, CEM). Unions were also created at the international level, with the [male] Union of Superiors General (USG), launched officially in 1957, and the [female] International Union Superiors General, (UISG), launched in 1965.[93] These two international unions had (and still hold) regular meetings, both for themselves and with the Congregation for Religious and Secular Institutes, and with the Secretariat of State. As we will see, hierarchical and horizontal structures had their own connections on the ground; in the case of Mozambique, this resulted in a dynamic of back-and-forth consultations between actors in Rome and pastoral leaders in Mozambique. Most of these dynamics took place formally, but some unfolded along informal networks based, among others, on nationality or friendship.[94]

We saw earlier that the Vatican intervened directly in the affairs of the Diocese of Beira on various occasions. It sent envoys to Mozambique late in 1971 after the expulsion of the White Fathers and in 1972 to evaluate the situation and nominate a new bishop for Beira. The result of the first visit was a secret report to the pope that recommended the removal or redeployment of the Portuguese bishops who had most strongly compromised their position with the colonial state. We also saw Mozambican bishops and congregations writing to, and consulting with, the nuncio in Lisbon who traveled to Mozambique on his own account too. In addition, there are incomplete and obscure references about confidential or secret Vatican interventions, such as a secret letter the pope is reported to have addressed to the bishop of Nampula in late 1971 when he was acting as apostolic administrator in Beira; or an equally secret letter that the bishop would have written to the pope in 1973 (the contents of both letters remain unknown).[95] Finally, we know that the pope received several bishops as well as Mozambicans and specifically missionaries from central Mozambique in *ad limina* and personal audiences. In 1970 the pope also received leaders of the main liberation movements from Portuguese Africa. Such involvement suggests that the Vatican was concerned with Mozambique and paid careful attention to the development of the church there. What is unclear, partly because we do not know the content of these meetings, is the consequences of these audiences, in particular in relation to shifts in policy.

Information about discussions and decisions made among religious orders in Rome in relation to Mozambique and Beira is sparse. The crisis triggered by the expulsion of the White Fathers in 1971, however, led to the disclosure of some information, including the minutes of USG meetings that took place between the congregations and between the USG and the Secretariat of State. I use this event as a case study to uncover how the USG worked in relation to Mozambique, how it related to the Vatican's dicasteries, and how it contributed to the making of Vatican policy.[96] It is worth remembering here that the exit of the White Fathers was a first, a type of event that had never before taken place in the history of the Catholic Church. It is also worth recalling that the White Fathers' council decided to leave Mozambique only after their superior general traveled to Mozambique and to Portugal to investigate the situation and to consult with his missionaries and secular authorities. Less well-known is the fact that the White Fathers consulted the Secretariat of State before making their decision, and held discussions with other superior generals represented in the USG. The secretary of state, Cardinal Villot, seems to have wanted to act, but was unsure how to do so.[97] In February he asked the superior general of the society, Théo van Asten, to postpone the decision until April, to which van Asten acceded. But in the face of the Vatican's extended indecision and lack of action, and seeing that the pope did not want to formally support a decision to leave Mozambique but also did not want to oppose it, the White Fathers decided to act unilaterally.[98] The White Fathers thus took the lead for the Vatican and marked the policies in relation to Mozambique, which created some unhappiness in relation to form but was eventually accepted in relation to content by most in the Vatican.[99]

In regard to the USG, the White Fathers wanted to consult and discuss the situation with their colleagues before making any final decision. They eventually held six meetings with their USG partners before and after their expulsion from Mozambique. The first meeting took place on February 4, 1971, to discuss the situation in Mozambique and to seek advice and support—not to persuade others to follow the course of the White Fathers, the Superior argued. Representatives of twelve congregations attended, among which the Burgos fathers, the Comboni fathers, the Franciscans, the Jesuits, the Marist Brothers, the Picpus fathers, and the White Fathers as well as the Blessed Sacrament fathers (who worked in Lourenço Marques), the Capuchins (who worked in Zambezia), the Consolata (who worked in Inhambane and Niassa) and the Montfort missionaries (who worked in Cabo Delgado). The superiors present agreed to write a document to the bishops of Mozambique denouncing the situation in the church (without attacking anybody, they specified) and setting conditions for work to continue there. They set up a commission (consisting of a White Father, a Montfort representative, a Spiritan, and a Consolata representative) to draft the text.[100] The second meeting took place on March 6, 1971, on the return of the superior general of the White Fathers from Portugal and Mozambique. Present were representatives of the Franciscans, the Capuchins, the Marist Brothers, the Jesuits, and the Comboni fathers. The superior of the White Fathers began by describing the state of affairs in Mozambique and his meetings there and in Portugal. The congregations considered whether they should all leave Mozambique. The majority opinion was that it would be wiser to be expelled from Mozambique than to leave, so that the missionaries who stayed in the country (secular clergy and other congregations) would not suffer any consequences.[101] No decision was made at this meeting, but before the next one the White Fathers made public their decision to leave Mozambique.

At the third USG meeting on May 14, Father van Asten simply announced that his society would leave the territory. Other congregations expressed discontent about this. One superior felt the decision had introduced a division between the religious institutes, and another thought the decision too extreme. Most superiors agreed, however, to publish a jointly authored document about Mozambique, as agreed at the previous meetings.[102] At the fourth and fifth meetings, in April and June 1971, no progress was made on the joint document. Most superiors now agreed with the denunciation the White Fathers had made when leaving Mozambique, but they themselves did not want to leave—some had even given orders to their men prohibiting them from leaving their missionary posts. Other superiors wanted to continue with their protest, but from within. As to the joint document, the superiors now disagreed and abandoned the first draft because "members of the different institutes are from different origins and experience the situation in widely diverging ways." But it was agreed to draft a new letter.[103] At the sixth meeting, a statement for the bishops of Mozambique was submitted to the congregations' representatives and, in spite of some disagreements and one abstention, the new draft letter was approved—unfortunately, I did not find a copy of the letter in any archive, and hence cannot report on its content. The USG members subsequently sent the letter to the Secretariat of State, which, without any explanation, blocked and archived it at once.[104]

This experience and the failure of the letter/statement did not mean an end to the congregations' discussion on Mozambique. On the contrary, meetings took place again in 1973, after the Macuti affair, the revelations about the Mukumbura and Wiriyamu Massacres, and the expulsion of several more missionaries. In July 1973, fourteen USG members (excluding the White Fathers since they had left Mozambique in the meantime) met Monsignor Agostino Casaroli from the Secretariat of State. The USG members declared that they were very concerned about the situation in Mozambique and wished the Holy See to take a public position. Casaroli, in turn, explained that he had recently made a declaration in favor of the right of people to independence and that "as clear as the problems of Mozambique may be, as difficult are the solutions."[105] The USG proposed three specific measures to the Holy See: first, to place pressure on the episcopate in Mozambique; second, to choose better bishops (to which the secretary of state highlighted a lack of good potential prelates); and third, to free the church from its economic ties to the Portuguese state. The two sides agreed on these demands and included them in a report that was sent to the pope in August 1973.[106] In November, a new meeting was held with roughly the same individuals. Casaroli represented the Secretariat of State and reported the latter agreed in general terms with the letter sent to the pope. When asked about the Holy See's position toward the liberation movements, Monsignor Casaroli explained:

The principle is clear: when human rights are violated (massacres, episodes of violence, etc.), the church cannot remain silent; it has to denounce.

Regarding the struggle of the liberation movements for independence, it does not seem that the church can intervene. Specifically, the church cannot undertake anything in favor [of] or against independence. It is not the role of the church to support either Portugal or FREMILLO [*sic*], or to participate actively and directly in the liberation movements.

One cannot forget that the Mozambican population itself is divided on the question of independence.[107]

On the question of the financial dependence of the church in Mozambique, the secretary of state explained:

The church will not initiate breaking up a convention that has been signed with a state [i.e., the Concordat and Missionary Accord]. It can revise certain clauses, for example, if subsidies that the church receives from the government hamper its liberty. But it is not enough for the religious to be prepared to renounce these subsidies; the prelate and the secular clergy also need to be prepared to do the same.[108]

With these words the secretary of state argued that the church never broke international agreements and that the Vatican could not and would not make a decision on any financial matters unless all clergy and the bishops agreed (it is unclear whether a majority would have been sufficient). At the end of the meeting, one superior general requested that the Holy See at least give some signal that it was preoccupied with the situation in Mozambique. He suggested that the Vatican publish a document clarifying the church's official position and encouraging the missionaries in Mozambique. The secretary of state indicated that he was disposed to examine the possibility of such a document, although he would have to ask the opinion of the pope first.[109]

The position of the Holy See did not prevent religious orders from following their own line of action. We saw this in relation to the White Fathers and it occurred again, spectacularly, when the Picpus fathers decided in March 1974 to leave Mozambique—taking the lead of the White Fathers. The decision resulted from problems the society had experienced at its Inhaminga mission where massacres had occurred in 1973 and 1974,[110] and where the fathers could no longer work due to the military situation and the white population's suspicions against them. Seeing no perspective for the situation to improve in the near future, the fathers not only withdrew from Inhaminga but decided to leave Mozambique altogether.[111] The decision to leave was made by the regional superior in Mozambique, after he was forced to close the Inhaminga mission. He asked permission from the superior general in the Netherlands who, in turn, asked the nuncio in Lisbon. The latter did not explicitly approve but implicitly made clear that he would not oppose the decision. Thus, on March 18, 1974, the Picpus superior general wrote a letter to his missionaries saying that he accepted the regional's proposal for a full withdrawal of all twelve missionaries from Mozambique, and communicated this decision to the Secretariat of State on the same day.[112]

It is worth comparing this decision process with that of the White Fathers. In 1971 the superior of the White Fathers had consulted with the nuncio in Lisbon just as the Picpus fathers did in 1974; but in the case of the White Fathers, the nuncio opposed the withdrawal from Mozambique. He suggested instead that the society remain in Mozambique to avoid strong reactions and to preserve the few openings the regime had provided.[113] It is possible that the White Fathers had created a precedent.

In addition, the situation of the church in Mozambique had deteriorated dramatically from 1971 to 1974, and the views of the Vatican had evolved. Apart from the difficulties already discussed, the bishop of Nampula, Dom Manuel Vieira Pinto (Beira's vicar-general in 1971–72), and several of his missionaries were also expelled *manu militari* by the Portuguese government in February 1974 after they published a letter saying they supported the independence of Mozambique—this was the first time the Portuguese expelled a bishop from an overseas territory. Regardless of the differences between the situation in 1971 and the one in 1974, the fact is that in both a religious congregation made a major decision in spite of an unwillingness by the Vatican to take a public position, thus taking a lead in setting the policy of the church.

To conclude this chapter, we note three important findings from our exploration of religious congregations, bishops, and the Vatican between 1967 and 1974. First, divisions and tensions between religious congregations not only continued after the death of Dom Sebastião Soares de Resende but deepened to the point that groups of missionaries openly fought against one another. The fight took on such proportions that one can talk of an implosion of the Diocese of Beira by 1971—a rare occurrence in the Catholic Church. Second, different styles of episcopal leadership had different outcomes, and not always those one would expect, since both conservative and progressive bishops failed to run the diocese smoothly while Dom Altino, a secular priest, succeeded. What seems to explain Dom Sebastião's and Dom Altino's success is their adoption of the position of mediator between the different congregations and the different theologies rather than trying to rule in a top-down fashion in favor of one pastoral line or another. Third, the chapter confirms that religious orders have an important role in shaping the orientation and history of the Roman Catholic Church, both at the local and diocesan levels and at the central level of the Vatican. Chapter 2 showed how religious orders shaped policies and politics locally, by shaping the diocese's policies downward toward the missionaries' presence on the ground, and upward by influencing the bishop's views and actions. The last section of this chapter has shown that religious congregations also shaped policies and politics at the level of the Vatican. In fact, we discovered that in relation to Mozambique, religious orders not only influenced the Holy See but actually took the lead twice in making Catholic politics between 1971 and 1974.

6

Independence

Revolution and Counterrevolution

The decolonization process in Mozambique began with a coup d'état in Lisbon on April 25, 1974. Military captains involved in the "colonial wars," tired of a conflict that they felt could not be won militarily, seized power in Lisbon and put an end to the Estado Novo. Decolonization did not follow immediately. The first transitional government was ambiguous about the empire, some factions, including the new president, showing an interest in an "imperial federation of states." After a few months and several transitional governments, the new regime eventually committed to a negotiated handover of power. Because Frelimo was the main nationalist movement in Mozambique and had not stopped fighting after the coup d'état, the Portuguese government agreed to enter negotiations on independence with it exclusively. Talks took place in Zambia, leading to an agreement in September 1974. Independence was to be formally granted in June 1975; until then, there was to be a period of transition during which Frelimo and the Portuguese army would together administer the territory. On June 25, 1975, power was duly transferred to Frelimo, and national independence ensued. A period of massive change followed as Portuguese settlers left the country en masse and Frelimo engaged the country on the path of a socialist revolution.

After 1975, all key institutions in Mozambique underwent massive change—the state, the churches, and society more broadly. This happened in a tense regional context, with two white settler regimes, Rhodesia and southern Africa, at its borders, allied to each other and opposed to African independence and socialism. This chapter investigates these radical changes in Mozambique in order to understand how the Catholic Church changed with independence, how it related to the new Frelimo government and its socialist project, and how it reacted to the eruption of a new war, launched by Rhodesia and the Resistência Nacional Moçambicana (Mozambican National Resistance, RENAMO) guerrilla movement. While the period is different, historical works often continue to operate under a "political paradigm" (see the introduction). Trying to break from it, the coming pages aim not to figure out whether the church supported the Revolution or the Counter-Revolution, but to understand how, within the limits of "possibility and constraint," the church carried on working, reorganized itself, and gave itself a new mission.

The Transition, 1974–1975

When the coup d'état against Marcello Caetano took place in Portugal in 1974, the church in the dioceses of Beira and Tete was in crisis. The White Fathers had left Mozambique, the Picpus missionaries were on their way out, and a significant number of Burgos missionaries and several other priests, brothers, and sisters had been expelled. Both dioceses were left with mainly Jesuits and Franciscans alongside the female congregations. Half the mission stations were now affected by the liberation war, some closed (see fig. 3.3), some taken over by religious sisters (e.g., Baruè) or administered from another mission (e.g., Chemba).[1] At a national level, the problems were equally severe. In April 1974, the bishop of Nampula (the former apostolic administrator of Beira) and the Comboni missionaries of his diocese wrote a document called "An Imperative of Conscience" to the episcopal conference by which they denounced, and personally renounced, the alliance between the church and the state. They demanded a revocation of the Concordat and the Missionary Accord and stated that they recognized the "claims of the liberation movements."[2] The document was leaked to the press and triggered a scandal that led to popular demonstrations. People in Nampula accused the bishop of being a "traitor" to Portugal and demanded that he and his priests be arrested. Rapidly, the governor-general and PIDE decided to expel the priests and repatriate the bishop to Portugal.[3] As the fathers and the bishop left, some missionaries organized a petition to support them. In their petition they declared that they fully agreed with the "Imperative of Conscience" declaration and that they were ready to leave Mozambique should they not be able to work according to these principles. They gave the petition to the nuncio in Lisbon during his visit to Mozambique in April 1974, only a few days before the coup d'état in Lisbon. At that point it had already been signed by three hundred religious men and women, 17 percent of the national clergy, with a good number of missionaries still to be contacted.[4]

The period of transition, from the coup in Lisbon on April 25, 1974, to the Declaration of Independence on June 25, 1975, can be divided into two periods. First, there was a four-month period of negotiations between the leftist transitional government in Lisbon and Frelimo. At this point, the "political game" was open and any outcome seemed possible. Exiled politicians of all parties and movements returned to Mozambique and tried to promote their views and interests, while Frelimo decided to keep on fighting militarily. Settlers, in turn, defended their own views and interest, with hardcore settlers organizing the FICO movement,[5] and pro-African whites, such as the Democrats, standing with Frelimo. Social unrest was strong, with strikes, riots, and ethnic clashes—not least in Beira. On September 7, the day the Lusaka decolonization agreement was signed between Portugal and Frelimo, settlers attempted a coup. Chaos reigned for a few days, but Frelimo and the Portuguese army soon managed to restore order and calm.[6]

The second period started after the signing of the Lusaka Accord. A formal ceasefire came into force, a mixed military commission was established, and a mixed Portuguese-Frelimo transitional government was appointed. During this period, Frelimo built up its structures within the country, creating "dynamizing groups" (political action cells) and beginning to assert its hold over power in the administration and other institutions. Left-wing army commanders supported Frelimo and turned a blind eye on several excesses. As this period was provisional, some areas of politics were not clearly defined, such as the relation between church and state (to be discussed in detail below). Frelimo took advantage of the transitional period to eliminate competitors, and arrested hundreds of dissidents and Mozambican "reactionaries" with the active or passive help of the Portuguese military. Realizing that a full African decolonization could no longer be stopped, an increasing number of settlers left the territory to "return" to Portugal (even if some had never been to Portugal before). Eventually, 90 percent of settlers left between 1974 and the first months of independence.[7]

During the transitional period, the Vatican and the Catholic Church in Mozambique prepared for independence. At the level of the clergy, African priests and sisters organized themselves into the União dos Sacerdotes e Religiosas de Moçambique (Union of Priests and Religious Women of Mozambique, USAREMO) to push for the Africanization of the Church. The organization emerged from a network of black priests from southern Mozambique who decided in June 1974 to launch a formal and national union. In July of the same year, they sent two African priests to Dar es Salaam to meet with Frelimo—they stayed there twenty-five days.[8] After returning, the two priests met Cardinal Mozzoni, a special envoy for the pope who was in Mozambique to evaluate the situation. Mozzoni subsequently traveled across the whole territory, meeting with bishops and missionaries, and ended his trip by attending USAREMO's inaugural meeting in Inhambane on August 24. After the envoy had returned to Rome, the Vatican announced the first changes to the church's hierarchy, starting with the withdrawal of the contested archbishop of Lourenço Marques, who opposed African nationalism. In December 1974 the Vatican announced the nomination of the first two African bishops (those who had traveled to Dar es Salaam): Dom Alexandre dos Santos for the Archdiocese of Lourenço Marques/Maputo and Dom Januário Machaze Nhamgumbe for the Diocese of Porto Amélia/Pemba.

Another area that saw change related to the official status of the church in Mozambique. With the forthcoming end of Portugal's rule, the Concordat and the Missionary Accord were about to become null and void. It seems that, in a compromise move, the church decided to approach Frelimo to discuss the issue. At the talks, Frelimo would have proposed to retain the Concordat as it was while the church wanted to update it. Eventually, the two parties could not come to an agreement and the church considered the negotiations to have failed and the Concordat as being null and void. Thus, when the Vatican announced the appointment of the first two African bishops in December, it did so without consulting Frelimo.[9]

The Diocese of Beira was still in turmoil in mid-1974. More than half of the male missionaries had been expelled by the Portuguese state (60 out of 104), a new bishop had still not been found, and many missionaries were simply discouraged.[10] Dom Francisco Teixeira was still in place as apostolic administrator, but he was contested and the diocese held together only thanks to the vicar-general, José Augusto Alves de Sousa. In July 1974, a diocesan assembly was held with 170 male and female missionaries, the main issue being the forthcoming travels of the vicar-general. The key issue was whether the diocese should replace the vicar-general or not, and whether the replacement should be permanent ot temporary until Sousa returned. Dom Francisco argued that it was his responsibility to choose a new vicar-general and demanded a list of three names to select from. The clergy considered it their prerogative to decide and the assembly held a vote, against the wishes of Dom Francisco. The result was an overwhelming majority (149 out of 169 votes) in favor of keeping Father Sousa in place, even during his prolonged forthcoming absence.[11] In November another clash took place between the bishop and his clergy when some missionaries published a declaration in the media without having consulted the prelate beforehand. In the declaration they refused to take sides, posited their intention to work for the good of all people, and recognized "Frelimo as a preponderant factor in the realization of the legitimate and inalienable aspiration [of working for the good of the people]."[12] The bishop wrote a strong rebuttal to the priests in which he contested the claim that they could make decisions and issue public statements without consulting him. He argued that this showed division within the institution. He concluded his letter by asking for respect, even if he was only a transition prelate.[13]

In the midst of these tensions, the Vatican announced on December 23, 1974, the nomination of Dom Ernesto Gonçalves Costa as the new bishop for Beira—a position clearly not intended to be permanent since the Portuguese Dom Ernesto was also given the role of apostolic administrator of the dioceses of Inhambane and Lourenço Marques. With three dioceses on his plate, Dom Ernesto was physically present in Beira only part of the time. Yet, as he was dynamic, he managed to visit all congregations and missions in the subsequent months. He attempted to convince the White Fathers to return to Mozambique, and seems to have had a successful term.[14] The only disagreement that existed during his tenure was one with the Burgos fathers whom he saw as too Marxist and not ecclesial enough.[15]

All the Catholic congregations in Beira were concerned about what would happen at independence. Abroad, the priests who had been expelled from Mozambique met at the Picpus headquarters in the Netherlands in April 1974 and in Madrid two months later to discuss the situation. At the second meeting, Picpus missionaries, Comboni priests, White Fathers, Missionary Daughters of Calvary, Burgos fathers, and the bishop of Nampula were present. The meeting lasted three days and focused in particular on how to work for the people of Mozambique, how to get to know Frelimo and its policies better, and how to purify the church in Mozambique—with a proposal by some members that the episcopal conference apologize to the nation for the quietist position it had taken in the past.[16] In Beira itself, the missionaries held several meetings too. In December 1974, seventy-two male missionaries from Nampula, Inhambane, and Cabo Delgado met— apparently the sisters were "mistakenly" not invited. Discussions were held about politics, neutrality, whether the clergy could or should join Frelimo's Dynamizing Group, and the reasons that some missionaries had left the country. The gathering ended with the suggestion of holding a pastoral week on faith and politics in January 1975—an event that does not seem to have taken place in the end. At all the Beira meetings, positions diverged significantly. Some missionaries advised caution and neutrality while others wanted to break open the existing structures and free the church, even in terms of the relationship with the Vatican.[17] These disparities reflected the distinctive approaches held by different congregations and individuals with varying interests, concerns, and views—ranging from pro-Portuguese positions to support for liberation theology.

Of the ordained African priests of the dioceses of Beira and Tete, Dom Jaime Pedro Gonçalves was still abroad during the transition period, as was Father Mucauro who was studying medicine at this point. In Tete, Father João de Deus Kamtedza continued as the superior of the mission of Fonte Boa, and Father Domingos Ferrão worked at the parish-mission of Saint Pedro in the city of Tete and now sat on the diocese's Curia. Father Mateus Gwenjere, in turn, had returned to Beira on August 3, 1974, but did not do any religious work. Instead, he formed the Frente Independente Africana (FREINA) political party, which, within days of arriving in Beira, merged with the Partido da Convenção Nacional (National Convention Party, PCN) led by his fellow countryman, Congregationalist pastor Uria Simango. As a result, Gwenjere was appointed as the PCN's national adviser. However in Beira, as elsewhere, Frelimo strove to dominate the African scene unchallenged. A few days after Gwenjere's return, a Frelimo delegation went to Murraça, Gwenjere's home mission, to organize a *banja* (popular meeting) where it denounced "false nationalists" who fostered disturbances—code name for Frelimo dissidents, and Gwenjere specifically.[18] On August 25, a day after Gwenjere had held his first press conference representing the PCN, white Frelimo supporters violently attacked him with a machete in the Beira hotel where he stayed (near the bishop's residence in Beira). He was saved at the last moment thanks to the arrival of a priest who put the attackers to flight. Gwenjere was brought to a hospital where he was in a coma for several hours and had to stay for several days.[19] As soon as he was discharged from the hospital, Gwenjere fled from Mozambique and went back into exile in Kenya.[20] This marked the end of the activities in the country of the most politicized African priest in Mozambique.

During the transition period, Frelimo's position toward religion was ambiguous. It was clear that the party would implement socialist policies after independence, but the movement treated religion with respect and argued that religion and the churches would do well after 1975. When the two African priests visited Frelimo in Dar es Salaam in July–August 1974, the liberation movement's leadership promised happy days after independence. In Lourenço Marques, all churches were given access to the national radio station, a first in the country, and the prime minister asked pastors to take turns coming to pray with the cabinet once a week.[21] In Beira, Frelimo nominated Alberto Cangela de Mendonça as governor, a civilian who had been jailed by PIDE in the 1960s and was part of Frelimo's clandestine network inside Mozambique. Mendonça was a devout Catholic and, with his family, sat in the front row of the Beira cathedral every Sunday.[22] In the countryside, too, Frelimo commanders showed a positive regard for the church, explaining that Frelimo expected the church to reopen all mission stations that had been closed due to the war and to continue their work as before independence. After touring the whole diocese and meeting with twelve Frelimo commanders in September 1974, a Picpus missionary wrote the following to a colleague: "I was devastated about the situation I encountered [at the mission] in Inhaminga and, even more, in Lundo. Everything is practically destroyed. The other missions operate at a slow rhythm. Much zeal and dedication, but a great lack of personnel. This is why everywhere Frelimo asked that the missions return to the same life they had before."[23]

In summary, at this point Frelimo gave the impression that things would go well for the churches after independence and that they would be able to continue work as before, if under a Socialist regime.

Church and State in Beira after 1975

After a nine-month transition period, Mozambique was granted independence on June 25, 1975. The new Mozambican constitution gave relatively positive first signs of what was to come. Article 33 stated: "In the People's Republic of Mozambique the state guarantees its citizens the freedom to believe or not to believe in a religion." Article 26 added that there could be no discrimination on the basis of religion. And Article 19 stated that "the People's Republic of Mozambique is a secular state, in which there exists an absolute distinction between the State and religious institutions."[24]

Within a month, however, Frelimo decreed the nationalization of all health, education, and justice services (on July 24, 1975), which affected the Catholic Church in particular since it controlled most of the health and educational institutions for Africans, thanks to the Concordat and the Missionary Accord. Within a few days, all schools, seminaries, dormitories, hospitals, clinics, and health posts were taken away from the church. What most shocked the clergy and the bishops was the extensiveness of the policy and the suddenness of its execution. Fathers José Augusto Alves de Sousa and Odilo Congil write that "the practical execution of these nationalizations turned them into something much more detailed and therefore much more radical. It affected all institutions and all goods, all that constituted the life of a mission."[25] Apart from buildings, Frelimo nationalized land, church funds, residences, cars, furniture, appliances, and, in some cases, the church buildings themselves. The application depended on which nationalizing commission was in charge, many of which were armed and had an encompassing understanding of the law. Unsurprisingly, most clergy saw this move as a direct attack against the church. Only a minority supported Frelimo in this venture, among them the Burgos fathers, adepts of liberation theology. On August 11, 1975, two weeks after the nationalization law was passed, the Burgos brothers issued a public statement of support for Frelimo and for nationalization (which was published in the main national newspaper):

2. We support the conquests of the people of Mozambique, in particular the measures taken by the Council of Minister on July 24, 1975 [i.e., nationalization]. . . .
5. We recognize Frelimo as the revolutionary vanguard and the only leader of the people of Mozambique.
6. In this context, we understand that our insertion within the Mozambican revolution is valid.
9. We are not in solidarity with any reactionary or reformist attitude or action within the church.
10. The Catholic Church is marked by a class struggle, hidden behind layers of false feelings of unity. By participating in the revolutionary struggle, we are preparing the true unity of the church, since this depends on the unity of humanity.[26]

This statement was not only radical within the context of Beira and Mozambique but also revolutionary within the global Catholic Church. Calling publicly for the waging of class struggle *within* the Catholic Church was probably another world premiere. This might have helped Frelimo and the revolutionary cause in Mozambique at the time, but it rang alarm bells in the Vatican, upon which it proceeded to organize a response (see below).

While nationalization and Catholic dissent unfolded, the Catholic hierarchy was further renewed. In November 1975, the African priest Alberto Setele was appointed as bishop of the Diocese of Inhambane. In December 1975 Jaime Pedro Gonçalves was nominated as coadjutor bishop of Beira (the assistant of a bishop with a right of succession to the position of bishop) (more details below). And on May 31, 1976, the bishops of Xai Xai, Tete, and Quelimane resigned and the Vatican replaced them with Júlio Duarte for Xai Xai, Paul Mandlate for Tete, and Bernardo Filipe Governo for Quelimane. These new appointments tipped the balance of power within the CEM, which thereupon began to dissociate itself from the quietist approach of the colonial church. While the Protestant Christian Council went on to adopt a "pastoral care" approach to the government, the CEM adopted a prophetic voice and began to publish critical pastoral documents. In June 1976, it issued a pastoral letter titled "Living Faith in Today's Mozambique" in which the bishops declared their support for nationalization, but posited that the process had gone too far by excluding the spiritual realm, by being too materialistic and atheist: "The atheism propagated publicly as well as the efforts that are seen to form a society without God, without any opening to the supernatural, constitutes one of the gravest errors of ours times."[27]

When the archbishop of Maputo met President Samora Machel in November of the same year, he handed him a Catholic report on reeducation camps. Machel's focus at the meeting was on the pastoral letter however: he declared that it would be better for the church to enter into consultation with the authorities rather than choosing the public "distribution of pamphlets." He explained: "Pamphlets bring confrontation between church and state. And we do not want this in our Republic. . . . Distributing pamphlets is reminiscent of the colonial times."[28] These warnings did not stop the CEM, however. In May 1977, it published a communiqué in which it discussed nationalization and Marxism, and introduced the issue of human rights, specifically critiquing a public execution of criminals (without a proper and fair trial) that had taken place in the Quelimane football stadium and that the bishop and clergy of Quelimane had been asked to attend.[29] By 1976, then, not only had the political context in Mozambique changed profoundly and the church has suffered extensive nationalization, but the Catholic hierarchy had been renewed and had made the strategic choice to adopt a prophetic voice (in contrast to the quietist tradition chosen during colonial times).

Independence brought major changes to the Diocese of Beira too. First, a new African bishop was chosen in 1975. The choice was not easy because possible candidates were few and several declined, notably the Jesuit fathers João de Deus Kamtedza and José Augusto Alves de Sousa (who remained vicar-general), insofar as their order discouraged its members from serving as bishops. The choice then fell on Father Jaime Pedro Gonçalves, a diocesan priest who returned to Mozambique on July 10, 1975. The Vatican nominated him as coadjutor bishop in December 1975, and instated him as full bishop a year later on December 12, 1976. As we saw in chapter 3, Dom Jaime was ordained in 1967 and went to Rome and Canada where he gained degrees in theology, education, and social leadership.[30] As fifth bishop of Beira, he was a proponent of USAREMO, whose aims he promoted among his clergy. His episcopal model seems to have been that of the late Bishop Sebastião Soares de Resende, with a stronger inclination toward deploying a prophetic voice—something he carried into the Episcopal Conference over which he presided between 1976 and 1986. For the position of vicar-general, he chose Father Guilherme da

Costa, an African Franciscan priest and cousin of his who was ordained in October 1975.

Among the clergy, the departure of religious personnel from Beira increased dramatically in 1975, with about two-thirds of the missionaries leaving. The Portuguese congregations were most affected by this, in particular the (male and female) Franciscan congregations (see table 6.1). This situation critically affected the diocese. It lost not only much of its infrastructure, due to nationalization, but also a significant number of its personnel. The number of catechists dropped even more radically, from 538 in 1974 to 10 in 1980, largely as a result of the government's antireligion drive (see below).[31] This led to a redistribution of power and workload. On the one hand, African personnel gained in importance: by 1983, Mozambicans constituted 50 percent of all clergy (priests, brothers, sisters, and employees) in Beira and held all the key positions of power.[32] On the other hand, the decline of the Jesuit clergy and the collapse of the male and female Franciscan orders led to a new balance between the congregations. With few personnel left and under enormous pressure, Dom Jaime decided to merge parishes (all missions were now called parishes) and to end the practice of allocating certain areas to particular congregations. He divided the diocese into four pastoral zones (Beira, Buzi, Zambeze, and Manica) and put a commission consisting of two priests, two female religious staff, and one lay person in charge of each.[33]

In view of the massive changes that independence brought, the bishop of Beira decided soon after his nomination to organize a Diocesan Pastoral Assembly, which took place in May 1977, four months before the first National Pastoral Assembly also held in Beira. The final document of the diocesan assembly focused on one sole point, namely, "the urgency in this period of time to concentrate all efforts on the formation and development of Christian communities." The document explained: "Under the impulse of the New Reality, all Christians should aim at living their faith in Jesus Christ with all its consequences, inserted in small [base] communities, like the primitive Christian communities that the Acts of the Apostles talk of."[34] By 1980, Beira's second Diocesan Pastoral Assembly reported on the changes that had happened since its first meeting: "Small [base] communities exist in almost all parishes. Some are already structured and organized, and others are still being formed, but all of them [perform] some essential ministries. . . . In some communities (Catandica, Murraça, Gorongosa), lay individuals hold the right solemnly to administer baptism and officially to testify at weddings as well as to [administer] Holy Communion, in the absence of a priest."[35]

Table 6.1. Catholic personnel in the Diocese of Beira, 1973 and 1981.

	1973	1981
Diocesan	5	5
Jesuits	13	5
Franciscans	46	10
White Fathers	—	3
Comboni	8	3
Picpus	5	4
Burgos	6	4
Marist Brothers	6	1
Priests of the Sacred Heart of Jesus (Dehonian)	—	1
Franciscan Sisters of Mary	23	5
Franciscan Hospitaller of the Immaculate Conception	12	3
Franciscan Sisters of Our Lady of Victories	54	8
Repairing Missionaries of the Sacred Heart of Jesus	5	4
Sisters of Saint Joseph of Cluny	4	4
Franciscan Missionaries of the Mother of the Divine Shepherd	17	4
Franciscan Missionaries of Our Lady	51	7
Daughters of Saint Paul	6	4
Mercedarian Missionary Sisters	15	3
Sisters of the Sacred Heart of Mary	6	3
Daughters of Charity of Saint Vincent de Paul	—	1
Pequenhas Filhas da Nossa Senhora [sic]	3	—
Comboni Missionary Sisters	—	4
Sisters of the Precious Blood	—	1
Missionary Daughters of Calvary	1	—
Total	286	87

Source: Diocese da Beira, "Resumo dos dados Estatísticos do Ano de 1973. Distritos da Beira e da Vila Pery" and Diocese da Beira, *Relatório Quinquenal*, Beira, 1982, p. 10.

In September, the National Assembly chose the same path. The "base community" model was adopted at the national level for various reasons. While some bishops (such as the bishop of Inhambane) saw it as a form of resistance against communism,[36] others (like the bishop of Nampula, Dom Manuel Vieira Pinto) thought it would make the Church less clerical and more engaged in the fight for justice.[37] Nevertheless, the church's new orientation had dire consequences: Frelimo considered the choice of a church of communities to mean that the church was choosing to resist the government option toward socialism. In the subsequent months, Frelimo (a party-state since its Third Congress in February 1977) therefore began to attack all religions, with a particular focus on the Catholic Church (see below).

While the church transformed itself into a "people's church," the Vatican moved to rein in the Burgos priests. The Burgos fathers were doubtless the most radical group of priests in Mozambique, having supported the Frelimo guerrillas before independence, doing the same for the Zimbabwean guerrillas in Mozambique and Rhodesia after 1975, and actively supporting the Frelimo revolution.[38] As mentioned earlier, they declared a class struggle within the church in 1975 and actively defended the socialist revolution. After a period of close surveillance by Propaganda Fide and an unfruitful exchange of letters, the Vatican decided in 1977 to counter the order's "deviance" by demanding the order's direction in Madrid to annul all "liberationist" decisions made since 1969, or else it would close down the institute at once. Eventually, it seems that the Vatican had to demote the whole Burgos leadership to make the changes it wanted. This led many priests to abandon not only their institute but also the church at large—in Mozambique, some of the missionaries went to work for the ministry of education.[39] In a less dramatic way, the episcopal conference introduced some measures to rein in prorevolutionary stances. At a 1977 meeting in Beira, with all male and female religious superiors present, the CEM discussed the clergy's involvement in the unfolding socialist revolution. In a presentation the leadership listed the advantages and disadvantages of getting involved in Frelimo's revolution and concluded with the following suggestion: "He who engages [in the revolution] should do it in communion with the local church and not dispense with direct action in pastoral work; bishops should say clearly what they think about those who engage themselves so as to avoid unnecessary conflict."[40] In other words, the CEM tried to make sure that, at the very least, any engagement with the Frelimo revolution occurred with the knowledge, if not authorization, of the hierarchy.

In July 1978, Frelimo held its first "Department of Ideological Works" conference, at which it closely analyzed religion and the works of the

Catholic Church. In relation to religion, the conference concluded that faith institutions in Mozambique were trying "to resist the political and ideological undertaking launched by Frelimo's ground structures" and critiqued the Catholic Church for having developed small base communities that were just like party cells, adapting its theology to the situation, appropriating revolutionary language, and presenting itself as defender of human rights.[41] The outcome of the conference was a major campaign by the party-state against religious organizations in all of Mozambique. In December 1978, a set of very restrictive norms was adopted to limit religious work while an offensive began to close religious buildings, place some religious staff under house arrest, and convert people to atheism. While the provinces of Manica and Sofala were not the worst affected by this, the situation nonetheless became very dire. Christians in Gorongosa, Chibabava, and Inhaminga were jailed because of their faith. Priests in Chimoio, Murraça, and Beira, accused of exercising religious influence or collaborating with the enemy, were arrested or placed under house arrest. And the bishop of Beira was jailed several times because his "travel authorization" was not correct (in 1979 the government introduced an internal travel pass, known as the *Guia de marcha*).[42] Catholic church buildings were closed down (ten in the Diocese of Beira between 1979 and 1981) and religious practice was actively discouraged among the population. Between nationalization and this offensive against religion, church attendance took a serious hit. Drawing from the official figures of the diocese, the church estimated in 1980 that it had not only lost 123,950 Catholics (mostly through the flight of white settlers), but that only 19,150 of the remaining 95,000 Catholics (i.e., 20 percent) were still practicing their faith. This means that 80 percent of the Catholics in Beira diocese would have stopped attending mass.[43]

What about the relation between congregations and the bishop after independence? As we saw, the Catholic Church had set up several national structures in Mozambique before 1975. The CEM was established in 1965, male religious congregations established FIRM in 1973. Before independence, there was tension between these bodies because all bishops were Portuguese, many of them conservatives, while FIRM was dominated by non-Portuguese missionaries, most of whom had fully embraced Vatican II and many of whom were inclined to support the independence of Mozambique. After 1975, some of these tensions continued, albeit in different forms. One of the new tensions related to the fact that many missionaries were ill at ease with USAREMO's demands for Africanization, which they saw as racially based and potentially undermining the progressive religious and political agenda the church had fought for up to independence.[44]

Otherwise, the relation between congregations and the bishop continued to be complex. In November 1978, the bishops and the heads of the male and female religious institutes held a three-day meeting in Beira to discuss their relations. Their final conclusions listed a number of obstacles to the good "insertion of religious [individuals] in the pastoral activities of the local church." These were presented as:

- A lack of coordination between pastoral agents
- A lack of dialogue between bishops and religious superiors
- A narrow conception and content of the [church's] pastoral approach
- Attitudes of distrust
- A lack of mutual deepening of charisms [that] led bishops and superiors to act beyond their respective competencies.[45]

The document proposed "communion" and "dialogue" as solutions. For communion, it suggested "planning and working together; accepting each other's personal and group limitations; creating an atmosphere of fraternal collaboration, in spite of the differences between us and even possible opposing characters; emphasizing the value of praying and reflection; always acting in accordance with the orientation of the bishop and the norms of one's congregation."[46] For dialogue, it recommended:

> defining the priorities of the local church; searching for the identity and incarnation of this church; accepting that no individuals or groups can on their own give a pastoral character to an activity; consulting the feeling of communities; recognizing that pastoral decisions depend on the bishop; evaluating the tasks at the level of the group by overcoming personal points of view; and giving particular attention to the elements that are in crisis.[47]

For all its details, what the document reveals is that, despite the radical changes that had taken place in the church and the profound shifts in the historical context of Mozambique, differences and tensions continued between the church hierarchy and the religious congregations. This serves as a reminder that, as Max Weber indicated, tensions are simply a structural feature of the Roman Catholic Church (see the introduction).

The Catholic Church, RENAMO, and War

In 1976, a year after Mozambique achieved independence, the white regime of Rhodesia decided to launch a war of destabilization against the country. There were several reasons for this: Frelimo had adopted the United Nations' sanctions against Rhodesia (which Portugal did not apply); it had been supporting the Zimbabwean African National Union (ZANU) since 1975, offering training camps and military bases within Mozambique and in areas bordering on Rhodesia; and it had adopted a communist political orientation.[48] The war of destabilization was low-level, mainly targeting key infrastructure (such as bridges, railway lines, or fuel depots) and ZANU's military camps. Because many ZANU camps were located in their area, the dioceses of Beira and Tete were directly affected by this war. They saw bombardments and incursions by Rhodesian troops, aided by the South African special reconnaissance forces under the ALCORA agreement. In a major operation in August 1976, the Rhodesians killed a Spanish Burgos priest and a boy who was accompanying him, and badly injured a Cluny sister and the vicar-general of the Diocese of Tete, Father Domingos Ferrão, when the four of them drove by and came face to face with the soldiers setting up explosives to blow up a bridge.[49]

During the same period, the Rhodesian secret service supported the formation of a Mozambican armed resistance movement, eventually known as RENAMO that for a number of years operated principally in central Mozambique. While the war of destabilization stopped with the independence of Rhodesia in 1980 (at which point it became Zimbabwe) and ZANU's coming to power, the guerrilla war waged by RENAMO not only continued but grew in intensity. Indeed, the Rhodesian and South African secret services and armies agreed to accommodate the RENAMO rear base and radio support structures in South Africa while RENAMO foot soldiers were told to settle more permanently inside Mozambique. After the apartheid regime expanded its support for the guerrilla movement, RENAMO began to expand into northern and southern Mozambique, eventually affecting the whole country from 1984 onward.[50]

While the government was already convinced that the Catholic Church opposed its socialist revolution, RENAMO's emergence led it to believe that the church was also allied to the guerrillas. On a general level, its argument rested on the simple dictum that anyone who is not unconditionally with us has to be against us. More specifically, its argument rested on two considerations. First, Frelimo posited that the church and RENAMO had similar origins and similar aims, and thus were objective allies. It saw both as products of colonialism and aligned with imperialism. Both formed what Frelimo called a "counterrevolutionary front" against the socialist revolution. Considering a call by the bishops in 1982 for peace negotiations with RENAMO (at a time when the government only wanted a military solution), President Machel explained:

For us, this kind of positioning [by the bishop] is not a surprise considering where it comes from. Ultimately [their] objective is to appear as the "heralds of peace," to confuse the people, to promote the armed bandits, and to give them credibility. They [the bishops] are the spiritual inheritors of colonialism in the same way as the armed bandits are a historical prolongation of the action of the colonial army.[51]

The argument that RENAMO stemmed from the Portuguese colonial army rested on the idea that RENAMO included men from the Portuguese African military troops, in particular the infamous GE and GEP African special forces trained in Beira by Jorges Jardim and the Flechas special forces launched by PIDE in early 1974, just weeks before the April "Carnation Revolution."[52] While the argument rested on a few particular cases (one or two Portuguese PIDE agents and former GE or GEPs who had indeed joined RENAMO), the truth is that most RENAMO soldiers came from Frelimo's own armed forces, including its first two leaders, André Matsangaiça and Alfonso Dhlakama.[53] In other words, this connection may have a small element of truth, but the genealogy is much more complicated and involves Frelimo's own history.

Regarding the Catholic institution, Frelimo's argument that it was the spiritual inheritor of colonialism rested on the idea that the hierarchy had not changed since independence. Machel argued that all the Vatican had done in 1974–75 was to appoint African bishops so as to avoid the decolonization of the church. In a speech in 1982, he explained in detail how he thought the Vatican had solely put a coat of black paint on the colonial church:

We say that that the enemy uses religion, in particular the Catholic Church. There are these bishops who have been promoted thanks to the sacrifice of our people. Before [in colonial times] they did not eat with the bishops, they did not eat with the superiors in the missions; they ate in the kitchen. [When] we proclaimed independence, they were promoted to bishops and transformed themselves into an operational force of political and ideological subversion (applause). Yesterday they were with the Portuguese colonialists. This association was not by chance. . . .

They refuse liberation, they do not have the personality of the Mozambican in our heroic people. Anti-patriots! They want to fight against us. They are subverting the people against socialism, against social wellbeing, [against] organized life. They recruit here using their cassock. But we have force, we have the people.

The ultimate objective of imperialism is to return to exploiting our labor using these agents camouflaged in cassocks.[54]

Needless to say, the accusation that the Catholic bishops were all disguised colonialists and imperialists is problematic. The majority of Mozambican bishops were in favor of independence when Machel made this speech in 1982. Six were Africans and two were Europeans (see fig. 6.1). Of the two Europeans, Dom Luis Gonzaga Ferreira da Silva had been bishop of Niassa before independence and had indeed been favorable to colonialism. Dom Manuel Vieira Pinto, however, the bishop of Nampula, had been pro-Frelimo and had been expelled from Mozambique in 1974 for this very reason. In fact, he and Dom Alexandre dos Santos, the archbishop of Maputo, were the bishops most supportive of the Frelimo government.[55] This makes clear that there was significant division between the Mozambican bishops. Even if the bishops were at times critical of the government (and some were hostile to its revolution), the majority favored independence and a minority supported a socialist independence as imagined by Frelimo. This brings nuance to the argument that all bishops were colonialists and imperialists. Indeed, it is exactly the bishops' diverse views that gave space to Frelimo to influence and benefit from division between

Figure 6.1. Mozambique's bishops at the National Pastoral Assembly, Beira, September 1977. Bishop Jaime Gonçalves is at the center. Reproduced by permission from the Archive of the Diocese of Beira.

them—something it did quite effectively.[56] In addition, religious congregations were equally marked by diversity and division, with a few of them openly and actively in favor of Frelimo's revolution, such as the Burgos fathers, the Comboni missionaries, the Picpus fathers, the Capuchins, and some sisters.

Apart from claiming that both RENAMO and the Catholic Church had the same colonial origins, Frelimo asserted that they were united in an objective to counter the socialist revolution. Both institutions were critical of, or even opposed to, Frelimo, but not for the same reasons. For one, neither the church hierarchy nor any of the religious congregations or their priests and sisters had the same political program as RENAMO. Clerics may have been opposed to Frelimo's revolution, if not to Frelimo itself, but in very few cases did Catholic clergyman (or religious women) actively support RENAMO. And the number who did so were fewer than the religious men and women who supported Frelimo—they were also nothing compared to the active (albeit marginal) support some fundamentalist Protestant movements gave to RENAMO in what they experienced as an "anti-Communist crusade."[57] Besides, while it is true that some priests worked in RENAMO-occupied areas, this was only during the late 1980s and primarily to cater to Catholics who had become divided by the war and separated from their clergy. In other words, the church and RENAMO did not share the same aim or work together.

The second discursive pillar that Frelimo deployed to accuse the Catholic Church of working with RENAMO related to the fact that the guerrillas had many Catholics in their midst. In his extensive analysis of RENAMO, Alex Vines elaborated on this view: "Many of RENAMO leaders originated from Catholic missions."[58] He goes on to explain that RENAMO's president Dhlakama studied at a Catholic mission, that the movement's late secretary-general Evo Fernandes attended a Catholic school, and that two RENAMO spokespersons were former Catholic seminarians. A general examination of the situation would lead one to agree that many leaders in RENAMO were indeed Catholic. But the significance of this fact is low when we take into account that in 1959 the church controlled 99.8 percent of all preprimary schools (called "adaptation schools") and the majority of primary schools *for Africans.*[59] It is thus not surprising that many RENAMO leaders were Catholics—like many Frelimo leaders. The claim that RENAMO had many former seminarians in its leadership has more substance but it is also more complicated and subtle than Vines's discussion suggests. First, until the 1960s the Catholic seminaries had been the only educational institutions that offered secondary education to Africans. Thus, finding Catholics in any leadership, let alone in RENAMO's leadership, is hardly surprising or significant. Second, and conversely, it is not Catholic seminarians who became important in RENAMO, but more specifically the group of seminarians who came out of one specific minor seminary—Zobuè.

Indeed, several Zobuè students who joined Frelimo in the 1960s (leaving just after the White Fathers were removed from the seminary) joined RENAMO after independence. Many of them became embroiled in the factional fight alongside Father Mateus Gwenjere. After the 1968 crisis, a significant number of them went into exile in Kenya and other countries from where they engaged in dissident anti-Frelimo politics.[60] After independence, the majority of them did not return to Mozambique—they were warned not to and the few who did return were arrested as they stepped off the plane and sent to reeducation camps. Some of these exiles went to work for Radio Voz da África Livre (aka Radio Quizumba) in Rhodesia (the anti-Frelimo radio station set up by the Rhodesians secret services in parallel to RENAMO) in 1976, and a few others began to work for RENAMO's external wing (as representatives for the party abroad). Only a few of this Zobuè group of men became active RENAMO members, but many passively supported RENAMO's politics. The existence and genealogy of the group was known to Frelimo and was even publicly acknowledged by Machel. At a meeting in 1982 with religious leaders, he declared:

> I have still not had the time to explain the origins of the armed bandits to you. Our fight against these armed bandits did not start today. Since 1962 when we founded Frelimo, our fight has always been against armed bandits: armed by the colonial army, armed by imperialism, always aiming to destroy Frelimo. . . .
>
> These are problems that Frelimo had to carry until victory and they were made thicker by these brain-dead who were here, the ultra-racists that were here. After April 25, 1974, more than 35 political parties emerged in Mozambique. Their seat was in Beira.[61]

Considering that President Machel was addressing this speech to religious leaders, there is little doubt that he was thinking of Father Gwenjere and the former seminarians of Zobuè when he made these comments. An important stream of the Frelimo dissidents was indeed constituted of elements of the Catholic elite of central Mozambique, and the political parties set up in Beira during the transition period included some of these very elements, not least Father Mateus Gwenjere, as we have seen.

While Frelimo accused and attacked the Catholic Church in the 1970s, the institution transformed further. Most importantly, it morphed its prophetic voice into a prophetic *mission* in the 1980s. In line with the neo-Thomist view that the church should be above politics, the CEM began to deploy a narrative whereby the church gave advice to the party-state, its enemies, and society. After it lost most of its infrastructure (an issue exacerbated by destruction due to the war), the CEM started to recommend negotiations to bring peace back to the country. In early 1982, the episcopal conference published a pastoral letter about peace and dialogue; and in late 1983, it issued a letter calling for a dialogue between what it called the "warring parties," thus breaking the official discourse in which RENAMO was referred to only as the "armed bandits." The words also equated Frelimo and RENAMO. Frelimo reacted angrily to these letters (see discussion above), but the church held firm, continued to make these recommendations, and even went on to promote peace in practical terms, offering itself as mediator.

After the Nkomati Accord of 1984 failed to stem the war,[62] the Franciscans began to build up contacts with the Mozambican government and RENAMO to try to launch peace negotiations. Leading the process was Father Manuel Carreira das Neves, a former missionary in Beira (between 1962 and 1974), at the time studying for a doctorate in Rome and linked to the Franciscan International Center for Peace among People in Assisi. After some first positive contacts with both sides, a member of the Assisi International Center traveled to Maputo in February 1985 to talk to President Machel. In December of the same year, representatives of the center met RENAMO's secretary-general in Lisbon. Things seemed to be going so well that the two sides agreed on an initial encounter for the summer of 1986. Yet before this could happen, the Mozambican government got cold feet and the process stalled. A few months later, President Machel died in a plane crash and the process died with him. According to one of the main actors on the government's side, the reason Frelimo withdrew from the process was the realization that the links the Franciscans had with RENAMO were with former Portuguese settlers from Beira rather than with the African leadership of RENAMO.[63] This shows, on the one hand, the continued angst the government had toward colonialists, particularly those from central Mozambique, and, on the other, how it actually did have a nuanced insight into the Catholic Church and the guerrilla movement. It opens the question of what would have happened if the congregation involved in these early contacts between Maputo and RENAMO had been the White Fathers with their intimate connections to RENAMO's African leadership, rather than the Franciscans. Nevertheless, three years later the Catholic Church and several Protestant leaders launched a new joint initiative that would eventually lead to the Rome Peace Process, starting in

1989 and eventually bringing peace to the country in 1992. This new process not only unfolded in Rome but had as its central mediator Dom Jaime Gonçalves, the archbishop of Beira, a leading figure in the development of a prophetic voice and mission in the church, and a man with roots in central Mozambique like the leadership of RENAMO.[64]

All in all, in less than a decade the Catholic Church in Beira (and in Mozambique more generally) underwent profound changes. It saw an Africanization of its leadership, lost about half of its religious personnel, lost most of its properties, and faced a destabilizing attack by the state while working in areas directly affected by the violence of Rhodesian aggression and a new guerrilla war. In the second half of the 1970s, the church transformed its structure to place base communities in its center, and developed a prophetic voice critical of the state's excesses and "errors." In the 1980s, the church further developed a neo-Thomist prophetic *mission* to give orientation to society, preach peace, and position itself as (potential/future) mediator in peace negotiations between the state and the guerrillas. Can we conclude that the church remained colonial or became neo-colonial after independence? It would seem more appropriate to say that the Catholic Church underwent its own revolution with independence and that it significantly changed its historical trajectory toward a Mozambique-centered and neo-Thomist identity.

Epilogue

In 1986, at the end of the period under study, the Catholic Church in central Mozambique was an institution facing difficult times. The government stood in a tense relation with it, and the civil war that had started in 1976 now engulfed state, society, and economy across the whole territory. By 1986, the church had completed its transition from an imperial institution into a fully national church and, even more importantly, had finished its transformation from an institution that engaged directly with the state, whether in alliance with or opposition to it, to an institution and moral force that stood above the Mozambican state and society. This was a typical neo-Thomist position, fully supported by the Vatican, which allowed the institution not only to advise all sides of the war to negotiate a political settlement but also to offer itself as an impartial and independent mediator in such negotiations. It attempted this, unsuccessfully, in 1985–86, and successfully in 1989 when talks between the Mozambican government and the armed guerrillas opened in Rome. The mediators during the negotiations, which were to last until 1992, were the Catholic community of Sant'Egidio, the Italian state, and the Catholic Church of Mozambique.

The man who represented the Mozambican Catholic Church as mediator was, surprisingly, not the highest cleric of the country, Cardinal Dom Alexandre dos Santos of Maputo, but Archbishop Jaime Gonçalves of Beira. The latter was chosen because apparently the guerrillas saw the cardinal as too favorable to the government and the archbishop as more impartial. Dom Jaime talked to both the government and the guerrillas, and traveled to the bush in 1988 to visit RENAMO's leadership, before the talks started.[1] The difference between these two postcolonial episcopal figures was one of personality, but it echoed colonial times when Dom Sebastião Soares de Resende of Beira stood in contrast to the prelates of Lourenço Marques. Dom Sebastião ran an open, internally diverse, and decentralized institution whereas the prelates in the southernmost diocese administered the church in a top-down fashion, and possibly even had a regal view of their role, with the cardinal of Lourenço Marques being chauffeured around his diocese in a Rolls-Royce. While Dom Alexandre dos Santos in the late 1980s had no regal pretensions, he adopted a much less critical and prophetic voice than his colleague, Dom Jaime, and this clearly made a difference in terms of his being seen as less impartial and less able to function as a mediator. This illustrates two broader points. The first is that there were, consciously or not, some continuities from the colonial to the postcolonial episcopacy. While men changed, some ideas and approaches remained with the new bishops—a certain diocesan Catholic culture. Second, it shows that diversity exists not just within dioceses but also between them. Beira and Maputo were quite different in relation to their episcopal leaders as well as their religious makeup, tradition, and history.

Understanding Catholic Politics

The chapters in this book offer an in-depth exploration of the diversity in the Roman Catholic Church in central Mozambique. As mentioned in the introduction and first suggested by Max Weber, it is not diversity as such that characterizes the Roman Catholic Church but the way the institution manages it. Whereas extreme diversity in Protestant organizations tends to lead to schism, the Catholic institution has developed an institutional mechanism to prevent schism and contain differences and disagreements. It did so, and still does today, by institutionalizing diversity within religious congregations and societies to whom it grants autonomy. The consequence of this distinctive way of managing diversity is that the global Catholic Church is uniquely diverse internally and has a large horizontal layer made up of congregations, religious orders, institutes, and societies that answer to the Vatican and cut across the top-down hierarchical dimension supposedly so typical of the church. Considering this characteristic, the challenge for historians and other social scientists lies in how to understand and explain the making of Catholic politics, since neither a purely top-down nor a wholly bottom-up analysis captures and manages to make sense of the internal diversity of the church, its decentralized nature, and its complex internal decision-making mechanisms.

Catholicism and the Making of Politics argues for the need to look at the church and its politics through the prism of religious congregations, thus from a horizontal perspective. Beira had no less than eighteen different religious congregations, with (sometimes significant) diversity in terms of history, sociology, culture, theology, and political outlook. Some differences were linked to their roles within the diocese, with religious orders specializing to various degrees in evangelization, education, health, and elite formation. Other differences resulted from the particular histories and cultures of each congregation. We saw that most Portuguese congregations in central Mozambique were sensitive to the imperial objectives of the Portuguese state while foreign congregations were not. Cutting across this, both foreign congregations and diocesan Portuguese clergy in particular were keen on Vatican II reforms while other congregations were more interested either in keeping the traditional, Portuguese-centered church or in searching for a compromise between the two positions. While nationality was an important element, particularly in relation to politics, the clergy was divided in various ways on most other issues. The Jesuits, Franciscans, and White Fathers, for example, shared a profound interest in training an African clergy while the Burgos fathers were more interested in forming base communities. The Jesuits had an obsession with nurturing and growing an elite while the Burgos and Picpus fathers were not interested in this at all.

In Beira and Tete, congregations worked along the same diocesan guidelines, captured in a rule book that was discussed and revised at diocesan synods. Yet congregations applied these regulations differently (sometimes choosing not to apply them at all), so that practices could actually differ quite significantly. The length of the catechumenate (preparation before baptism) was a significant marker of these differences and probably one of the most debated issues within the central Mozambican church before independence. While the bishop tried to develop a unified practice, his clergy disagreed until the very end of the colonial period. Congregations had different approaches to conversion and resisted a unification of practice because this would have meant aligning with views that did not correlate with their own theological position. The length of the catechumenate was indeed fundamentally linked to understandings of conversion and practices of faith—giving rise to the question of whether congregations gave priority to orthodoxy or to orthopraxis. The first bishop of Beira, Dom Sebastião, was wise enough not to use his authority to impose a decision, but his skills at negotiating and compromising and his choice to focus on incremental change did not lead to any profound shifts. The point here is that congregations had the freedom to apply a policy or not, and were thus able to shape policy in practice. Religious congregations thus influenced (and still influence) Catholic policy *downward* by the way they chose to apply (or not) decisions made by the hierarchy, the first of three ways, as this book argues, that congregations influence and shape Catholic politics.

The previous pages have also shown how religious orders can influence Catholic politics *upward*, whether at the diocesan or Vatican level—a second way in which congregations influence and shape Catholic policy. At the diocesan level, the best example was the influence the White Fathers had on Dom Sebastião in relation to the catechumenate, "inculturation," and African nationalism and independence. Later, it was the turn of the Franciscans to influence Dom Manuel Ferreira Cabral, Dom Sebastião's successor as bishop of Beira. In Rome, we saw the White Fathers discussing the situation in Mozambique and their thoughts of leaving the territory in 1971 with other congregations. Two years later, the same congregations (without the White Fathers) not only discussed the situation but decided to press the Vatican and the pope into taking action. The analysis of these meetings revealed differences not just between but also within congregations, notably between individual provinces and the superior-general. This was the case among the Franciscans whose general in Rome was very critical of Portuguese colonialism while his Portuguese province actively supported the regime. Even more important, we saw two congregations, the White Fathers and the Picpus congregations, making the decision to leave Mozambique, in 1971 and 1974, respectively, without the explicit support of, or even in opposition to the pope and the Secretariat of State, meaning both congregations took a lead in making Catholic policy worldwide.

A third way congregations shape Catholic policy is *laterally*. Congregations influence each other, both formally and informally. They do so by socializing together and, more formally, by gathering at diocesan meetings or synods set up by a bishop or by themselves to discuss a particular topic, a new policy, or new directions in theology. Synods take place in dioceses and in Rome, and the ultimate synod that took place during the period under consideration was the Second Vatican Council, which took place between 1962 and 1965 in Rome. In Beira, we saw Dom Sebastião Soares de Resende organize diocesan synods where the bishop gave particular congregations space to influence others on specific points. In the 1970s, we saw congregations taking the lead in organizing meetings to set up official diocesan policies in the face of inaction on the part of a new bishop. Less formally, there are affinities that straddle congregations and other divides. The Jesuits were very influential in this respect in Beira, with the bishop showing great respect toward them after having studied at their university in Rome and with the White Fathers (whose society is modeled on that of the Jesuits) emulating them in many respects. Institutionally, an important moment for congregations to influence each other came in the 1950s when male religious organizations launched the worldwide Union of Superiors General and, a few years later, female superiors established the International Union Superiors Generals. Similarly, male congregations in Mozambique created a federation of male religious institutes in 1965 whereas female religious congregations did so just after independence. These unions brought congregations together to better engage with the hierarchy, thus providing them with the opportunity to influence each other more than ever before.

While congregations wielded influence and pressure downward, upward, and laterally, their relationships with each other and with the hierarchy were, of course, marked even more strongly by collaboration. Unity is indeed what makes the church stand and what makes it move forward. One could argue that institutionalizing internal diversity is what makes the Catholic Church unique and also makes all sorts of futures possible for the church. The point here is not to emphasize difference *over* unity (the Catholic motto is difference *in* unity), but rather to highlight that both difference and unity coexist and that congregations, which embody much of the diversity in the church, need to be recognized as a fundamental element in Catholic politics. Congregations need to be studied thoroughly, in themselves, in relation to each other, as well as in their relation to the hierarchy, in order to understand the nuances and complexities involved in how the church sets policies and puts them into practice, and in how they have diverse influences on the ground.

As a final example, I return to the peace negotiations between the Mozambican government and the RENAMO guerrilla movement in the late 1980s and early 1990s. Most of the historiography has focused on the role of the Sant'Egidio community, which hosted the talks and acted as mediator at the peace talks between 1989 and 1992.[2] But it goes without saying that the community could not have proceeded had it not received the authorization to do so from the Vatican. It is equally clear that Sant'Egidio could not have succeeded if it had not worked hand in hand with the Mozambican Catholic Church. In other words, if we are to fully understand the role of the Catholic Church in Mozambique's peace process, we need to move beyond the study of Sant'Egidio (and/or the bishop of Beira) to analyze the different parts of the church that were involved, their relations to each other, and their relations (individually and collectively) with the other actors in the process.

The Historical Trajectory of the Church in Mozambique

Many scholars divide the history of the Catholic Church in Mozambique (and elsewhere in Africa) into two discreet periods—the colonial and the postcolonial. They qualify the church accordingly, distinguishing between a colonial church and a postcolonial church. Based on that distinction, many proceed to analyze the transition from one to the other, with debates focusing on the nature and depth of the change that took place. Some argue that the church became African or national after independence, others that the institution remained colonial, and still others that it became neocolonial. The debate takes place among academics, politicians, and activists who reproduce what I called a "political paradigm" (see the introduction). Actors conflate political and religious categories, apply a political periodization onto the Catholic Church, and try to figure out on whose side the church placed itself. While it is true that decolonization/national independence was a major break in the history of African nations, and equally true, as Jean-Marie Bouron has noted, that political changes at independence profoundly shaped the organization and dynamics of Catholicism after independence,[3] it remains inadequate to describe the church on the sole basis of a categorization rooted in a narrow political realm.

Moving beyond the political paradigm, *Catholicism and the Making of Politics* investigates the role of the church in spite of, as well as thanks to, its political alliances. It also analyzes the church across the colonial and postcolonial periods, bridging the independence divide, to trace the development of the institution over more than four decades. Following Fred Cooper and others,[4] the approach adopted here focuses on the historical trajectory of the church, with its shifts, turns, and ruptures. A first outcome of this approach has been to uncover that the church in Mozambique—ranging from the bishop of Beira to many missionaries, including conservative ones—began to prepare for independence (usually understood as a single radical rupture in 1975) and what it would mean for the African clergy from the early 1960s onward, and that the consequences of independence were only fully absorbed and appropriated by the Catholic institution by the early 1980s. In this manner, the issue of decolonization and independence straddled the colonial and postcolonial periods, with the church reorganizing and redefining its priorities between 1960 and 1980. This means that the model of the church established with the Concordat and Missionary Accord in 1940 began to be undone from 1960 onward and that a new model of the postcolonial church was only fully realized in the early 1980s. It also means that we can speak of three periods for the Catholic Church in Mozambique between 1940 and 1986: a full concordarian period after 1940, a period of transition between 1960 and 1980, and a new era since 1980.

How should we characterize the Catholic institution between 1940 and 1986 if we are to avoid the political adjectives of "colonial" and "postcolonial"? Historians and social scientists usually consider two aspects when seeking to define a religious institution: its relation to political power and its internal organization. In relation to the first, we may advance that the church was a "church of power" between 1940 and 1975. It was allied to the state through the Concordat, the Missionary Accord, and the Missionary

Agreement; or as Dom Sebastião put it, the church fitted into "the general organization of the state services." During this period the church actively supported colonialism and imperialism—at least until 1960. Between 1960 and 1980, the church transformed and different projects competed until the end of the 1970s. While some priests, not least the Burgos fathers, pushed for an approach in support of the new socialist state (in a new version of a "church of power"), the bishops developed a prophetic voice and worked at positioning the church along renewed neo-Thomist lines above state and society. After a period of transition, the church thus became what I would call a church of the *magisterium*, one that assumed for itself the church's authority to give authentic interpretation of the Word of God. The Mozambican church became a *magister* (teacher) who seeks to announce and teach the Gospel and the social doctrine of the church, denounces what goes against the doctrine of the church, and stands above all state politics. This stance placed the church at a distance from the state as well as from other social actors. It also allowed the institution to extract itself discursively from the conflict and the war, on the basis of which it was able to demand negotiations to resolve the armed conflict and transform itself into a mediator.

Looking at the internal organization of the church in central Mozambique between 1940 and 1986, the two decades between 1940 and 1960 can be characterized as imperial and missionary in nature: the church relied overwhelmingly on Portuguese and European staff, depended on the colonial state for funds, and invested heavily in infrastructure, in particular schools and health facilities. The institution was hierarchical, patriarchal, paternal, and focused on the conversion of Africans into Christian and Portuguese subjects. Some congregations were more interested than others in the colonization of Mozambique, and some were more concerned than others about infrastructure. Vatican II and political events in the 1960s led to some change in this model. In the Dioceses of Beira and Tete, many congregations modified their approaches while one or two (such as the Burgos order) used it to introduce profound changes. While it is possible to say that the dominant model was being questioned and challenged in the 1960s, a significant change of official church only came with independence. After 1975, African elements took over the leadership of the Catholic institution and set new objectives at a new pace. Nationalization and a postcolonial war critically shaped the church's options and choices. Africanization and inculturation were two key elements. Institutionally, the church transformed into a less hierarchical and less clerical organization, developing Christian base communities and shifting some power to the laity. Catholic historians and theologians in Mozambique talk of a shift toward a "ministerial church" or a "church of the huts."[5] The extent and success of the transformation toward base communities and the laity remains to be investigated fully, but the church certainly did become less clerical and more African and national after 1975.

The trajectory of the church in Mozambique is similar to that of many other churches in Africa after 1940. Most Catholic institutions on the continent were missionary and imperial in the first half of the twentieth century. Within this general categorization, the Diocese of Beira was unique in that it was very diverse (most dioceses had much less diversity) and the bishop of Beira reigned in an unusually collegial fashion, along the lines of an inclusive and transformational leadership style. The conflict that followed upon the bishop's death in 1967 and the appointment of a number of less collegial replacements was also unique for its depth and violence, exacerbated as it was by the liberation war. As a result, the church in central Mozambique saw two global firsts taking place: the departure of a congregation from a territory as a sign of protest (the White Fathers in 1971) and a declaration of class struggle within the church (the Burgos fathers in 1975). After independence in 1975, the situation of the church in Mozambique became less dissimilar to most Catholic institutions in Africa. The church faced an authoritarian regime, was affected by nationalization, and saw the departure of a large number of its European missionaries. While this meant that the church was no longer able to provide the extensive social and educational services it had offered in the past, it also no longer depended on the state and thus had more freedom to remain distant from it. What the Mozambican church did more than most other churches on the continent is to abandon its old imperial and missionary model and transform into a less hierarchical, more community-oriented, and more prophetic institution. While Beira was the dissident voice in the colonial church in Mozambique, after independence its bishop became the vanguard of a new institutional model that became dominant after 1977 and reached its zenith in the late 1980s when the Catholic Church became a mediator in the peace talks between Frelimo and RENAMO.

Notes

Note on Translations

1. For a history of racial categories in the Portuguese Empire and their practice, see Bender, *Angola under the Portuguese*.
2. *Divisão Adminstrativa da Província de Moçambique*.

Introduction

1. Kuhn, *Structure of Scientific Revolutions*, 10.
2. Tiberondwa, *Missionary Teachers*; Porter, *Religion versus Empire?*
3. Comaroff and Comaroff, *Of Revelation and Revolution*.
4. Cooper, "Possibility and Constraint," 168.
5. Majeke, *Role of the Missionaries*; Tiberondwa, *Missionary Teachers*.
6. Idowu, "Predicament of the Church." 417–19.
7. Mandelbaum, *Missionary as a Cultural Interpreter*.
8. Said, *Orientalism*; and Said, *Culture and Imperialism*.
9. Comaroff and Comaroff, *Of Revelation and Revolution*.
10. Comaroff and Comaroff, *Christianity, Colonialism and Consciousness*, 88.
11. Porter, "'Cultural Imperialism.'"
12. Among others, see Cruz e Silva, *Protestant Churches*; Cruz e Silva, "Igrejas protestantes"; and Helgesson, "Church, State and People."
13. Cruz e Silva, *Protestant Churches*, 79. The colonial state outsourced African education to the Catholic Church. The term "Portuguese 'nationalist' education" in the quote thus means education by the Catholic Church.
14. Schubert, *A guerra e as igrejas*, 84.
15. Peterson, *Ethnic Patriotism*; Peterson, "Conversion"; see also Peterson, *Creative Writing*.
16. There are several Catholic histories of Mozambique (at the country, diocesan, and congregational levels). Among others, see Sousa and Correia, *500 anos*; Marime, *Arquidiocese do Maputo*; and Baritussio, *Mozambico*.
17. Sousa and Correira, *500 anos*.
18. Cooper, *Colonialism in Question*, introduction.
19. Lloyd, *Structures of History*, 89, and more generally chaps. 3 and 4.
20. Bayart, "Comparing from Below," 8. See also Bayart, *State in Africa*; and Bayart, "Fait missionnaire."
21. Abrams, *Historical Sociology*, x.
22. Reese, *Inside the Vatican*.

23. See, for example, Dunkerley, *Power in the Isthmus*, 275–76; or Martin, *Jesuits*.

24. Among others, see Léonard, *Salazarisme et fascisme*, 114; Braga da Cruz, *O Estado Novo*, chap. 5; Newitt, *History of Mozambique*, 534–35; Souto, *Caetano*, chap. 9; and Cabaço, *Moçambique*, 197–207.

25. Bruneau, "Church and Politics," 286–89; Neuhouser, "Radicalization of the Brazilian Catholic Church."

26. For reasons of clarity, I use the terms "order" and "congregation" interchangeably, and avoid the terms "society" or "institute." For a definition and discussion of these terms, see section "Defining and Historicizing the Horizontal Church" in this chapter.

27. The figures are extracted from McKensie, *Roman Catholic Church*, 102. For more recent figures and a list of orders, see Foy, *Our Sunday Visitor's Catholic Almanac*; and the yearly publication *Annuario Pontifico* published by the Vatican.

28. See Soullard, "Le pouvoir des religieux"; Moulin, "Le pouvoir"; and Creuzen, *Religious Men*.

29. Hanson, *Catholic Church in World Politics*, 85, and Cava, "Financing the Faith," 43–45. See also Seidler and Meyer, *Conflict and Change*, 12–15.

30. Weber, *Sociologie des religions*, 368. Surprisingly, I have not found an English translation of the texts cited here. The translation is my own.

31. Weber, *Sociologie des religions*, 251.

32. Weber, *Sociologie des religions*, 251–52.

33. Weber, *Sociologie des religions*, 265 and 255, respectively.

34. Michael Hill explains that if a charismatic movement splits from the institution, by definition it becomes a "sect." Thus, religious orders are always part of a church while sects are separate from it. See Hill, *Religious Order*, chap. 3.

35. Among others, see Creary, *Domesticating a Religious Import*; and Denis, *Dominican Friars*.

36. Among others, see McNamara, *Sisters in Arms*; Wittberg, *Rise and Decline*.

37. Francis, "Toward a Typology," 438–39.

38. Goffman, *Asylums*.

39. Hill, *Religious Order*, chap. 3. See also Goddijn, "Sociology of Religious Orders"; and Servais and Hambye, "Structure et signification." The latter set of authors seems to have been the first to adopt Goffman's categories to analyze religious orders.

40. Moulin, *Le monde vivant des religieux*, 272.

41. Moulin, *Le monde vivant des religieux*, 14.

42. Moulin, "Pour une sociologie"; Moulin, "Les origines religieuses"; Moulin, "Aux sources des libertés."

43. Moulin, *Le monde vivant des religieux*, chap. 4.

44. Soullard, "Le pouvoir des religieux," 121.

45. The only exceptions to this are diocesan congregations and monasteries that are answerable to diocesan bishops.

46. Hostie, *Vie et mort*, chap. 1.

47. The main vows are to obedience, chastity, and poverty, but can also include silence and confinement.

48. Rocca, "La fabrication d'une sociologie."

49. According to Canon Law 207, "there are among the Christian faithful in the Church sacred ministers who in law are also called clerics; the other members of the Christian faithful are called lay persons." Among the clergy (the body of clerics, also called "priests") who are entitled to give all sacraments, the church distinguishes between "secular clerics" who stand under the exclusive orders of a bishop and "religious" or "regular" clerics who belong to a religious order. Religious orders have a second category of members, namely, "consecrated religious," called "brothers." Like all sisters, the latter are not ordained and are unable to administer the sacraments. Finally, the terms "monks" and "nuns" refer to religious men and women who live in a monastery or a convent, respectively, secluded from society in order to better worship God.

50. Hostie, *Vie et mort.*

51. Hostie, *Vie et mort,* 344, 348–49, 355.

52. Cita-Malard, *Religious Orders.*

53. McKensie, *Roman Catholic Church,* 102; Hostie, *Vie et mort,* 16–17.

Chapter 1

1. As an interdisciplinary and qualitative investigation, this study is informed by the methodologies of history and sociology. It draws on research in state and church archives in Mozambique, Portugal, the Netherlands, Spain, and Italy, indepth interviews with affected parties, oral histories, and fieldwork. For a detailed discussion of the sources used and the insights they granted, but also the limits they imposed, see Morier-Genoud, "Catholic Church," appendix 1.

2. Boxer, *Portuguese Seaborne Empire,* 180.

3. See Morier-Genoud, "Vatican vs. Lisbon"; Duffy, *Portuguese Africa,* chap. 5; and Pinto Rema, "A actividade missionária."

4. Alexandre, "O império português"; Alexandre, *Velho Brasil;* Clarence-Smith, *Third Portuguese Empire;* and Jerónimo, *A diplomacia do império.*

5. On the Companhia de Moçambique, see Universidade Eduardo Mondlane, *Moçambique no auge do colonialismo,* chap. 5; Newitt, *Portugal in Africa,* chap. 4; Vail, "Mozambique's Chartered Companies"; and Neil-Tomlinson, "Mozambique Chartered Company."

6. Birmingham, *Concise History of Portugal,* chap. 4; and Sardica, "150 anos da regeneração."

7. Cruz Correia, "Moçambique," 242–43.

8. Dores, *A missão da República.*

9. Officially, the British and German governments exerted pressure in order to defend religious freedom, but unofficially they also coveted the Portuguese colonies. See Schebesta, *Portugals Konquistamission,* 327–29.

10. Marques, *Breve história de Portugal,* chaps. 13–14; and Simpson, *A igreja católica,* chap. 1.

11. Léonard, *Salazarisme et fascisme,* chap. 2; and Braga da Cruz, "O Estado Novo."

12. Carvalho, "Salazar e a concordata."

13. The Padroado was a set of privileges and duties to administer the church in the East, granted by the Holy See to the Portuguese crown (the West was granted to the Spanish crown). See Rego, *Le patronage portugais.*

14. Braga da Cruz, "O Estado Novo, 204; and Leite, "Enquadramento legal," 51.

15. Cited in Braga da Cruz, *O Estado Novo,* 62. See also Reis, "A concordata de Salazar?"

16. For the details of the negotiations, see Reis, *Salazar e o Vaticano;* and Carvalho, "Salazar e a concordata."

17. Cruz, *Anuário católico de Portugal 1941,* 405. Duncan Simpson similarly advances the formula of "*pax salazarista* and Catholic revivalism"; see Simpson, *A igreja católica,* 82–83.

18. Authors have debated whether the church was made subordinate to the state or the state became subservient to the papacy. It is my contention that it was neither but rather a reciprocal alliance. Among others, see Cahen, "L'état nouveau," 312n4. The expression "agreed separation" comes from Braga da Cruz, *O Estado Novo,* chap. 2.

19. Paragraph 1 of the Missionary Status of April 5, 1941, cited in Wenzel, *Portugal und der Heilige Stuhl,* 409.

20. Wenzel, *Portugal und der Heilige Stuhl,* 343–54; and more generally, Ferreira, "Acordo missionário."

21. Portuguese Legate to the Holy See to the Minister of Foreign Affairs, Rome, March 23, 1936, most confidential, A48, 2° Piso, M195, Secção Especial/Special section, Ministério dos Negócios Estrangeiros (Archive of the Ministry of Foreign Affairs), Lisbon (hereafter cited as MNE-SE). More generally, see Lopes, *Missões franciscanas,* chap. 9.

22. Lopes, *Missões franciscanas,* 408. The area Dom Rafael hoped to gain for his order was the area of Lourenço Marques and Beira, which would cover two of the three dioceses to be created. For the differences between a vicariate and a diocese, see Bowen, "Diocese (Eparchy)." Note that the head of a vicariate is a vicar or delegate of the pope.

23. Lopes, *Missões franciscanas,* 408.

24. *Boletim mensal das missões franciscanas e Ordem Terceira* (Braga) (July 1941): 161–92.

25. Comment written by Salazar, dated March 16, 1943, on letter by Minister of Colonies to Salazar, February 18, 1943, M195, A48, 2° Piso, MNE-SE. The comment reveals that Salazar knew the details of the matter and was sensitive to the politics between Catholic congregations.

26. Sebastião Soares de Resende, Bishop of Beira, diary entry December 1, 1943, Private Archives of the Bishop of Beira, Library of the Center of African

Studies, University of Oporto, Portugal (hereafter cited as PABB). OFM stands for Ordem Friar Minor (Franciscan) and SJ stands for Society of Jesus (Jesuit).

27. Azevedo, "Perfil biográfico," 393.

28. Resende, *O sacrifício da missa*, viii–xvi.

29. Matos, "Os bispos portugueses."

30. Matos, "Os bispos portugueses," 340.

31. Barreto, *Religião e sociedade*, 172.

32. Barreto, *Religião e sociedade*. More generally, see Rodrigues, "Teologia."

33. Ultramontanism longs for a strong Catholic institution centralized under the pope, with a united and homogeneous Catholic community able to face the modern world. On this subject, see O'Malley, *Vatican I*, especially chap. 2.

34. Resende, *O sacrifício da missa*, viii–xvi.

35. On the development of neo-Thomism in Portugal, see Cruz Pontes, "Tomismo." More generally, see Taveneaux, "Le catholicisme post-tridentin," esp. 1129–30. On intransigent Catholicism, see Malheiro da Silva, "Tradicionalismo."

36. Resende, *O sacrifício da missa*, xiii.

37. Resende, *Profeta em Moçambique*, 92.

38. Resende, *Profeta em Moçambique*, 99.

39. Resende, *Profeta em Moçambique*, 102.

40. Alexandre, "A África"; and Machado Pires, "Messianismo."

41. Resende, *Profeta em Moçambique*, 132.

42. Resende, *Profeta em Moçambique*, 121.

43. Resende, *Profeta em Moçambique*, 122.

44. On this subject, see Allina, *Slavery by Any Other Name*; Isaacman, *Cotton Is the Mother of Poverty*; and Isaacman and Roberts, *Cotton, Colonialism, and Social History*.

45. Bishop of Beira, diary entry October 19, 1944, PABB. On this question, see also Tajú, "Dom Sebastião Soares de Resende."

46. Bishop of Beira, diary entry June 22, 1945, PABB.

47. Resende, *Profeta em Moçambique*, chap. 6. More generally, see Isaacman, *Cotton Iis the Mother of Poverty*; and Pitcher, "From Coercion to Incentives."

48. Bishop of Beira, diary entries April 11, 1950, and April 28, 1950, PABB.

49. Bishop of Beira, diary entries April 10, 1950, and April 13, 1950, PABB.

50. Léonard, "Salazarisme et Franc-Maçonnerie"; and Marques, *A maçonaria portuguesa*. For Moçambique, see Rocha, *A imprensa de Moçambique*, and Serrão, "Contributos para a história."

51. Bishop of Beira to the Minister of the Colonies, January 3, 1950; Bishop of Beira to the Patriarch of Goa, February 6, 1950; and Bishop of Beira to Mr. Patavina, August 3, 1950; all in PABB.

52. About the laity, see Dom Sebastião's pastoral letter "Responsabilidade dos leigos" (1956) in Resende, *Profeta em Moçambique*, chap. 12. For his intervention at Vatican II, see Resende, *Profeta em Moçambique*, chap. 4.

53. Castelo, "*O modo português*," chap. 3. See also the special issue, "Luso-tropicalisme: Idéologies coloniales et identités nationales dans les mondes lusophones," published by the journal *Lusotopie* in 1997.

54. On Adriano Moreira, see Lucena, "Adriano Moreira," 537.

55. The calculations are based on Azevedo, "Perfil biográfico," 410.

56. Bishop of Beira to the Minister of the Colonies, January 3, 1950; Bishop of Beira to the Patriarch of Goa, February 6, 1950; and Bishop of Beira to Mr. Patavina, August 3, 1950; all in PABB.

57. Diocese da Beira, "Relátorio missionário relativo ao ano de 1944," Beira, March 19, 1945, p. 26, Arquivo Histórico de Moçambique (Historical Archive of Mozambique), Maputo, Mozambique (hereafter cited as AHM).

58. Among others, Bishop of Beira, diary entry November 17, 1948, PABB. I have not been able to discover why the Diocese of Beira received (comparatively) less money than other dioceses, at least during the bishop's first decade in Beira (1944–54).

59. See, for example, Bishop of Beira, diary entries April 30, 1947, November 10, 1947, and September 30, 1951; all in PABB.

60. See Bishop of Beira, diary entry November 10, 1949, PABB. The last districts occupied were Miruro and Maravia (in the extreme west of the Tete district) in 1953 when Burgos fathers went to occupy mission stations there.

61. Pereira, "Os Jésuitas em Moçambique," 87–88.

62. See, for example, Bishop of Beira, "Relatório da diocese da Beira de 1947," 22; "Relatório de 1948," 23–24; and "Relatório de 1957," 11; all in AHM.

63. Bishop of Beira, "Relatório da diocese da Beira de 1950," 22, AHM.

64. Ferreira, "A acção católica," 282. See also Fontes, "A acção católica portuguesa . . . (1940–1974)"; and Fontes, "A acção católica portuguesa (1933–1974)."

65. Bishop of Beira, diary entry October 22, 1945, PABB.

66. Bishop of Beira to Mr. David Barrote, March 7, 1950; and Bishop of Beira to Dr. Marcelo Caetano, April 6, 1949; both in PABB.

67. For the name *Adeante*, see Bishop of Beira to Dr. Costa Nunes, April 25, 1949; and Bishop of Beira to Dom Rafael, August 6, 1949; both in PABB.

68. For a history of the newspaper, see Capela, "Para a história," and Rocha, *A imprensa de Moçambique*, 169–70.

69. Rocha, *A imprensa de Moçambique*, 159–60, 213.

70. Moreir-Genoud, "José Capela"; and Júlio Meneses Rodrigues Ribeiro, multiple interviews, Maputo, April and May 1997.

71. Capela, "Para a história"; and Lima, *Caso do Bispo da Beira*.

72. Capela, "Para a história."

73. "Relatório da diocese da Beira de 1944," 33, Relatório no. 166, Fundo do Governo Geral, AHM.

74. Pereira, "Os Jésuitas em Moçambique," 51.

Chapter 2

1. Pedro, *Anuário católico . . . 1964*; and Pinheiro, *Na entrega do testemunho*. Note that the Diocese of Beira became smaller between the bishop's arrival in 1943 and independence in 1975 because the dioceses of Quelimane and Tete were split off from it, in 1954 and 1962, respectively.

2. Woodrow, *Jesuits*, chap. 2.

3. Cruz Correia, *O método missionário*.

4. Pereira, "Jésuitas em Moçambique," chap. 2.

5. Sousa, *Os Jesuítas em Moçambique*. The four periods defined by the author are: 1560–72, 1610–1759, 1881–1910, and from 1941 onward.

6. Franciscan fathers, notably from Goa, had visited Mozambique earlier, but their missions either failed outright or did not last. See Montes Moreira, "Bibliografia dos franciscanos em Moçambique."

7. Lopes, *Missões franciscanas*, 2; Montes Moreira, "A restauração da provincia Franciscana"; Cunha, *Jornadas e outros trabalhos*, 73.

8. Liesegang, "Sofala, Beira e a sua zona"; Vail and White, "The Struggle for Mozambique," 243–75; and Vail, "The Making of an Imperial Slum."

9. Correia, *Missões franciscanas portuguesas*, 2.

10. Franco, "A visão do outro."

11. Morier-Genoud, "Vatican vs. Lisbon," 11–13.

12. See Dom Rafael's biography in Azevedo et al., *Franciscanos em Moçambique*, 340–42. For his role in the negotiations between the Vatican and Lisbon, see Reis, "Portugal e a Santé Sé," 1042–43.

13. Montes Moreira, "Franciscanos," 279.

14. Lopes, *Missões franciscanas*, 330–35.

15. Linden, *Catholics, Peasants, and Chewa Resistance*.

16. Duffy, *Portuguese Africa*, ch. 5; and Newitt, *A History of Mozambique*, 352–55.

17. Linden, *Catholics, Peasants, and Chewa Resistance*, 31.

18. Sacra Congregazione degli Affari Ecclesiastica Straordinari, no. di protocolo 355/45, Vaticano, January 26, 1945, Doc. 306.265, Box 306 (3), Archives Générales des Missionnaires de l'Afrique (General Archives of Missionaries of Africa [White Fathers]), Rome (hereafter cited as AGMAfr.). See also Sebastião Soares de Resende, Bishop of Beira, diary entries for April 21, 1944; November 28, 1944; December 5, 1944; July 16, 1945; and July 21, 1945; all in the Private Archives of the Bishop of Beira, Library of the Center of African Studies, University of Oporto, Portugal (hereafter cited as PABB).

19. Bishop of Beira to P. Guerreiro, March 29, 1950; and Bishop of Beira to P. Viegas, April 29, 1950; both in PABB.

20. Bishop of Beira to P. Viegas, April 29, 1950, PABB.

21. Ilundáin, *Gozo y lágrimas*, 13, 16.

22. Bishop of Beira, diary entry, November 20, 1954, PABB.

23. Rademaker, *Called to Serve*. See also Vasconcelos, *Religiosos*, 195–200.

24. Report on a meeting between the Provincial Superior and the Picpus local council of Lisbon, V.C.M.I no. 6, 1956, 3 pp., Folder "Divers," Box Prov. 6.21, Archives of the Picpus Congregation, Breda, The Netherlands (hereafter cited as APICC).

25. José Verhoeven, "Arquivo da história da missão do Sagrado Coração," July 18, 1960, 16 pp., Folder "Divers/épars," Box Doc. 6.26, APICC; José Verhoeven, Picpus missionary, interview, Breda, September 15, 1999.

26. Baritussio, *Mozambico*, 167–72.

27. Baritussio, *Mozambico*, 184; and Pinheiro, *Na entrega do testemunho*, 472.

28. *Cem anos de presença das irmãs*, 7.

29. Azevedo, "Perfil biográfico," 400; and Lavado, *Franciscanas Missionárias de Maria*.

30. Nóbrega, "A Congregação das Irmãs Franciscanas."

31. Azevedo, "Perfil biográfico," 400; and Pedro, *Anuário católico*, 492.

32. Soares Tomás, *Irmãs Franciscanas missionárias*.

33. Pedro, *Anuário católico*. For the Missionárias Reparadoras do Sagrado Coração de Jesus, see their webpage, accessed June 1, 2018, http://www.mrscj. org/index.php/mocambiques.

34. A "comity agreement" is an agreement of mutual exclusion to avoid the duplication of churches and missions in a specific area.

35. Report on a meeting between the Provincial Superior and the Picpus local council of Lisbon, V.C.M.I no. 6, 1956, 3 pp., Folder "Divers," Box Prov 6.21, APICC.

36. Blommaert, *Mozambique*, 9.

37. Letter to Bishop of Beira, January 27, 1961, Folder "Correspondente P. Provincial met Roberto Bucken Nov 59/Dec 61," Box Prov. 6.21, no. 40, APICC.

38. Father Antonius Petrus Joseph Martens, Picpus missionary, interview, Beira, September 26, 2001. See also Rogier van Rossum, Picpus priest, interview, Valkenburg, September 13 and 14, 1999.

39. Woodrow, *Jesuits*, 12; and Lacouture, *Les Jésuites*, 192.

40. See, for example, Van Volsem (SG) to Father Garin (Superior of the Mission), November 5, 1947, 548(2), AGMAfr. In the letter, Van Volsem talks about authorized hairstyles and reports on one father's bedtime: "Father Marostica did not write [to] us to ask [for] permission to keep awake at night. You are right in prohibiting [this]; you have provisionally allowed him to remain awake until 10 pm: this is the latest; he has to be in bed by this time. He will have to ask authorization for this from the Superior Regional when the latter comes to visit."

41. See, for example, Superior of Mozambique to the Superior General, Annex, November 25, 1949, 548(5), "Vie régulière," AGMAfr.

42. Cyprien d'Alger, "Ordres mendiants," 1162.

43. Van Dijk, "Le franciscanisme comme contestation"; Boff, *Saint Francis*. In 1948, the Franciscan superior, Frei Joaquim de Sousa Violante, noted in his circular of December 16 that a Mozambican bishop had told one of the

fathers, "I am surprised that the Franciscan fathers live and work in the missions as independently as if they were secular priests, something which one actually does not see with other religious congregations." See Box 1 "Correspondência de e para a Custódia (1921–1980)," Archives of the Franciscan Custódia of Mozambique, Maputo, Mozambique (hereafter cited as AFCM).

44. Pereira, "Les Jésuites"; and Pereira, "Jésuitas em Moçambique."

45. Orradre, "Origen y evolución historica."

46. Pinheiro, *Na entrega do testemunho.*

47. Silva, *As missões católicas femininas*, 49, 52.

48. Pasquier, "Lavigerie et le renouveau."

49. It goes without saying that a few Franciscan missionaries did invest significantly in learning local languages and they engaged in the translation of different religious works. See, for example, the case of Frei António José Ribeiro, in Azevedo et al., *Franciscanos em Moçambique*, 373.

50. Bishop of Beira to Snr. P. Larreira, August 31, 1950, PABB.

51. Bishop of Beira, diary entry for April 19, 1947, PABB.

52. Bishop of Beira to the superior of the "C. de Maria," August 23, 1950, PABB. See also Diocese da Beira, Relatório de 1946, 12, Arquivo Histórico de Moçambique (Historical Archive of Mozambique), Maputo (hereafter cited as AHM).

53. Diaire de la Mission des Pères Blancs au Mozambique, May 1946 [Gorongosa], entry dated June 17, 1946, AGMAfr.

54. Durrieu au Pe.Van Volsem, October 21, 1948, Beira, Box 548 (5), AGMAfr.

55. Durrieu au Pe.Van Volsem, October 21, 1948, Beira, Box 548 (5), AGMAfr.

56. P. Garin to the Regional Superior, Gorogonsa, January 11, 1948; and Garin to the Regional Superior, January 19, 1948; both in Box 548(2), AGMAfr.

57. Jesuit Superior to Bishop of Beira, June 23, 1946, File 14, "Correspondência com o Bispo," Box 323, Archives of the Portuguese Province of the Company of Jesus (hereafter cited as APPCJ).

58. Bishop of Beira to Snr. P. Ernesto, April 2, 1952, PABB.

59. Bishop of Beira, diary entry, February 4, 1952, PABB. The exact quote reads: "Foram para minhas ultimas desilusões."

60. The encyclical ambiguously talks of the "training of local clergy." See Benedict XV, *Maximum Illud.*

61. "Dados históricos e Situação judídica," [1960], 2, Dossier "Amatongas," Custódia de Moçambique, Ordem Franciscana, Box 9, AFCM.

62. "Dados históricos e Situação judídica," [1960], 2, Dossier "Amatongas," Custódia de Moçambique, Ordem Franciscana, Box 9, AFCM.

63. Bishop of Beira, diary entry, January 7, 1944, PABB.

64. "Conselho da Custodia, Actas 1953 à 1972," 14 (Council meeting, Inhambane, August 1, 1958), AFCM.

65. I have not found any documents showing why Dom Sebastião accepted the opening of this seminary. But, considering the previous concern of the

bishop, it seems clear that one reason was the fact that the diocesan seminary was fully operating.

66. Bishop of Beira, diary entry January 30, 1947, PABB.

67. Bishop of Beira to Dom Rafael [de Assunção], January 24, 1950, PABB.

68. To date, I have found only one example of such a bilateral agreement between a congregation and the bishop. This has precluded a detailed comparison and analysis of these agreements.

69. Willis, "Men on the Spot."

70. Relatório do ano de 1949 do Bispo da Beira, pp. 13–14, Direcção Geral de Educação—SSC: Repartição da Cultura e das Missões, AHU/ACL-MU/ DGE/RCM/000/Mç1442, SC, MU, Overseas Historical Archive, Lisbon (hereafter cited as AHU).

71. Bishop of Beira, diary entry January 18, 1954, PABB; and "Conselho da Custódia: Actas," entries for May 13, 1954, and December 13, 1954, AFCM.

72. The bishop wrote in his diary on June 10, 1956 (PABB): "Holy day at the Cathedral of the Sacred Heart of Jesus. Father Neves, a Franciscan from Inhambane, preached. His sermon is twenty years out of date. Worse is that the sermon does not teach Christian doctrine. One loses time, gets bored and I don't know what more . . . and eventually the people remain ignorant of the things of God and Heaven. How can we correct this? We launched a campaign, we, the newer clergy, to re-educate in this fashion so that we may begin a new era."

73. Relatório do ano de 1951 do Bispo da Beira, p. 31, Missões—actividades missionárias das congregações, 1946–63, AHU/ACL-MU/DGE/RCM/000/ Mç1438, SR, SC-SSC, AHU.

74. Letter from the bishop and forty-five priests to Salazar, October 18, 1953, 3 pp. [read by Salazar on February 23, 1954], Repartição da Cultura e das Missões, SR, Missões-Assuntos comuns, Actividade missiónaria, 1946–63, AHU/ACL-MU/DGE/RCM/000/Mç1439, SC-SSC, AHU.

75. Relatório do ano de 1953 do Bispo da Beira, p. 15, Missões—actividades missionárias das congregações, 1946–63, AHU/ACL-MU/DGE/RCM/000/ Mç1438, SR, SC-SSC, AHU.

76. Moçambique, "Directrizes missionárias," 1940, 13 pp., CP 15, Instituto Nacional dos Arquivos Nacionais/Torre de Tombo (Institute of National Archives/Torre de Tombo), Lisbon (IAN/TT), Archive of Oliveria Salazar (hereafter cited as AOS).

77. Bishop of Beira, diary entry November 11, 15, and 16, 1944, and December 14, 1944, PABB. I have been unable to find a copy of this document in any archive. The bishop's diary reveals only that the document was published in early 1945 after the bishop worked on it during the months of November and December 1944.

78. In the absence of a copy of the 1945 document, I am unable to trace whether this was already a concern for the bishop at this time.

79. The Burgos and Picpus orders had not arrived in Beira yet.

80. Monsignor Durrieu à Prein, December 2, 1953, 548 (2), AGMAfr.

81. Prein to Monsignor Durrieu, letter received in Rome on February 5, 1953, 548(2), AGMAfr.

82. Prein to Monsignor Durrieu, letter received in Rome on February 5, 1953, 548(2), AGMAfr. See also letter no. 1336 (n.d.); letter sent on November 8, 1953; and letters of Monsignor Durrieu to Prein, February 6, 1953, and December 2, 1953; all in 548(2), AGMAfr.

83. Resende, *Profeta em Moçambique.*

84. Resende, *Profeta em Moçambique,* 26 (canon 296 §2).

85. Letter from [Superior?] to Bishop of Beira, July 17, 1951, Box 323/14, APPCJ. In his letter, the superior also argued that his instructions to his men were not an act of disrespect for the authority of the bishop insofar as the bishop had to agree to these orders for them to take effect.

86. Diocese da Beira e Quelimane, *Regulamento dos Missionários,* 6.

87. Among others, see José Verhoeven, picpus missionary, interview, Breda, September 15, 1999; Bishop António Montes Moreira, Franciscan superior, interview, Lisbon, April 28, 2001; and Laurinda Baptista, Franciscan sister of Calais, interview, Chimoio, September 20, 2001.

Chapter 3

1. The best example of this approach is Neill, *History of Christian Missions.*

2. Among others, see Gray, "Problems of Historical Perspective"; and Ranger and Weller, *Themes.* More recently, see Comaroff and Comaroff, *Of Revelation and Revolution.*

3. Peterson and Allman, "Introduction."

4. For reasons of coherence, I counted the province of Tete in my calculation of 1974. Calculations have been made on the basis of data from Pedro, *Anuário católico do ultramar português 1960,* 203; and Pedro, *Anuário católico . . . 1964,* 177, 217. (The figure given on page 177 for the total population is lower than the number of Catholics. I have corrected it to 1,500,000. This figure produces the percentages of Catholics provided here. If my assumption is incorrect, then the percentage of Catholics in the population would be even higher).

5. Diocese da Beira e Quelimane, *Regulamento dos missionários,* 36–37.

6. Pedro, *Anuário católico . . . 1960;* Pedro, *Anuário católico . . . 1964.*

7. Brandão, *A igreja católica,* 111. For a critique of the book, see Morier-Genoud, "Review of Brandão, *A igreja católica.*"

8. Wilson, *Religion,* chap. 1. Within the European context, this argument has been used to explain secularization in cities while in Africa it has been used to explain high rates of conversion to Christianity in urban areas; see Cox, *Secular City* and, for a more modern perspective, Bielo, "Urban Christianities."

9. *Cidade da Beira,* 65–66. Whereas the proportion of Africans in Beira was 73.5 percent in 1940, it had dropped to 70 percent by 1964. See Direcção provincial dos Serviços de Estatística Geral, *Anuário estatístico 1964,* 34. We also

note here that 90 percent of all those baptized in the Diocese of Beira in 1969 were Africans; whites constituted only 4.5 percent of all baptisms.

10. Dom Teodosio, "Relatório dos trabalhos missionários, ano de 1941," Lourenço-Marques, 1942, p. 3, Fundo do Governo Geral (hereafter cited as FGG), Arquivo Histórico de Moçambique (Historical Archive of Mozambique), Maputo, Mozambique (hereafter cited as AHM).

11. Dom Teodosio, "Relatório dos trabalhos missionários no ano de 1942," Lourenço-Marques, 1942, p. 13, FGG, AHM.

12. Bishop of Beira, "Relatório missionário relativo ao ano de 1944," Beira, 1945, p. 8, FGG, AHM. See also Schebesta, *Portugals Konquistamission*, 327–29.

13. Bishop of Beira, "Relatório dos trabalhos missionários no ano de 1942," Lourenço-Marques, 1943, pp. 13–14, FGG, AHM.

14. Bishop of Beira, "Relatório missionário relativo ao ano de 1945," Beira, 1946, p. 8, FGG, AHM.

15. Pereira, "Jésuitas em Moçambique," 58–71. See also, for example, Bishop of Beira, "Relatório dos trabalhos missionários no ano de 1944," Beira, 1945, p. 8, FGG, AHM.

16. Alberto, *Os angonis*, 65.

17. Linden, "Chewa Initiation Rites," 30–44.

18. Nota confidential n°23/E/10-1 do Administrador de Macanga ao Director da Admnistração civil de Manica e Sofala, January 9, 1953, file E/7/1, Box 793, Secção Administrativa, Fundo do Governo do Distrito da Beira, AHM.

19. For a history of the area, see Allina, *Slavery by Any Other Name*; and Neves, "Economy, Society and Labour."

20. P. José Miguel Vieira, "Monografia da Paroquia de Nossa Senhora do Rosario de Macequece (Missão sucursal)," February 11, 1934, p. 3, Cx 9, Archives of the Franciscan Custódia of Mozambique, Maputo, Mozambique (hereafter cited as AFCM).

21. Bishop of Beira, "Relátorio 1943," 6, Fundo do Governo da Beira, "Missões religiosas," AHM.

22. A minor seminary is a secondary boarding school for boys who wish to become priests.

23. It was an early hypothesis of mine that Catholic congregations provided networks that Africans drew on. My interviews proved this hypothesis largely wrong. In fact, only a weak Franciscan or White Fathers' network existed; most of my interviewees saw no particular difference between congregations, and they said they switched without even thinking about which order might run a certain church, parish, or mission.

24. "Orthopraxis" is a theological term meaning "correct practice." "Orthodoxy" means "right belief."

25. Antoine Vergote defines "folk Catholicism" as a Catholicism that is tightly bound to the cultural traditions of a society and followed by the majority of its members. Vergote, "Folk Catholicism," 6.

26. Father Pollet to Superior General (SG), April 23, 1954, 548(4), Archives Générales des Missionnaires de l'Afrique (General Archives of Missionaries

of Africa [White Fathers]), Rome, Italy (hereafter cited as AGMAfr.). See also Father Pollet to SG, June 5, 1955, 548(4), AGMAfr.

27. Louis Durrieu (SG) to Father Naedts (Vila Gouveia), February 25, 1950, 548(3) Baruè, AGMAfr.

28. Entry July 10, 1946, Diaire de la Mission des Pères Blancs au Mozambique [Gorongosa], AGMAfr.

29. Diaire de la mission de Gorongosa, 1946–60, entry July 11, 1946, Carnet de Conseil, AGMAfr.

30. Father Philippe Pattavina, "Mozambique missionnaire," 1949, p. 10, file Q 29/15, AGMAfr.

31. Interviews were held, among others, with Vitorino Mendes dos Reis, Chimoio, September 18, 2001; Alberto Jequessene Soro, Chimoio, September 19, 2001; Nicolau da Barca, Chimoio, September 20, 2001; Agostinhio Cufa dos Muchangos, Manica, September 21, 2001; Benjamin Taramba Manhoca, Manica, September 21, 2001; Maria and Gustavo Lukas Mozinho, Dondo, October 4 and 5, 2001; António Dina Cardos, Beira, September 30 and October 6, 2001; Margarida Lopes Rodrigues, Beira, October 3, 2001; and Lukas Bizeque Quembo de Raposo, Dondo, October 4, 2001.

32. Dom Jaime Gonçalves, bishop of Beira, interview, Beira, July 7, 2009.

33. "Relatório da diocese da Beira relativo ao ano de 1944," 33, Relatório n°166, FGG, AHM.

34. Diocese da Beira e Quelimane, "Regulamento dos Missionários," 30–31.

35. "Seminário de S. João de Brito do Zóbuè."

36. Diary entry January 7, 1944, Private Archives of the Bishop of Beira, Library of the Center of African Studies, University of Oporto, Portugal (hereafter cited as PABB).

37. "Relatório da Diocese da Beira de 1942," 7, Relatório n°166, FGG, AHM; "Relatório da Diocese da Beira de 1944," 33, Relatório n°141, FGG, AHM. The Franciscans admitted privately that their seminary faced numerous difficulties. After closing down Amatongas, the Franciscans sent their current students to a Franciscan seminary in Nyasaland and to Portugal (Zobuè had only just opened and could not yet accommodate advanced students) and they focused their hopes on opening a minor seminary in the southern parts of Mozambique. One of their students, Alexandre F. Lopes became the first African priest in Mozambique in late 1953 under the name of Alexandre José Maria dos Santos. At independence he became bishop of Maputo and was appointed as cardinal in 1988. On his early career, see *Missões Franciscanas* 121 (October 1953): 7.

38. Dom Sebastião Soares de Resende, "Relatório da Diocese da Beira de 1950," 19, FGG, AHM.

39. No comprehensive history of the Namaacha seminary exists. Elements can be gleaned from Marime, *Arquidiocese do Maputo*, 50–51; and Veloso, *D. Teodósio Clemente*, 273–76.

40. André de Bels, former White Father missionary, interview, Baltimore, June 18–19, 1999; and Jaime Gonçalves, archbishop of Beira, interview, Beira, September 13, 2001.

41. Father Theodore Prein, "Seminário diocesano de Zobuè: Relatório do ano lectivo 1950–1951," July 15, 1952, p. 2, Folder "Zobuè," Box "Missões de Tete 1949–51," Arquivo da Diocese de Beira (Archive of the Diocese of Beira), Beira, Mozambique (hereafter cited as ADB).

42. Father Theodore Prein, "Seminário diocesano de Zobuè: Relatório do aano lectivo 1950–1951," July 15, 1952, p. 2, Folder "Zobuè," Box "Missões de Tete 1949–51," ADB; and Mabunda, "A C. E. M. na luta armada."

43. Father Theodore Prein, "Seminario diocesano de Zobue: Relatorio do ano lectivo 1950–1951," July 1, 1952, p. 2, Folder "Zobuè," Box "Missões de Tete 1949–51," ADB.

44. Bishop of Beira to Rector of the Seminary, March 20, 1954, ADB.

45. Jaime Gonçalves, archbishop of Beira, interview, Beira, September 13, 2001; Samuel Abudo Mucauro, Catholic priest, interview, Beira, September 11, 2001; and André de Bels, former White Father missionary, interview, Baltimore, June 18–19, 1999. The head of the tribunal had to report to the superior of the seminary who thus exercised indirect control.

46. Father Theodore Prein, "Seminário Diocesano de Zobuè: Relatoório do ano lectivo 1950–1951," July 1, 1952, p. 2, Folder "Zobuè," Box "Missões de Tete 1949–51," ADB.

47. "Seminário de S. João de Brito," 146.

48. Creary, *Domesticating a Religious Import*, 90.

49. The first African priest was ordained in 1953. He came from southern Mozambique and studied at the Franciscan seminary of Amatongas. See footnote 37.

50. Hastings, "Vocation for the Priesthood."

51. Father Cras (Regional Superior) to Dom Sebastião, November 21, 1956, 548(5), "Vie régulière," AGMAfr.

52. Bishop of Beira, diary entry August 10, 1953, PABB.

53. Technically FRELIMO is written with all caps for the liberation front and Frelimo, uncapped, for the political party, which was founded out of the liberation movement in 1977. For reasons of coherence and ease of reading, I use lowercase in this book.

54. PIDE-LM to Lisbon, Radio n°312/68-Gab, recebido 3.4.68 [p. 151] and PIDE-LM to Lisbon, Radio n°315/68-Gab, received April 4, 1968 [p. 150], both in NT 244 "Domingos Gonçalo Ferrão," Processo 9296-CI(2), PIDE archive, Instituto Nacional dos Arquivos Nacionais/Torre de Tombo (Institute of National Archives/Torre de Tombo), Lisbon, Portugal (hereafter cited as IAN/TT). Students from Zobuè were jailed in the same period and the bishop did not help them either. Today some students think that the bishop did not have the power to help them. See Paulo Cuvaca, former seminarian in Zobuè, interview, Beira, September 8, 2015.

55. Dhada, *Portuguese Massacre*, chap. 7; and Hastings, *Wiriyamu*. While Wiriyamu led to a significant international crisis between the United Kingdom and Portugal, the 1971 massacre of Mukumbura played a more important role in

politically realigning the various sectors of the Mozambican church (see chapter 5 in this volume).

56. Officio no.454/65SR of March 12, 1965, Sub-Inspector Francisco Bartolomeu da Costa to Sub-Director of PIDE in Lourenço Marques, "Pe Mauricio Charles Pollet e Mateus Pinho Guengere," Processo 3894-CI(2), PIDE archive, IAN/TT.

57. Radio no. 7/65/GAB (Interpol Lisbon to Interpol Lourenço Marques), IAN/TT, PIDE archive, Processo 3894-CI(2), "Pe Mauricio Charles Pollet e Mateus Pinho Guengere," and Letter of Dom Sebastião to Salazar, October 6, 1965, IAN/TT, PIDE archive, Processo (SC)-CI(2) 1734, vol. 3, "Missionários no Ultramar."

58. Gwenjere's flight from Mozambique was remarkable. Before leaving, he informed the vicar-general of his intention, upon which the vicar-general informed the authorities. PIDE immediately sent an agent to follow Gwenjere while seeking authorization from Lisbon to arrest him. On July 25, Gwenjere crossed the border on foot, alone and in civilian clothes, just as the police, on order from the overseas minister, drove to Murraça to arrest him. See Ministério do Ultramar, gabinete dos Negócios Politicos, Apontamentos, Assunto: "Actividades do padre Mateus da Missão de Nossa Senhora de Fátima da Muraça-Sena," March 31, 1967; and PIDE, rádio n°285/67/Gab de ?/4.7.67 [pp. 287–88], Processo 3894-CI(2), "Pe. Mauricio Charles Pollet e Mateus Pinho Guengere"; both in PIDE/DGS Archive, IAN/TT. See also Lukas Alfandegas Zingue (who helped him across the border), former catechist, interview, Murraça, July 13, 2009.

59. Report of Father Mondor (July 6–27, 1965) in White Fathers, *Mozambique*, 192; and Father André van Zon, Blessed Sacrament missionary, interview, Maputo, April 19, 1996.

60. White Fathers, "Mozambique," 192; Mabunda, "A C. E. M. na luta armada," 2–3; and Lawe Laweki, former Zobuè seminarian, interview, Maputo, April 6, 2012.

61. Azevedo et al., *Franciscanos em Moçambique*, 301–10, 460–61. Interestingly, the Franciscans placed two African priests from the south of the territory to work in central Mozambique. Frei Vasco Pedro Machonice worked in three different missions in central Mozambique between 1959 and 1961, and Frei Fernando do Carmo Ribeiro served at the cathedral in Beira from 1971 to 1978; see Azevedo et al., *Franciscanos em Moçambique*, 431, 455.

62. Soares Tomás, *Irmãs franciscanas missionárias*, 175.

63. Lavado, *Franciscanas missionárias de Maria*, 219–21.

64. Sousa, *As franciscanas missionárias*, 266; Fernanda Jesus Rodrigues, Franciscan sister of Calais, interview, Chimoio, September 20, 2001.

65. *Cem anos de presença das irmãs*, 43.

Chapter 4

1. Cheza, "Le franciscan Placide Tempels."

2. Prudhomme, "Mission et religions."

3. Charles, *Prayer for all Men*; Bishop of Beira, diary entry, December 3, 1956, Private Archives of the Bishop of Beira, Library of the Center of African Studies, University of Oporto, Portugal (hereafter cited as PABB). In his 1955 report to the state, the bishop wrote: "Catholicism can incarnate in any civilization, in what it has of truth; and therefore to become Christian, all and any men will not feel the need to abandon, in our case, his African identity. . . . The African can perfectly well become Christian without having to abandon being an African and being in the truth, beauty, and generosity of African civilization." See Bishop of Beira, Relatório da Diocese da Beira 1955, p. 11, Fundo do Governo Geral (hereafter cited as FGG), Arquivo Histórico de Moçambique (Historical Archive of Mozambique), Maputo, Mozambique (hereafter cited as AHM).

4. Rego, *Temas sociomissionológicos*, 29. See also Rego, *Alguns problemas*.

5. On Vatican II, see Linden, *Global Catholicism*, chaps. 3–4; Wilde, *Vatican II*; and Antunes, "Concílio Vaticano II."

6. Antunes, "Concílio Vaticano II," 61–63, 244–47. Dom Sebastião intervened in this discussion to propose that religious men and women should be better integrated into diocesan structures, in particular into the diocesan presbyteries (the advisory bodies to a bishop).

7. Luciano da Costa Ferreira writes, mistakenly, that the missionary weeks began in 1968; see Ferreira, *Igreja ministerial*, 84. But he conflates missionary weeks and pastoral weeks. While the latter started in 1968, the former began in 1963 (the first taking place on August 4–8, 1963, in Quelimane), at the beginning of Vatican II. See Júlio Meneses Rodrigues Ribeiro, Catholic layman, multiple interviews, Maputo, April and May 1997.

8. Ferreira, *Igreja ministerial*, 84.

9. Júlio Meneses Rodrigues Ribeiro, Catholic layman, multiple interviews, Maputo, April and May 1997. Documentation on the weeks can be found in Fundo do Júlio Meneses Rodrigues Ribeiro, AHM.

10. Ferreira, *Igreja ministerial*, 84–85. Again, Ferreira gets his dates wrong: Nazaré was opened in 1968 and not 1969. Among others, see Sousa and Correia, *500 anos*, 110.

11. Perez, "Memórias dos missionários"; and Sousa, *Memórias de um jesuíta missionário*, 271–75.

12. Father José Maria Moreira Pereira de Faria, Franciscan missionary, interview, Lisbon, May 1, 2001; and Júlio Meneses Rodrigues Ribeiro, Catholic layman, multiple interviews, Maputo, April and May 1997.

13. Pereira, "Les Jésuites," 106–7.

14. Bishop of Beira, diary entry, June 18, 1963, PABB.

15. See, for example, *Diário de Moçambique*, September 17 and 29, 1967, and October 1, 4, 7, 9, 13, 15, and 21, 1967.

16. On economic policy, see Leite, "Colonial, politica"; Pereira, "A economia do império"; and Pitcher, *Politics*, chap. 7. On white settlers, see Castelo, "Colonial Migration"; Middlemas, "Twentieth Century White Society"; and Clarence-Smith, *Third Portuguese Empire*, 177–80.

17. Rosas, *História de Portugal,* 371–449; and Wheeler, "'Estado presente de tranquilidade.'"

18. Among others, see Pitcher, "From Coercion to Incentives"; and Isaacman, *Cotton Is the Mother of Poverty.*

19. Keese, "Bloqueios no sistema"; and Keese, *Living with Ambiguity,* esp. chap. 4.

20. Clarence-Smith, *Third Portuguese Empire,* 179–84.

21. Cahen, "Corporatisme et colonialisme."

22. Cahen, "L'état nouveau," 342.

23. Liesegang and Tembe, "Subsídios para a história."

24. Tembe, "Uhuru na Kazi"; Cahen, "Mueda Case"; and Adam, "Mueda," 24–28.

25. On UNAMI, see Borges Coelho, *O início da luta armada,* chap. 2. Oddly there is not a single publication on MANC yet. For some preliminary elements, see Freitas, "Movimentos subversivos," 320–21, and Neves, "Economy, Society and Labour," 298–303.

26. Cahen, "Mueda Case," 45.

27. Borges Coelho, *O início da luta armada,* 62; Marcum, *Conceiving Mozambique,* 55–56.

28. Cabrita, *Mozambique,* ch. 6; Marcum, *Conceiving Mozambique,* 65–67; and Couto, *Moçambique 1974,* 146–54.

29. COREMO saw a first group splinter off in 1967 when Amos Sumane left the organization to create the União Nacional Africana da Rombezia (African National Union of Rombezia), a secessionist movement aimed at gaining independence for northern Mozambique. See Borges Coelho, *O início da luta armada,* 63.

30. Marcum, *Conceiving Mozambique,* 65–67.

31. One of the most recent versions of this argument can be found in Chabal et al., *History of Postcolonial Lusophone Africa,* 5–7.

32. For the latest incarnation of this argument, see Tembe and Gaspar, "O contexto colonial." In English, see, for example, Hall and Young, *Confronting Leviathan,* 12.

33. Cahen, "Nationalism and Ethnicities," 166. See also Brito, "Une re-lecture nécessaire."

34. Cahen, "Nationalism and Ethnicities"; Cahen, "Anticolonialisme identitaire"; and Cahen, "Mueda Case." This argument is also made in Adam, *Escapar aos dentes,* 70–77; and in Brito, "Une re-lecture nécessaire."

35. Though he did not look specifically at the nationalist elite from central Mozambique, the first scholar who examined the social origins of Frelimo's factional fights is Walter C. Opello Jr. See Opello, "Pluralism and Elite Conflict"; and Opello, "Internal War."

36. Borges Coelho, *O início da luta armada,* 52, 61. For the Portuguese machinations against Changonga, using his family left behind in Mozambique, see Ivens-Ferraz de Freitas, SCCI-L. M., *Informação* n°64/962, secreto, October 4, 1962, Box 340, Serviço coordenação e centalização da informação de Moçambique (hereafter cited as SCCIM), Instituto Nacional dos Arquivos Nacionais/

Torre de Tombo (Institute of National Archives/Torre de Tombo), Lisbon, Portugal (hereafter cited as IAN/TT).

37. Joel da Neves for some reason writes that MANC was created in 1959; this may have to do with the fact that his narrative is based primarily on oral interviews. His thesis contains the only existing history of the party. See Neves, "Economy, Society and Labour," 298–303.

38. Minutes of the interrogation by PIDE of Peter Edward Nthawira Balamanja and Minizhu Jack Ntundumula Bande, June 17, 1963, Box 67, SCCIM, IAN/TT.

39. Consulado Geral de Portugal, Salisbury, Pr. 16, N°104, confidential, à dir. PIDE Lourenço Marques, January 16, 1963, Processo SC/SR 417/63, "Congresso Nacional African de Moçambique," IAN/TT.

40. Ministério dos Negócios Estrangeiros, Direcção-Geral dos Negócios Políticos e da Administração Interna, Proc. 940, 1(8)D, UL 209, April 3, 1963; and Oficial de Comando so Special Branch BSA Police GHQ, Causeway, Rodésia do Sul, ào Rogério Morais Coelho Dias, director da PIDE, May 23, 1963, personal and secret, réf. XY2266 (tradução); both in Processo SC/SR 417/63 "Congresso Nacional African de Moçambique," IAN/TT. On the Chikunda, see Isaacman and Peterson, "Making the Chikunda"; and Isaacman and Isaacman, *Slavery and Beyond.*

41. PIDE, Informação n°81-SC/CI(2), April 2, 1963, 2 pp., secret, p.1, SC/SR 417/63, PIDE/DGS Archive, IAN/TT.

42. Minutes of the interrogation by PIDE of Peter Edward Nthawira Balamanja, SC/SR 417/63: passim, PIDE/DGS Archive, IAN/TT; and in Box 67, SCCIM, IAN/TT.

43. Cahen, "Les mutineries."

44. Spencer, *Toward an African Church.*

45. Ncomo, *Uria Simango;* and Liesegang and Tembe, "Subsídios para a historia."

46. See Gundana's autobiography in Mussanhane, *Protagonistas,* 345–51. For Inácio António Nunes, see his interview on Mozambican television on the occasion of the fiftieth anniversary of the founding of Frelimo. See Nunes, "50 anos da Frelimo."

47. André de Bels, former White Father missionary, interview, Baltimore, June 18–19, 1999; and Benjamin Serapião, former seminarian in Zobuè and Namaacha, interview, Chicago, November 1, 1998. See also Borges Coelho, "Entrevista," 152; and various documents in P.161-CI(2), "André Léo de Bels," Serviço Centrais P.161-CI(2), "André Léo de Bels," PIDE/DGS Archives IAN/TT.

48. For the US side, see Schneidman, *Engaging Africa,* 23–24.

49. PIDE-Moçambique, Relatório imediato n°911/67/GAB, P°19/GAB, July 10, 1967, secret; and PIDE-Moçambique, Relatório n°1509/67-GAB, P°19/GAB, September 17, 1967, confidential; both in SCCIM Box 156, PIDE/DGS Archives, IAN/TT. Lukas A. Zingue, a former cathechist and student at Murraça, calculated that 144 individuals left for the liberation struggle with the

help of Father Pollet and Father Gwenjere. Lukas A. Zingue, former cathechist, interview, Murraca, July 18, 2009.

50. United Nations General Assembly, "Provisional Summary Record of the One Thousand Seven Hundred and Twelfth Meeting, New York," November 6, 1967, p. 25.

51. Opello, "Pluralism and Elite Conflict"; and Cabrita, *Mozambique*, chap. 8.

52. Panzer, "Pedagogy of Revolution"; and Cabrita, *Mozambique*, chap. 8. See also Laweki, "Sérgio Vieira"; and Laweki, "A crise de 1968," 6. See also the memoirs of former student Francisco Moises, *Daring to Survive*, chaps. 28–29; and, from the other side of the conflict, the memoirs of Martins, *Porquê Sakrani?* chap. 20.

53. Panzer, "Pedagogy of Revolution"; and Cabrita, *Mozambique*, chap. 8; Laweki, "Sérgio Vieira"; Laweki, "A crise de 1968," 6; Moises, *Daring to Survive*, chaps. 28–29; and Martins, *Porquê Sakrani?* chap. 20.

54. Moises, *Daring to Survive*, chaps. 28–29; Tembe Ndelana, *From UDENAMO to FRELIMO*, 95–96; Lawe Laweki, former seminarian of Zobuè, interview, Maputo, July 5, 2012; Benjamin T. Majambe, former liberation fighter and Frelimo dissenter, interview, Beira, May 29, 2015; and Manuel João Favor, former liberation fighter and Frelimo dissenter, interview, Caia, July 17, 2009.

55. Newitt, *History of Mozambique*, 525–26; and Cabrita, *Mozambique*, chap. 10.

56. After Mondlane's death, Uria Simango should have taken over Frelimo's leadership. Instead, a triumvirate was instituted. Soon after, Frelimo expelled Simango from the Central Committee and the leadership. He left Frelimo and Tanzania soon after, leaving behind in Frelimo very few members of the (Protestant or Catholic) elite of Manica and Sofala.

57. See, among others, Martins, *Porquê Sakrani?* 309; Christie, *Samora*, chap. 5; and Marcelino dos Santos, key Frelimo leader, interview, Maputo, April 24, 1997.

58. PIDE devised various plans to bring Gwenjere back on the Portuguese side after he left Frelimo. Gwenjere considered the proposal only once, in 1973, but did not follow up on it. The documentation contained in the PIDE archive indicates that Gwenjere never worked with PIDE or passed information on to it. See his file in Processo 3894-CI(2), "Pe. Mauricio Charles Pollet e Mateus Pinho Guenguere," PIDE/DGS Archive, IAN/TT.

59. Buendia, *Educação moçambicana*, 180n52. For Father Mateus Gwenjere's biography, see Benjamin António Gwenjere, interview, Inharugué, July 17, 2009; and personal correspondence with Lawe Laweki.

60. Ncomo, *Uria Simango*, 343n493; and Lawe Laweki, former seminarian of Zobuè, interview, Maputo, July 5, 2012; personal correspondence with Lawe Laweki; and Manuel João Favor, former liberation fighter and Frelimo dissenter, interview, Caia, July 17, 2009. See also Gwenjere's own declaration denying racism in Joaquim Furtado, *A guerra*.

61. Derluguian, "Social Origins," esp. 90–98.

62. Cruz e Silva, "Igrejas protestantes"; and Cruz e Silva, *Protestant Churches*. The Swiss Mission, from which the local Presbyterian Church grew, perceived itself as the church of the Tsonga people.

63. Cardinal of Lourenço Marques to the Bishop of Beira, letter, December 9, 1960, PABB.

64. Bishop of Beira, diary entry, July 26, 1959, PABB: "I received the grades [from Namaacha] and those of Tomé, Ferrão and André are the best. The vice-rector said Tomé would be a good student for the Gregorian [University]. Above all of them must be André Saene." See also Father André de Bels, former White Father missionary, interview, Baltimore, June 18, 1999.

65. Transcription of *Informação*, [n/d], confidential, Caixa 319, SCCIM, IAN/TT; Bishop of Beira, diary entry, December 27, 1963, PABB; and André Saene to Mr. Abel Sazuze, UDENAMO office, Lusaka, July 13, 1965, Processo 3894-CI(2), "Filipe Masquil," NT, PIDE/DGS, IAN/TT.

66. Reproduced from Serapião, "Preaching of Portuguese Colonialism," 36. Bracketed text appears in the original.

67. Frelimo referred to the instructions on its radio programs and Eduardo Mondlane reproduced them in his book *Struggle for Mozambique*, 74–75. For the history of the policies, see Bishop Alberto Setele, bishop of Inhambane, interview, February 26, 1996. For a description of the event, see the memoirs of António Disse Zengazenga, *Memórias*, 26–42. In an interview in 2001 with the author, Dom Custódio insisted that he had never been against independence, merely against immediate independence. Dom Custódio Alvim Pereira, interview, Rome, June 26, 2001.

68. Bishop of Beira, diary entry, February 25, 1963, PABB.

69. Bishop of Beira, diary entry, February 26, 1963, PABB.

70. Ferreira, *Carisma vicentino*, chap. 3.

71. Report of the visit of Father Mondor to Mozambique, July 1965, cited in White Fathers, "Mozambique," 192. See also Father André van Zon, Blessed Sacrament priest, interview, Maputo, April 19, 1996.

72. Bishop of Beira, diary entry, June 20, 1964, PABB. The White Fathers Society only accepted Africans in their society with the explicit authorization of the prelate of the diocese. As far as I know, only one or two Africans tried to enter the society. See François Van Volsem, "Note du Conseil Généralice," January 15, 1962, 446(1), Archives Générales des Missionnaires de l'Afrique (White Fathers), Rome (hereafter cited as AGMAfr).

73. Bishop of Beira, diary entry, December 27, 1963, PABB. The last sentence is unclear in Portuguese. It reads: "Ele disse que havia algo de verdade mas não era tudo verdade. Inclusive disse que não sabia se o colégio ficaria la, pois, não tenho confiança neles, se isto é verdade."

74. Father Pollet to Bishop of Beira, February 9, 1966, cited in White Fathers, "Mozambique," 195.

75. Bishop of Beira, diary entry, January 15, 1963, PABB.

76. This quote is from the Letter to the Hebrews 5.1, and it means "in order to offer gifts and sacrifices for sins."

77. White Fathers, "Mozambique," 167.

78. Nolan, *Departure of the Missionaries*, 73–74.

79. Ilundáin, *Proyeccion misionera*, 397; *Anuário pontifico per l'anno 1964*; and *Anuário pontifico per l'anno 1970*.

80. Rodriguez, "Sintesis y evaluacion," 488.

81. On the second assembly of the Burgos brothers in Mozambique, see Orradre, "Origen y evolucion historica," 388–89; Miguel Buendia, former Burgos missionary, interview, Maputo, April 1, 1997; and Father Mateus Carbonell Rodrigues, Burgos missionary, interview, Beira, September 15, 2001.

82. Albert Font, interview in *Notícias* (Maputo) (January 29, 1983); and Miguel Buendia, former Burgos missionary, interview, Maputo, May 26, 1997.

83. Miguel Buendia, former Burgos missionary, interview, Maputo, May 26, 1997.

84. "Assembleia Regional em Moçambique (PP. de BURGOS), 1970," 4, Box 32(9)/9, Archives of the Portuguese Province of the Company of Jesus (hereafter cited as APPCJ).

85. "Reunion del grupo IEME en Mozambique," 4, Box 32(9)/9, APPCJ. The document is reproduced in *Misiones Extranjeras* 6 (November–December 1971): 71–76.

86. The debate then shifted to whether they should work in the Frelimo liberated areas in Tete province or collaborate from their mission stations only. See Miguel Buendia, former Burgos missionary, interview, Maputo, April 1, 1997.

87. Letter of Jorge Jardim to Salazar, May 20, 1961, CP 144, Archive of Oliveria Salazar, IAN/TT; and Letter of Superior of the Picpus fathers(?) to the Bishop of Beira, November 10, 1961, Prov. 8.11, Archives of the Picpus Congregation, Breda, The Netherlands (hereafter cited as APICC).

88. "Notícias das nossas casas. Informações da Vice-Provincia de Portugal," n°8, October 1, 1969, p. 2, Prov. 3.04, Folder "Verslag–Vice Prov. Indonesia & Vice-Prov. Portugal," APICC.

89. Document n°8, Superior General of the Picpus Fathers, "Pro Memoria" [to the Vatican], February 20, 1970, Prov. 6.22, "Dossier Portugal na uitwijziing," APICC; see also Documents n°17, n°19, n°26, n°106, n°107, etc., in Prov. 6.22, "Dossier Portugal na uitwijziing," APICC.

90. António Sopa, personal communication, April 3, 1997.

91. Miguel Buendia, former Burgos missionary, interview, Maputo, April 1, 1997.

92. White Fathers, *Mozambique*, 237–38.

93. Father Montes Moreira, Franciscan priest and superior of the Portuguese province, interview, Lisbon, April 28, 2001.

94. Frei José Maria Moreira Pereira de Faria, Franciscan missionary, interview, Varatojo, May 1, 2001. See also Document n°3, "Rapport sur l'origine de certaines difficultés dans le diocèse de Beira et conséquences qui en ont résultés pour le personnel et pour notre propre groupe," 2, Doc. 6.26 "Dossier Mozambique 1971-I," APICC.

95. "Actas dos Capitulos da *Custódia*," 54: Acta 2° Capitulo, Lourenço Marques, January 23, 1973, Archives of the Franciscan Custódia in

Mozambique, Maputo, Mozambique (hereafter cited as AFCM). The previous year, the same *Custódia* noted: "The majority of missionaries ask that we do not create conflict with the authorities, so that we do not prejudice the work of the missions"; see "Conselho da *Custódia*: Actas, 1953 à 1972": Reunião do Conselho, Amatongas, June 22, 1972, AFCM.

96. Miguel Buendia, former Burgos missionary, interview, Maputo, April 1, 1997.

97. Bertulli, *A cruz e a espada*, 65n23.

98. Director PIDE-Moçambique ào Directo-Geral em Lisboa, oficio n°233/71/DI/1-SR, confidential, January 28, 1971, Processo 16.541-CI(2), "Ordem dos Padres Franciscanos ou ordem dos padres Franciscanos," PIDE/DGS Archives, IAN/TT.

99. Woodrow, *Jesuits*, 213–29.

100. Pereira, "Les jésuites," 110n95.

101. Pereira, "Jésuitas em Moçambique," 160–62, 167–70.

102. P. Joaquim Ferreira Leão, "Panorama actual de Moçambique, 19 June 1971," 1, Box 32(9)/9, APPCJ.

103. Pereira, "Jésuitas em Moçambique," 175. Interestingly, the superior of the Jesuits deemed the archbishop of Lourenço Marques a "Bishop of the Middle Ages." See Pereira, "Jésuitas em Moçambique," 175.

104. Pereira, "Jésuitas em Moçambique," 176.

105. A study of Father Albano should be done. He was given the mission of Metolola in Zambezia for his experiment in 1963–64. He placed his work under the motto "patria morena" (brown fatherland). See Júlio Meneses Rodrigues Ribeiro, multiple interviews, Maputo, April and May 1997; and Lobiano do Regò (pseudonym for Father Albano), *Pátria Morena* (with a letter and preface by Gilberto Freyre).

106. Pereira, "Jésuitas em Moçambique," sections 4.4 and 4.5.

Chapter 5

1. Middlemas, *Cabora Bassa*; Henriksen, *Revolution and Counterrevolution*.

2. For a general analysis, see Henriksen, *Revolution and Counterrevolution*. For specifics on Tete, see Coelho, *O início da luta armada*.

3. Cann, *Counterinsurgency in Africa*.

4. Cann, *Counterinsurgency in Africa*, 156.

5. Borges Coelho, *O início da luta armada*, chap. 1.

6. Meneses and McNamara, "Origins of Exercise ALCORA"; and Meneses and McNamara, *White Redoubt*. See also Meneses and Martins, *As guerras de libertação*.

7. Bertulli, *A cruz e a espada*, 287–97; and Dhada, *Portuguese Massacre*, chap. 6.

8. Dhada, *Portuguese Massacre*.

9. Antunes, *Jorge Jardim*.

10. By 1967, Radio Pax was broadcasting programs for seventeen hours a day, some in local languages, across the whole of central Mozambique. See Costa, "Radio Pax"; Lopes, *Missões franciscanas*, 560–62; and "Rádio Pax—posto emissor da Beira."

11. The incident Jardim referred to here was an article about cars being stolen and abandoned near the military barracks of Beira that was published without having been submitted to the state's censorship process. The newspaper was suspended for thirty days for this misdemeanor. See Rocha, *A imprensa de Moçambique*, 170–71. More generally, see Capela, "Para a história." For an earlier suspension and the legal process that developed from it, see Lima, *Aspectos da liberdade religiosa*; and Lima, *Caso do Bispo da Beira*.

12. Jorge Jardim, letter to Salazar, February 23, 1968, CP-144, 4.2.11/1, Instituto Nacional dos Arquivos Nacionais/Torre de Tombo (Institute of National Archives/Torre de Tombo), Lisbon (hereafter cited as IAN/TT).

13. Brandão, "Os padres de Macúti"; Sousa, *500 anos*, 125–27; interview of Teles Sampaio in Antunes, *A guerra*, 791–98.

14. Santos et al., *O julgamento dos padres*, 53–63.

15. Santos et al., *O julgamento dos padres*, 200–249.

16. "Memória: A bandeira do Macúti."

17. Jorge Jardim, letter to Prime Minister Caetano, February 22, 1973, cited in Antunes, *Cartas particulares*, 31.

18. Antunes, "Jorge Jardim," 57, 67–68.

19. The scope of Caetano's decentralization, through the constitutional reform of 1971–72, proved rather cosmetic: overseas provinces were given little more than legislative assemblies, governors-general, and a consultative junta. See Souto, *Caetano*, and Tajú, "O projecto do engenheiro," 15–27.

20. Miguel Murrupa was from Pebane district in Zambezia. He studied at Zobuè Seminary; in 1958, he worked at the *Diário de Notícias*. After becoming a member of Frelimo, he joined Radio Ghana in June 1962. He left Frelimo in 1970, crossed the border back into Mozambique, where he turned himself over to the Portuguese authorities. Júlio Meneses Rodrigues Ribeiro, Catholic layman, multiple interviews, Maputo, April and May 1997; and "Interview with Miguel Murrupa." in *Tempo* (Lourenço Marques) (December 13, 1970). Another person working for Jardim was Gilberto Waya, also a former Zobuè seminiarian. Jardim appointed him as vice-consul of Malawi in Nacala.

21. The newspaper originally belonged to the Centro Africano de Manica e Sofala, the organization that represented the mestiço elite of central Mozambique. The church bought it in 1962 and sold it to Jardim in 1970, together with the *Diário de Moçambique*. See Rocha, *A imprensa de Moçambique*, 190–93; and Capela, "Preface." See also the next section "Episcopal Death, Succession, and Crisis" in this chapter.

22. Cann, *Counterinsurgency in Africa*, chap. 5; Borges Coelho, "Da violência colonial ordenada"; and Couto, *Moçambique 1974*, 66–72.

23. Guerra, *Memória das guerras coloniais*, chap. 26; and Antunes, "Jorge Jardim," 321–26.

24. Tajú, *O projecto do engenheiro*, chap. 2; Couto, *Moçambique 1974*, chap. 4; Antunes, "Jorge Jardim," 476–86, chap. 17; and Jardim, *Moçambique*.

25. Father Guilherme da Costa Gonçalves, Franciscan priest, interview, Inhambane, August 23, 2017.

26. Pereira, "Jésuitas em Moçambique," 171–72.

27. Miguel Buendia, former Burgos missionary, interview, Maputo, April 1, 1997, and May 26, 1997.

28. This was the first time that female religious members entered into the private quarters of the episcopal seat. Before that, employees in the house had been only men. See Sister Henriquetta Teixeira, sister of the Franciscan Missionaries of Our Lady (Calais), interview, Chimoio, September 24, 2001.

29. Tajú, "Dom Sebastião Soares de Resende," 167.

30. PIDE, Subdeleg. da Beira, oficio secreto n°47/67-GAB, secret, February 28, 1967, NT 7254 "Francisco Nunes Teixeira," 3196-CI(2), PIDE/DGS Archives, IAN/TT.

31. The letter is reproduced in White Fathers, *Mozambique*, 201–2.

32. Pereira, "Jésuitas em Moçambique," 154–56; Sousa, *Memórias*, 184–85.

33. Father Francisco Augusto da Cruz Correia, interview, August 26, 1995; Sousa, *Memórias*, 185. See also Sousa, *Os jesuítas em Moçambique*, 181; White Fathers, *Mozambique*, 203–4; Pedro, "A missionação jesuíta," 126.

34. Pereira, "Les Jésuites," 112n99.

35. Trindade, *Memórias de um bispo*, 291; Ministério dos Negócios Estrangeiros, Direcção-Geral dos Negócios Políticos, Proc. 905, PAA 129, very urgent, confidential, 17 de Março de 1967, Processo 3895-CI(2), "Eurico Dias Nogueira," PIDE archive, IAN/TT; see also Sebastião Braz, personal communication, Ermesinde, February 26, 2001. On the papal visit to Goa, see Braga da Cruz, *O Estado Novo*, 165–75.

36. In September 1967, the Vatican nominated Ribeiro as auxiliary bishop of the Diocese of Braga, in place of Dom Manuel. Lisbon accepted the nomination: in 1969 he was made auxiliary bishop of Lisbon and in 1971 became the cardinal patriarch of Lisbon. See Almeida, *A Oposição Católica*, 236–39.

37. PIDE sub PIDE BR, oficio n°128/67-GAB, 18 de Agosto de 1967, secreto, Processo SC-CI(2) 8445, "Manuel Ferreira Cabral Júnior," PIDE/DGS Archives, IAN/TT.

38. PIDE, oficio n°504/68-GAB, April 3, 1968, secreto, Processo SC-CI(2) 8445, "Manuel Ferreira Cabral Júnior" (NP:7530), PIDE/DGS archives, IAN/TT.

39. A Franciscan missionary of Our Lady (Calais) recalled that she had no issues with Dom Manuel, but that he had difficulties entering in dialogue with his clergy. She contrasted this to Dom Sebastião's approachability, noting his episcopal seat was open to all and that he would receive everyone. See Sister Henriquetta Teixeira, sister of the Franciscan Missionaries of Our Lady (Calais), interview, Chimoio, September 24, 2001.

40. Letter reproduced in White Fathers, *Mozambique*, 217–19. A presbyterium is a group of priests within a diocese that advises the bishop.

41. White Fathers, *Mozambique*, 217–19.

42. In his memoirs, Father José Augusto Alves de Sousa argues that the bishop actually tried to defend his missionaries but did not succeed because he lacked prestige, connections, and flexibility. See Sousa, *Memórias de um jesuíta missionário*, 343–58.

43. White Fathers, *Mozambique*, 220–21.

44. Rocha, *A imprensa de Moçambique*, 214–15. For a history of the newspaper, see Capela, "Para a história." About Jorge Jardim, see Tajú, *O projecto do engenheiro*.

45. Document n°3, "Rapport sur l'origine de certaines difficultés dans le diocèse de Beira et conséquences qui en ont résultés pour le personnel et pour notre propre groupe," 3 pp., Doc. 6.26 "Dossier Mozambique 1971-I," Archives of the Picpus Congregation, Breda, The Netherlands (hereafter cited as APICC).

46. Document n°3, "Rapport sur l'origine de certaines difficultés dans le diocèse de Beira et conséquences qui en ont résultés pour le personnel et pour notre propre groupe," 3 pp., Doc. 6.26 "Dossier Mozambique 1971-I," APICC.

47. Document n°3, "Rapport sur l'origine de certaines difficultés dans le diocèse de Beira et conséquences qui en ont résultés pour le personnel et pour notre propre groupe," 3 pp., Doc. 6.26 "Dossier Mozambique 1971-I," p. 3, APICC.

48. Cited in Batalha, "Os Franciscanos," 178–79.

49. White Fathers, *Mozambique*, 286–88. The missionary was accused of having made anti-Portuguese comments. But this was the first time the man had drawn attention to himself and an expulsion did not seem very appropriate.

50. White Fathers, *Mozambique*, 286–88. For details on the meeting with the Mozambican Episcopal Conference, see Teixeira, *A igreja em Moçambique*, chap. 1.

51. White Fathers, *Mozambique*, 298.

52. White Fathers, *Mozambique*, 225.

53. Letter of Duarte Almeida to Pe. José Augusto de Sousa, Coimbra, August 4, 1971, Processo SC/CI(2) 6137, "Alberto Tavares," PIDE/DGS, IAN/TT.

54. PIDE Moçambique to PIDE Lisbon, report n°233/71/DI/1-SR, confidential, January 28, 1971, processo 16.541-CI(2), "Ordem dos Padres Franciscanos ou ordem dos padres Franciscanos," PIDE/DGS, IAN/TT.

55. Azevedo et al., *Franciscanos em Moçambique*, 416–17.

56. Gabinete dos Negócios Políticos, Ministry of Ultramar, Extraído do Oficio n°6224 of October 15, 1971, SCCIM Box 123, PIDE/DGS Archives, IAN/TT; Ministerio do Ultramar, Gabinete dos Negócios Políticos 6059/D-1-13/242, 8.10.1971, secret [transcription of a communication from the embassy at the Holy See], SCCIM Box 157, PIDE/DGS Archives, IAN/TT. See also the version of Cesar Bertulli, superior of the White Fathers, in Bertulli, *A cruz e a espada*, 264–67, 280.

57. Borges, *D. Manuel Vieira Pinto*, and Luzia, *Manuel Vieira Pinto*.

58. Pinto, "Dez meses de presença apostólica."

59. DGS-Moçambique, *Informação* n°69/71/DI/SC/G.G., July 19, 1971, Processo SC/CI(2) 6137, "Alberto Tavares," PIDE/DGS, IAN/TT.

60. DGS-Moçambique, *Informação* n°71/71/DI/2/SC G.G, July 23, 1971, "Padres de Burgos," P. Inf. 14.42 A/7, PIDE/DGS, PIDE/DGS Archives, IAN/TT.

61. Pinto, "Dez meses de presença apostólica"; *Informação* n°2431/71/DI/2/SC, September 1, 1971, secret, DGS-Moçambique, PIDE/DGS, IAN/TT; also see Sousa's memoir, *Memórias de um jesuíta missionário*, 371–72.

62. Bertulli, *A cruz e a espada*, chaps. 7–8.

63. Conselho dos Presbíteros da Beira, *Mensagem do Conselho*, 5.

64. DGS-Moçambique, *Informação* n° 2719/71/DI/2/SC, September 25, 1971, secret, "Missionários no Ultramar," vol. 1, Processo SC-CI(2) 1734, PIDE/DGS Archives, IAN/TT; DGS-Moçambique, *Informação* n°2773/73/DI/2/SC, June 25, 1973, confidential, "Missionários no Ultramar," vol. 1, Processo SC-CI(2) 1734, PIDE/DGS Archives, IAN/TT.

65. Tellingly, PIDE adopted the Francsican line of explanation, declaring that "the message of the council of the presbyterium of Beira of AGO71, signed by 5 Franciscan members of this same council, was a subtle maneuver by D. Manuel Vieira Pinto; [it was] communicated to the nuncio's office in Lisbon by the representative of the regional superior, Father Afonso Simões Frade." See DGS-Moçambique, *Informação* n°86/73/DI/2/SC-G.G. (ào Governador-Geral), secreto, Processo 17.869-CI(2), "Ordem dos Padres de Burgos ou Padres de Burgos ou Congregação S. Francisco Xavier de Burgos," PIDE/DGS Archives, IAN/TT.

66. DGS-Moçambique, *Informação* n°3591/71/2/SC, December 6, 1971, secreto, "Missionários no Ultramar," vol. 1, Processo SC-CI(2) 1734, PIDE/DGS Archives, IAN/TT.

67. D. Manuel Vieira Pinto, *Ponto de estudos para o conselho plenário*, n.d., 1p, Processo 16.541-CI(2), "Ordem dos Padres Franciscanos ou ordem dos padres Franciscanos," PIDE Archives, IAN/TT.

68. PIDE-Moçambique, *Informação* n° 739/72/DI/2/SC, March 9, 1972, confidential, "Missionários no Ultramar," vol. 1, Processo SC-CI(2) 1734, PIDE/DGS Archives, IAN/TT. If PIDE understood this particular situation well (probably because the Franciscans explained it to them), it usually did not understand the Church with much subtlety. For a good analysis of PIDE, see Mateus, *A PIDE/DGS*.

69. Bertulli, *A cruz e a espada*, 265.

70. "Os principais acontecimentos."

71. *Diário de Notícias* (Lisbon), February 25, 1972.

72. The name of the seminary changed from Namaacha to Pio X when Archbishop Custódio Alvim Pereira moved it to Lourenço Marques in 1964; see chapter 4 in this volume.

73. Antonius Petrus Joseph Martens, Picpus missionary, interview, Beira, September 26, 2001.

74. Corpo de Policia de Segurança da Provincia de Moçambique, Serviço de informação, Relatório imediato n°39/73, confidential, Box 127, SCCIM, PIDE/DGS archives, IAN/TT.

75. Antonius Petrus Joseph Martens, Picpus missionary, interview, Beira, September 26, 2001. Bishop Altino died in Martens's arms.

76. *Informação* n°2598/73/DI/2/SC, June 15, 1973, secreto, P° 23.26.01/ SR-1, DGS-Moçambique, PIDE/DGS, IAN/TT; *Informação* n° 759/72/DI/2/ SC, March 10, 1972, secreto, P° SR/1, PIDE/DGS-Moçambique, IAN/TT.

77. Father João de Brito, letter to the Vice-Provincial, April 2, 1973, document n°18, Prov. 6.23, APICC.

78. Cited in Aguirre, *Padawa*, 197.

79. Dhada, *Portuguese Massacre*, 81.

80. DGS-Moçambique, *Informação* n°86/73/DI/2/SC-G.G., "Panorâmica actual da igreja católica, apostólica romana, no estado de Moçambique e suas implicações com a segurança," n.d., secreto, Processo 17.869-CI(2), "Ordem dos Padres de Burgos ou Padres de Burgos," PIDE/DGS archive, IAN/TT. The quote reads: "O Prelado D. Felix Niza Ribeiro, quando Bispo de Tete, era considerado 'todo nosso' por manter boas relações com as autoridades civis."

81. "Os principais acontecimentos." Luís Gonzaga was the rector of Zobuè after the White Fathers left Mozambique. In late 1972 he was nominated bishop of Vila Cabral, where he stayed until after independence. PIDE described him as "the bishop in Mozambique who best identifies with our actual political system. He collaborates ostensibly with our services, because he believes 'in the good disposition of men and in the good results of organizations as long as they work well.'" See DGS-Moçambique, *Informação* n°86/73/ DI/2/SC-G.G., "Panorâmica actual da igreja católica, apostólica romana, no estado de Moçambique e suas implicações com a segurança," n.d., secreto, Processo 17.869-CI(2), "Ordem dos Padres de Burgos ou Padres de Burgos ou Congregação S. Francisco Xavier de Burgos," PIDE/DGS Archives, IAN/TT.

82. Pereira, "Jésuitas em Moçambique," 186–87.

83. White Fathers, *Mozambique*, 358–61.

84. See, for example, Braga da Cruz, *O Estado Novo*, chap. 5; Cerqueira, "L'église catholique portugaise"; and Guerra, *Memória das guerras coloniais*, chap. 31.

85. See, for example, Reis, *Salazar e o Vaticano*; Couto, *Moçambique 1974*, 271–77; Souto, *Caetano*, chap. 9; and Mbembe, "Rome et les églises africaines," chap. 4.

86. The meeting was of course with representatives from the Movimento Popular de Libertação de Angola (MPLA), the Frente de Libertação de Moçambique (Frelimo), and the Partido Africano da Independência da Guiné e Cabo Verde (PAIGC).

87. Reis, *Salazar e o Vaticano*, 327.

88. Souto, *Caetano*, 412.

89. Letter from [Superior?] to Bishop of Beira, July 17, 1951, Box 323/14, Archives of the Portuguese Province of the Company of Jesus (hereafter cited as APPCJ).

90. Reese, *Inside the Vatican*, chap. 5.

91. Sousa, "A conferência nacional," 683–87; Brito, "A federação nacional," 677–827.

92. DGS-Moçambique, *Informação* n°57/73/DI/SC.G.G, April 27, 1973, secret, "Reunião da FIRM," SC/CI(2) 1164/73, "Federação dos Institutos Religiosos Masculinos de Moçambique (F.I.R.M.)," PIDE/DGS Archives, IAN/ TT. For the statutes, see Federação dos Institutos Religiosos Masculinos de Moçambique, *Estatutos*, n.d., 2 pp., Box 81, Archives of the Franciscan Custódia in Mozambique, Maputo, Mozambique (hereafter cited as AFCM). For the female union in Mozambique, see Conferência dos Institutos Religiosos de Moçambique, "Acta da reunião realizada em Quelimane, de 26 a 29 de Novembro de 1974," 7, Box 81, AFCM.

93. Systermans and Gendrot, "Unione dei Superiori Generali"; Nardin and Rocca, "Unione internazionale."

94. Thomas Reese noted the existence, for example, of an American network in the Vatican. See Reese, *Inside the Vatican*, 158.

95. Direcção Geral de Segurança, Delegação em Moçambique, *Informação* n° 3812/71/DI/2/SC, December 30, 1971, confidential, "Missionários no Ultramar," Assunto: "Reunião de sacerdotes presidida pelo prelado diocesano, Nampula," vol. 1, Processo SC-CI(2) 1734, PIDE/DGS Archives, IAN/TT. For the letter, see Bertulli, *A cruz e a espada*, 330.

96. I have not found any information or documentation on the UISG's role in relation to Beira or Mozambique. Therefore, I do not deal with the female unions and their action or inaction.

97. Father Sousa, at the time vicar-general, says that Cardinal Jean-Marie Villot, the secretary of state, was opposed to the exit of the White Fathers. On the other hand, Sousa says that Cardinal Maurice Roy, from the Pontifical Council for Justice and Peace (another Vatican dicastery), was in favor and would have written to the pope to support them. Father José Augusto Alves de Sousa, Jesuit missionary, interview, Beira, September 9, 2001.

98. Nolan, *Departure of the Missionaries*, 117.

99. For the reaction of all religious actors, including the Vatican, see Nolan, *Departure of the Missionaries*, chap. 6.

100. White Fathers, *Mozambique*, 284–85; Nolan, *Departure of the Missionaries*, 111.

101. White Fathers, *Mozambique*, 302–3.

102. White Fathers, *Mozambique*, 293–94.

103. White Fathers, *Mozambique*, 333. See also Bertulli, *A cruz e a espada*, 339–46, although this author tends to underplay divisions and defends the White Fathers' official position.

104. Nolan, *Departure of the Missionaries*, 113–14.

105. White Fathers, *Mozambique*, 333. See also Bertulli, *A cruz e a espada*, 339–46.

106. Document 18, Unione Superiori Generali, "Seconda riunione dei superiorir generali e (o) loro assistente che hanno missionari nel Mozambico, con. S. E. R. Mons. Agostino Casaroli," confidenziale, November 22, 1973, p. 1, Box 6.25, "Reakties van missionaissen of religieuzen na de publikatie over Inhaminha von 10 mai 1974," 2–3, APICC. See also *Ephemerides Notitiarum* (Rome) 3 (September 12, 1973): 2.

107. Document 18, Unione Superiori Generali, "Seconda riunione dei superiorir generali e (o) loro assistente che hanno missionari nel Mozambico, con. S. E. R. Mons. Agostino Casaroli," confidenziale, November 22, 1973, p. 1, Box 6.25, "Reakties van missionaissen of religieuzen na de publikatie over Inhaminha von 10 mai 1974," APICC.

108. Document 18, Unione Superiori Generali, "Seconda riunione dei superiorir generali e (o) loro assistente che hanno missionari nel Mozambico, con. S. E. R. Mons. Agostino Casaroli," confidenziale, November 22, 1973, p. 1, Box 6.25, "Reakties van missionaissen of religieuzen na de publikatie over Inhaminha von 10 mai 1974," 2, APICC.

109. Document 18, Unione Superiori Generali, "Seconda riunione dei superiorir generali e (o) loro assistente che hanno missionari nel Mozambico, con. S. E. R. Mons. Agostino Casaroli," confidenziale, November 22, 1973, p. 1, Box 6.25, "Reakties van missionaissen of religieuzen na de publikatie over Inhaminha von 10 mai 1974," 3, APICC.

110. Ribeiro, *Inhaminga*.

111. Document n°139, Assembleia Regional, Nazaré, August 20–24, 1973, Box Prov. 6.26, "Correspontie II," APICC; Document n°155, Superior General, letter to all missionaries in Mozambique, March 28, 1974, Box Prov. 6.26, "Correspontie III," APICC; and Superior General, letter to the Vatican's Secretariat of State, March 28, 1974, Box Prov. 1.01, APICC.

112. Document n°155, Superior General, letter to all missionaries in Mozambique, March 28, 1974, Prov. 6.26 "Correspondentie III," APICC; and Superior General, letter to Cardinal Jean Villot, Secretary of State, March 28, 1974, Prov. 1.01, APICC.

113. White Fathers, *Mozambique*, 288.

Chapter 6

1. Pinheiro, *Na entrega do testemunho*.

2. The document is reproduced in Borges, *D. Manuel Vieira Pinto*, 53–59.

3. Duarte, "Entre évangélisation et lutte politique."

4. Severino Paeno, [Letter] "Aos superiores Gerais directamente interessado no problema de Moçambique como preparação para a reunião de 19 de Abril a 16 horas na Cúria generalítica dos Combonianos," [1974—document in the author's possession].

5. "Fico" in Portuguese means "I stay." The word was used as an acronym as an afterthought. Some argued it stood for "Frente Independente de Convergência Occidental (Independent Front for Western Convergence) while others maintained that it stood for "ficar convivendo" (to remain living together).

6. Couto, *Moçambique 1974*, chaps. 7–10; and Cardoso, *O fim do império*.

7. On Beira during the transition, see Darch and Hedges, "Political Rhetoric"; and Couto, *Moçambique 1974*, 445–54. About the "return" of white settlers to Portugal, see Castelo, "Colonial Migration."

8. Mabuiange, "União dos Sacerdotes Negros." For the visit to Dar es Salaam, see *Notícias* (Lourenço Marques), August 8, 1974; and Dom Januário Machaze Nhamgumbe, bishop of Pemba, interview, Maputo, June 1, 1994. A report of the visit can be found in USAREMO, *1a Reunião dos Sacerdotes*, 17–22.

9. Bishop Alberto Setele, bishop of Inhambane interview, Inhambane, February 24, 1996; Marcelino dos Santos, Frelimo leader, interview, Maputo, April 24, 1997. Marcelino dos Santos was the key player in this matter and traveled to Rome during this very period (*Notícias da Beira*, December 27, 1974). But he insists that Frelimo and he did not negotiate with the Vatican over the Concordat. In fact, he claims there were no negotiations.

10. "Visite au Mozambique du 3 au 10 juillet 1974," 4, Prov. 2.05, "Correspondentie Generaat J. Scheeper/Provinciaal G. Sporketl," 1973–75, no. 37, Archives of the Picpus Congregation, Breda, The Netherlands (hereafter cited as APICC).

11. "Assembleia Diocesana da Beira presidida por D. Francisco Nunes Teixeira," document 80, Folder "Documenten mit . . . III," Doc. 6.24, APICC. An issue playing in favor of Father Sousa was the fear that the Vatican would not nominate a new bishop should a wholly new and permanent vicar-general be nominated.

12. Comuniqué reproduced in *Palavra e Sinal* (Beira), no. 11, November 1974, pp. 2–3, Document 116, Folder "Documenten mit . . . III," Doc. 6.24, APICC.

13. Dom Francisco, letter, November 5, 1974, Doc. 114, Folder "Documenten mit . . . III," Doc. 6.24, APICC.

14. Costa, *Chamados à missão*, 85.

15. Dom Ernesto Gonçalves Costa, diary, cited in Costa, *Chamados à missão*, 84.

16. "Reunião de diversos Grupos Missionários, de Moçambique, em Madrid, 12–14 de Junho de 1974," Doc. 1, Folder "Kontakt mit missionarissen," Prov. 6.27, APICC. The same organizations met again in Lisbon on October 9, 1974; see *Notícias da Beira*, October 10, 1974.

17. "9 de Dezembro 1974: Reunião do clero da zona da BEIRA," December 21, 1974, 9 pp., no. 91, Folder "Documenten uit III," Prov. 6.27, APICC.

18. *Notícias* (Lourenço Marques), August 11, 1974; Lukas Bizeque Quembo de Raposo, Catholic layman, interview, Dondo, October 4, 2001; and Lukas A. Zingue, former cathechist, interview, Murraça, July 18, 2009.

19. *Notícias* (Lourenço Marques), August 27, 1974; "Comunicado No. 2 do PCN," *Notícias da Beira*, August 27, 1974; and Gwenjere's interview from his hospital bed in Furtado, *A guerra*.

20. Father Gwenjere lived in Kenya until 1976 when he was kidnapped and brought back to Mozambique by force. He was apparently killed by the state in secret, probably in 1977. See Cabrita, *Mozambique*, 83–84; and Ncomo, *Uria Simango*, 316, 342–43.

21. Morier-Genoud, "Of God and Caesar," 24.

22. Morier-Genoud, "Alberto Cangela de Mendonça."

23. Letter from P. João de Brito to P. José Martens, October 4, 1974, Divers, Doc. 6.27, APICC.

24. "Constituição da Republica Popular."

25. Sousa and Congil, *Arquidiocese da Beira*, 139, and chap. 14 for an exhaustive list of the nationalized properties.

26. *Notícias* (Lourenço Marques), August 14, 1975; also reproduced in Spanish in *Misiones Extranjeras* (Madrid), nos. 34–35, 1976, p. 507. For a description of how the letter was drafted, see Aguirre, *Padawa*, 243–45.

27. CEM, "Viver a fé."

28. "Encontro de D. Alexandre com o Senhor President, 25/10/1976," document in the author's possession.

29. CEM, "Comunicado da Conferência Episcopal."

30. For more biographical details, see Bié, "Foi A FRELIMO," 18–19; and Dom Jaime Gonçalves, archbishop of Beira, interview, Beira, August 15, 2001, September 13, 2001, and July 7, 2009.

31. Sousa and Congil, *Arquidiocese da Beira*. For 1974, see Pinheiro, *Na entrega do testemunho*, 177–216.

32. Diocese da Beira, "Pessoal Missionário da Diocese da Beira," October 15, 1983, Folder "Correspondentie bettrefende het . . . ," Prov. 6.28, APICC.

33. Diocese da Beira, *Relatório Quinquenal*, 9.

34. Sousa and Congil, *Arquidiocese da Beira*, 48–49.

35. Sousa and Congil, *Arquidiocese da Beira*, 50–51.

36. Bishop Alberto Setele, bishop of Inhambane, interview, Inhambane, February 26, 1996.

37. Pinto, "Como ser Cristão." More generally, see Luzia, *A igreja das Palhotas*.

38. Linden, *Catholic Church*, 270; and email communication with Father Vicente Berenguer, Burgos missionary, April 26, 2018. Father Berenguer confirms contact but is unsure whether there was more. He says that if it happened, this was not official policy but a priest's own initiative.

39. Miguel Buendia, former Burgos missionary, interview, April 1, 1997, and May 26, 1997; and Marques, "Anexo A. Dados biográficos." See also the dossier in *Misiones Extranjeras* (Madrid), no. 34–35, 1976. This is also described in euphemistic terms in the official history of the institute; see Ilundáin, *Proyeccion misionera*, 404–5.

40. *Intercambio* (Breda, the Netherlands), no. 21 (July 1979): 5.

41. Morier-Genoud, "Of God and Caesar," 49–50.

42. Diocese da Beira, *Relatório quinquenal*, 13–14; SAAR-Manica, "Relatório 23/5/79," National Directorate of Religious Affairs, Ministry of Justice, Maputo, Mozambique (hereafter cited as DNAR); and Sousa and Congil, *Arquidiocese da Beira*, 142–46.

43. Diocese da Beira, *Relatório Quinquenal 1982*, Beira, July 1982, p. 4.

44. Father Filipe José Couto, interview, Beira, August 14, 2017.

45. "Encontro dos Bispos com os Superiores Maiores dos Institutos Masculinos e Femininos de Moçambique, Beira 30 de Outubro-3 de Novembro

de 1978," 2–3, Box 81, Archives of the Franciscan Custódia in Mozambique, Maputo, Mozambique (herafter cited as AFCM).

46. "Encontro dos Bispos com os Superiores Maiores dos Institutos Masculinos e Femininos de Moçambique, Beira 30 de Outubro-3 de Novembro de 1978," 2–3, Box 81, AFCM.

47. "Encontro dos Bispos com os Superiores Maiores dos Institutos Masculinos e Femininos de Moçambique, Beira 30 de Outubro-3 de Novembro de 1978," 2–3, Box 81, AFCM.

48. Hall and Young, *Confronting Leviathan*, 115–16; and Adam, *Escapar aos dentes*, 152.

49. Stiff, *Silent War*, and Sousa, *Memórias de um jesuíta missionário*, 693. For the Spanish priest, see Ilundáin, *Gozo y lágrimas*, 300; Aguirre, *Padawa*, 246–47; and Chung, *Re-living the Second Chimurenga*, 142–43. For a biography of the priest who was killed, see Garcia, "Señor, en tu nombre echaré las redes."

50. Morier-Genoud, Cahen, and Rosário, *War Within*, esp. chap. 4.

51. FRELIMO, "*Consolidemos aquilo que nos une*," 64.

52. Borges Coelho, "Da violência colonial," 191; and Tajú, "RENAMO," 16.

53. The latest research on RENAMO seems to confirm this. See Cahen, "The War as Seen by Renamo."

54. "Venha o inimigo donde vier."

55. Borges, *D. Manuel Vieira Pinto*.

56. Morier-Genoud, "Y-a-t-il une spécificité," 414–16.

57. Askin, "Mission to RENAMO."

58. Vines, *RENAMO*, 104.

59. Calculations made on the basis of Ferreira, *Le colonialisme portugais*, 78–79.

60. See, for example, Zengazenga, *Memórias de um rebelde*; and Moises, *Daring to Survive*.

61. FRELIMO, "*Consolidemos aquilo que nos une*," 62.

62. The Nkomati Accord was a nonaggression pact between South Africa and Mozambique, signed on March 16, 1984. Frelimo agreed to stop supporting the ANC in exchange for which the South African state agreed to stop supporting RENAMO.

63. Pacheco, "A paz na rota"; and Neves, *São Franciscao de Assis*, 8–9. For a biography of Father Manuel Carreira das Neves, see Azevedo et al., *Franciscanos em Moçambique*, 441–42.

64. Gonçalves, *A paz dos Moçambicanos*.

Epilogue

1. Sousa, *A igreja e a paz*, 33–34; and Sousa, *Memórias de um jesuíta missionário*, 723–24.

2. Morozzo Della Rocca, *Mozambique de la guerre*, and, more critically, Anouilh, "From 'Charity' to 'Mediation'"; and Anouilh, "Des pauvres à la paix."

3. Bouron, "Itinéraires ecclésiaux."

4. See, for example, Cooper, *Colonialism in Question*, 3–32.

5. Ferreira, *Igreja ministerial*; and Luzia, "A igreja das Palhotas."

Bibliography

Interviews

Baptista, Laurinda, Franciscan sister of Calais. Chimoio, September 20, 2001.

Barca, Nicolau da, Catholic believer. Chimoio, September 20, 2001.

Bels, André de, former White Father missionary. Baltimore, June 18–19, 1999.

Buendia, Miguel, former Burgos missionary. Maputo, April 1 and May 26, 1997.

Cardos, António Dina, former catechist. Beira, September 30 and October 6, 2001.

Couto, Father Filipe José, Consolata priest. Beira, September 10, 2001 and Maputo, August 14, 2017.

Correia, Father Francisco Augusto da Cruz, Jesuit missionary. Maputo, August 26, 1995.

Cuvaca, Paulo, former seminarian in Zobuè. Beira, September 8, 2015. Interview in the presence of and with contributions by Ossumane Domingos and J. Mafequiz, also former seminarians.

Faria, José Maria Moreira Pereira de, Franciscan missionary. Varatojo (Portugal), May 1, 2001.

Favor, Manuel João, former liberation fighter and Frelimo dissenter. Caia (Mozambique), July 17, 2009.

Gonçalves, Guilherme da Costa, Franciscan priest. Inhambane (Mozambique), August 23, 2017.

Gonçalves, Jaime, Archbishop of Beira. Beira, August 15, 2001, September 13, 2001, and July 7, 2009.

Gwenjere, Benjamin António, nephew of Mateus Gwenjere. Inharugué (Mozambique), July 17, 2009.

Laweki, Lawe, former seminarian of Zobuè. Maputo, April 6, 2012, and July 5, 2012.

Majambe, Benjamin Tomocene, former liberation fighter and Frelimo dissenter. Beira, May 29, 2015.

Manhoca, Benjamin Taramba, former Catholic teacher. Manica (Mozambique), September 21, 2001.

Martens, Father Antonius Petrus Joseph, Picpus missionary. Beira, September 26, 2001.

Massinga, José Chicuara, former seminarian in Namaacha. Maputo, November 10 and 17, 1994.

Matsinhe, Alfredo Arnaldo, Catholic believer. Beira, September 12, 2001.

Molina Molina, Antonio, White Father missionary. Madrid, April 8 and 10–11, 2013.

Moreira, Bishop António Montes, Franciscan priest and superior of the Portuguese province. Lisbon, April 28, 2001.

Mozinho, Gustavo Lukas and Maria, Catholic believers. Dondo (Mozambique), October 4 and 5, 2001.

Mucauro, Father Samuel Abudo, Catholic secular priest. Beira, September 11 and 30, 2001.

Muchangos, Agostinhio Cufa dos, former Catholic teacher and catechist. Manica (Mozambique), September 21, 2001.

Nhangumbe, Januário Machaze, former bishop of Pemba. Maputo, June 1, 1994.

Nhongo, João Sozinho, former Catholic catechist. Beira, September 28, 2001.

Pereira, Custódio Alvim, former Archbishop of Lourenço Marques. Rome, June 26, 2001.

Perez, Fernando Pietro, White Father missionary. Beira, September 6 and 7, 2001.

Pollet, Charles Maurice, White Father missionary. Voreppes (France), June 18–19, 2001.

Raposo, Lukas Bizeque Quembo de, former Catholic teacher and catechist. Dondo (Mozambique), October 4, 2001.

Reis, Vitorino Mendes dos, Catholic believer. Chimoio (Mozambique), September 18, 2001.

Ribeiro, Júlio Meneses Rodrigues, Catholic layman. Maputo, multiple interviews, April and May 1997.

Rodrigues, Fernanda Jesus, Franciscan sister of Calais. Chimoio (Mozambique), September 20, 2001.

Rodrigues, Margarida Lopes, Catholic believer. Beira, October 3, 2001.

Rodrigues, Mateus Carbonelli, Burgos missionary. Beira, September 15, 2001.

Rosa, Maria Joana Araujo, Catholic believer. Manga, Beira, October 3, 2001.

Rossum, Rogier van, Picpus priest and professor of theology. Valkenburg (The Netherlands), September 13 and 14, 1999.

Santos, Marcelino dos Santos, key Frelimo leader, Maputo, April 24, 1997.

Serapião, Benjamin, former seminarian in Zobuè and Namaacha. Chicago, November 1, 1998.

Setele, Alberto, bishop of Inhambane. Inhambane (Mozambique), February 26, 1996.

Soro, Alberto Jequessene, Catholic believer. Chimoio (Mozambique), September 19, 2001.

Sousa, Father José Augusto Alves de, Jesuit missionary. Maputo, November 24 and December 1, 1994; and Beira, October 9, 2001.

Teixeira, Henriquetta, sister of the Franciscan Missionaries of Our Lady (Calais). Chimoio (Mozambique), September 24, 2001.

Verhoeven, José, Picpus missionary. Breda (The Netherlands), September 15, 1999.

Zingue, Lukas Alfandegas, former Catholic catechist. Murraça (Mozambique), July 13 and 18, 2009.
Zon, André van, Blessed Sacrament missionary. Maputo, April 19 and 27, 1996.

Newspapers

Diário de Moçambique (Beira)
Diário de Notícias (Lisbon)
Notícias (Lourenço-Marques/Maputo)
Notícias da Beira (Beira)
Savana (Maputo)

Periodicals and Magazines

Acção dos Franciscanos em Moçambique (Inhambane, Mozambique)
Boletim Mensal das Missões Franciscanas & Ordem Terceiras (Braga, Portugal)
Ephemerides Notitiarum (Union Superior General, Rome)
Grands Lacs (by the White Fathers in Namur, Belgium)
Igreja e Missão (Cucujães, Portugal)
Intercambio (Picpus in Breda, the Netherlands)
Miraduro: Revista dos Alunos do Seminário Maior de S. Pio X (Lourenço Marques, Mozambique)
Misiones Extranjeras (Spanish Institute of Missions, Burgos, Spain)
Missões Franciscanas (Franciscans in Braga, Portugal)
Petits Echos (by the White Fathers, Rome)
Tempo (Lourenço Marques/Maputo)
Vivant Univers (formerly *Grands Lacs*) (by the White Fathers in Namur, Belgium)

Primary Sources

Archives Générales des Missionnaires de l'Afrique (General Archives of the Missionaries of Africa) (White Fathers), Rome (AGMAfr)

Casiers verticaux, Casier 224 ("Carnet de Conseil de Murraça (1946–64)")
Casiers verticaux, Casier 224 ("Diaire de Gorongosa (1946–60/1961–71)")
Fonds Birraux, dossier 242 ("Lettres du Procureur, Fonds Procure Rome")
Fonds Birraux, dossier 275 ("Provinces Espagne, Portugal, USA, Ethiopi")
Fonds Birraux, dossier 306 ("Urundi, Mozambique")
Fonds Durrieu, dossier 361 ("Relations St. Père, dicastères, cardinal protecteur")
Fonds Durrieu, dossier 373 ("Maison Mère et annexes (Espagne, Portugal)")

Fonds Durrieu, dossier 446 ("Missions in genere")
Fonds Durrieu, dossier 548 ("Mozambique")
Phototèque

Archives of the Franciscan Custódia in Mozambique, Maputo (AFCM)

All boxes and books (archive not classified)

Archives of the Picpus Congregation, Breda, the Netherlands (APICC)

Box Prov. 1.01, Folder "Divers"
Box Prov. 2.04, Folder "Correspondentie met het Generaal Bertur"
Box Prov. 2.05, Folder "Correspondentie met de Generaal en de General Raad, okt. 1970–dec. 1972"; and Folder "Correspondentie Generaal J. Scheepen/Provincial G. Sprokel, 1973–75"
Box Prov. 2.22, Folder "Provinciale Commissie ler bestudering grandslagen Kloosterleven . . . , 1963–1964"; and Folder "Voobereiding Kapitel '64"
Box Prov. 3.04, Folder "Kerslag Vice-Prov. Portugal et Indonesia"
Box Prov. 6.21, Folder "Divers"; Folder "Correspondentie P. Provincial met Broeken, nov 59–dec 61"; and Folder "Correspondentie P. Provincial met Broeken, jan 62–nov 64"
Box Prov. 6.22, Folder "Correspondentie met Modesto Broeken"; Folder "Correspondentie Confraters vice-provincie met J. W. Westerhoven"; Folder "Portugal na uitwijzing"; and Folder "Divers"
Box Prov. 6.23, Folder "Corr. Sprokel mit confraters"; Folder "Corr. G. Spokel/M. Verwey"; Folder "Corr. G. Spokel/H. Scheepens (vice-prov.)"; and Folder "Divers"
Box Prov. 6.24, Folder "Doc uit I"; Folder "Doc uit II"; Folder "Doc uit III"; and Folder "Documenten uit maatschappelijk leven Portugal, Angola, Moz. III"
Box Prov. 6.25, Folder "Publiciteit van 10 mai 1974"; Folder "Reackties van mimssionaissen of religieuzen na publikatie over Inhaminha ban 10 mai 1974"; Folder "Publiciteit van 10 mai 1974"; Folder "Pater Provincia"; Folder "Dokumente betreffende Moz"; Folder "Corr. Spokel met Confraters"; and Folder "Lettres diverses";
Box Prov. 6.26, Folder "Divers"; Folder "Dossier Moz 1971-I"; Folder "Dossier Moz 1971-II"; Folder "Dossier Moz 1971-I"; Folder "Correspondentie I"; Folder "Correspondentie II"; Folder "Correspondentie III"; and Folder "Keker in Mozambique"
Box Prov. 6.27, Folder "Documenten uit het maatsdappelijk leven Angola en Mozambique"; older "Kontakt van missionarissen, die uit Mozambique vertrokken em andere missionaire instituten"; Folder "Oecumenische Kontaketn m. b. t. Mozambique"; and Folder "Divers"

Box Prov. 6.28, Folder "Divers"; Folder "Financien en financiele transacties in Nederlands"; and Folder "Addressen en Verzending," Box Prov. 6.29 [no title]
Box Prov. 8.11 [no title]

Archives of the Portuguese Province of the Company of Jesus (APPCJ)

Box 32, folder 9 ("Situation in Mozambique")
Box 323, folder 14 ("Correspondence with Bishops")
Box 327, folder 7 (7) ("Meeting with missionaries")
Box 328, folder 5

Arquivo da Diocese de Beira (Archive of the Diocese of Beira), Beira (ADB)

All boxes (archive not classified)

Arquivo Histórico de Moçambique (Historical Archive of Mozambique), Maputo (AHM)

Fundo da Inspecção dos Serviços Administrativos e dos Negócios Indigenas
Fundo do Governo da Beira
Fundo do Governo Geral
Fundo do Júlio Meneses Rodrigues Ribeiro
Fundo Fotográfico

Direcção Nacional dos Assuntos Religiosos, Ministry of Justice, Maputo (DNAR)

Various files (Archive not organized)

Instituto Nacional dos Arquivos Nacionais/Torre de Tombo (Institute of National Archives/Torre de Tombo), Lisbon (IAN/TT)

Fundo da Policia Internacional da Defesa do Estado (PIDE/DGS)
Fundo dos Arquivos da Companhia de Moçambique (ACM)
Fundo dos Arquivos de António Salazar (AOS)
Fundo dos Arquivos de Marcello Caetano (AMC)
Fundo dos Serviços de Centralização da Informação de Moçambique (SCCIM)

Ministério dos Negócios Estrangeiros (Archive of the Ministry of Foreign Affairs), Lisbon (MNE)

Secção Especial, 2 Piso, A48, M195

Overseas Historical Archives, Lisbon (AHU)

Fundo dos Ministério do Ultramar

Private Archive of the Bishop of Beira, Library of the Center of African Studies, Oporto, Portugal (PABB)

Diary, 1943–67 (22 volumes)
Letters, 1943–58

Secondary Sources

Abrams, Philip. *Historical Sociology*. Ithaca, NY: Cornell University Press, 1982.
Adam, Yussuf. "A Frente de Manica e Sofala." Unpublished paper, n.d.
———. *Escapar aos dentes do crocodilo e cair na boca do leopardo: Trajectória de Moçambique pós-colonial (1975–1990)*. Maputo: Promédia, 2005.
———. "Mueda, 1917–1990: Resistência, colonialismo, libertação e desenvolvi-mento." *Arquivo: Boletim do Arquivo Histórico de Moçambique* 14 (1993): 4–102.
Aguirre, José Javier Rotellar. *Padawa: História del Grupo del IEME en Mozambique, para andar por casa*. Tete-Beira-Maputo, 1996.
Alberto, Manuel Simões. *Os Angónis: Elementos para uma monografia*. Lourenço Marques: Instituto de Investigação Científica de Moçambique, 1967/1968.
Alexandre, Valentim. "A África no imaginário político portugês (séculos XIX–XX)." In *Velho Brasil, novas Áfricas: Portugal e o império (1808–1975)*, 219–29. Oporto: Edições Afrontamento, 2000.
———. "O império português (1825–1890): Ideologia e economia." *Analise Social* 38, no. 169 (2004): 959–79.
———. *Velho Brasil, novas Africas: Portugal e o império (1808–1975)*. Oporto: Edições Afrontamento, 2000.
Allina, Eric. *Slavery by Any Other Name: African Life under Company Rule in Colonial Mozambique*. Charlottesville: University of Virginia Press, 2012.
Almeida, João Miguel. *A Oposição Católica ao Estado Novo, 1958–1974*. Lisbon: Nelson de Matos, 2008.
Alves, José da Felicidade, ed. *Católicos e política: De Humberto Delgado à Marcelo Caetano*. Lisbon: Typografia Leandro, n.d.

Anouilh, Pierre. "Des pauvres à la paix: Aspects de l'action pacificatrice de Sant'Egidio au Mozambique." *Le Fait Missionaire: Social Sciences and Missions* 17, no. 1 (2005): 11–40.

———. "From 'Charity' to 'Mediation,' from the Roman Suburbs to UNESCO: The Rise of the 'Peace Brokers' of the Community to Sant'Egidio." In *Mediation in Political Conflicts: Soft Power or Counter Culture?* edited by Jacques Faget, 89–114. Oxford: Hart, 2011.

Antunes, Diamantino Guapo. "Concílio Vaticano II o contributo do episcopado de África e Madagáscar: Para a teologia da igreja local/particular e a sua recepção em alguns Sínodos dos Bispos." PhD diss., Pontificia Universitas Gregoriana, 2001.

Antunes, José Freire, ed. *Cartas particulares à Marcello Caetano.* Lisbon: Publicações Dom Quixote, 1985.

———. *Jorge Jardim: Agente secreto.* Venda Nova, Portugal: Bertrand, 1996.

Anuário estatistico da provincia de Moçambique. Lourenco Marques: Imprensa Nacional de Moçambique, 1943–69.

Anuário pontifico per l'anno 1963. Vatican City: Tipografia Poliflotta Vaticana, 1964.

Anuário pontifico per l'anno 1964. Vatican City: Tipografia Poliflotta Vaticana, 1964.

Anuário pontifico per l'anno 1970. Vatican City: Tipografia Poliflotta Vaticana, 1970.

Askin, Steve. "Mission to RENAMO: The Militarisation of the Religious Right." *Journal of Theology for Southern Africa* 69 (1989): 106–16. (Republished in *Journal of Opinion* 43, no. 2 [1990]: 29–38.)

Azevedo, Carlos A. Moreira. "Perfil biográfico de D. Sebastião Soares de Resende." *Lusitania Sacra* 2, no. 6 (1994): 391–415.

Azevedo, Carlos Moreira, ed. *Dicionário de história religiosa de Portugal,* 4 vols. Lisbon: Círculo de Leitores, 2000–2002.

Azevedo, David de, Manuel Marques Novo, José António Coreia Pereira, and Américo Montes Moreira. *Franciscanos em Moçambique: 100 anos de missão.* Braga: Editorial Franciscana, 1998.

Baëta, C. G., ed. *Christianity in Tropical Africa: Studies Presented and Discussed at the Seventh International African Seminar, University of Ghana, April 1965.* London: Oxford University Press, 1968.

Baritussio, Arnaldo. *Mozambico: 50 anni di presenza dei missionari comboniani.* Bologna: Editrice Missionaria Italiana, 1997.

Barreto, António, and Maria Filomena Mónica, eds. *Dicionário de história de Portugal,* vols. 7–9. Oporto: Figueirinhas, 1992.

Barreto, José. *Religião e sociedade: Dois ensaios.* Lisbon: Imprensa de Ciências Sociais, 2002.

Barroso, Dom António. *Padroado de Portugal em África: Relatório da prelazia de Moçambique.* Lisbon: Imprensa Nacional, 1895.

Batalha, M. L. L. "Os Franciscanos em Moçambique: 1940–1974: Acção social, cívica e religiosa." PhD diss., Universidade Portucalense, 2007.

Bayart, Jean-François. "Comparing from Below." *Sociétés politiques comparées* 1 (2008): 1–25.

———. "Fait missionnaire et politique du ventre: Une lecture foucaldienne." *Le Fait Missionnaire* 6 (1998): 9–38.

———. *The State in Africa: The Politics of the Belly.* London: Longman, 1993.

Bender, Gerald J. *Angola under the Portuguese: The Myth and the Reality.* Berkeley: University of California Press, 1978.

Benedict XV. *Maximum Illud: On the Propagation of the Faith throughout the World.* Apostolic Letter. November 30, 1919. http://www.svdcuria.org/public/mission/docs/encycl/mi-en.htm.

Bertulli, Cesar. *A cruz e a espada em Moçambique.* Lisbon: Portugália Editora, 1974.

Bié, Rafael. "Foi a FRELIMO quem agrediu o povo e depois foi agredida: Dom Jaime Gonçalves, arcebipo da Beira." *Savana* (Maputo), October 28, 2005: 18–19.

Bielo, James S. "Urban Christianities: Place-Making in Late Modernity." *Religion* 43, no. 3 (2013): 301–11.

Birmingham, David. *A Concise History of Portugal.* Cambridge: Cambridge University Press, 1993.

Blommaert, Edmund. *Mozambique: A Hopeful Return? A Suffering Nation . . . People with a Mission.* Breda: Missiecentrum Pater Damiaan, [1993].

Boff, Leonardo. *Saint Francis: A Model for Human Liberation.* New York: Crossroad, 1982.

Borges, Anselmo, ed. *D. Manuel Vieira Pinto, arcebispo de Nampula: Cristianismo, política e mística.* Oporto: Edições ASA, 1992.

Borges Coelho, João Paulo. "Da violência colonial ordenada à ordem pós-colonial violenta. Sobre um legado das guerras coloniais nas ex-colónias portuguesas." *Lusotopie* 10 (2003): 175–93.

———. "Entrevista com Celestino de Sousa: A actividade da Frelimo em Tete, 1964–1967." *Arquivo. Boletim do arquivo histórico de Moçambique* 10 (1991): 130–69.

———. *O início da luta armada em Tete, 1968–1969: A primeira fase da guerra e a reacção colonial.* Maputo: Arquivo Histórico de Moçambique, Núcleo Editorial da Universidade Eduardo Mondlane, 1989.

Borges Grainha, Manuel. *História da franco-maçonaria em Portugal (1733–1912).* Lisbon: Vega, 1976.

Bouniol, Joseph. *The White Fathers and their Missions.* London: Sands, 1929.

Bouron, Jean-Marie. "Itinéraires ecclésiaux en situation postcoloniale: L'indépendance des états africains a-t-elle contribué à l'implantation des églises catholiques locales?" In *Autonomie et autochtonie des églises: Logiques de localisation et d'universalisation en diverses situations missionnaires et post-missionnaires,* edited by Salvador Eyezo'o and Jean-François Zorn, 157–69. Paris: Karthala, 2015.

Bowen, H. G. "Diocese (Eparchy)." In *New Catholic Encyclopedia,* 4: 871. New York: McGraw-Hill, 1967.

Boxer, Charles. *The Church Militant and Iberian Expansion, 1440–1770*. Baltimore: Johns Hopkins University Press, 1978.

———. *The Portuguese Seaborn Empire, 1415–1825*. Harmondsworth: Penguin, 1969.

Braga da Cruz, Manuel. "O Estado Novo e a Igreja Católica." In *Portugal e o Estado Novo (1930–1969)*, edited by Fernando Rosas, 201–21. Lisbon: Editorial Presença, 1992.

———. *O Estado Novo e a Igreja Católica*. Lisbon: Editorial Bizâncio, 1999.

Branco, Frei Bento. *Missão cumprida: Impressões vividas e sentidas nos caminhos da vida—II*. Olaia, Torres Novas, Portugal: 1989.

Brandão, Pedro Ramos. *A Igreja Católica e o "Estado Novo" em Moçambique, 1960–1974*. Lisbon: Editorial Notícias, 2004.

———. "Os padres de Macúti." *História* (Lisbon) 67 (2004): 44–49.

Bretell, Caroline. "Archives and Informants: Reflection on Juxtaposing the Method of Anthropology and History." *Historical Method* 25, no. 1 (1992): 28–36.

Brito, Luis de. "Une re-lecture nécessaire: La genèse du parti-État FRELIMO." *Politique Africaine* 29 (1988): 15–27.

Brito, Maria Manuela de. "A federação nacional dos institutos religiosos femininos." In *I Congresso nacional de religiosos: Trabalhos apresentados ao congresso, Lisboa 8 a 13 de abril de 1958*, 677–82. [1958].

Bruneau, Thomas C. "Church and Politics in Brazil: The Genesis of Change." *Journal of Latin American Studies* 17, no. 2 (1985): 271–93.

Buendia Gomez, Miguel. *Educação moçambicana: História de um processo, 1962–1984*. Maputo: Livraria Universitária, 1999.

Byrnes, Timothy A. *Transnational Catholicism in Postcommunist Europe*. Lanham, MD: Rowman and Littlefield, 2001.

Cabaço, José Luís. *Moçambique: Identidades, colonialismo e libertação*. Maputo: Marimbique, 2010.

Cabrita, João M. *Mozambique: The Tortuous Road to Democracy*. New York: St. Martin's Press, 2000.

Cahen, Michel. "Anticolonialisme identitaire: Conscience ethnique et mobilisation anti-portugaise au Mozambique (1930–1965)." In *Frontières plurielles, frontières conflictuelles et Afrique subsaharienne: Actes du colloque "Etats et frontières en Afrique subsaharienne,"* edited by Colette Dubois, Marc Michel, and Pierre Soumille, 319–33. Paris: L'Harmattan, 2000.

———. "Corporatisme et colonialisme: Approche du cas mozambicain (1933–1979): II. Crise et survivance du corporatisme colonial, 1960–1979." *Cahiers d'Études Africaines* 24, no. 93 (1984): 5–24.

———. "The War as Seen by Renamo: Guerrilla politics and the 'move to the North' at the time of the Nkomati Accord (1983–1985)" In *The War Within: New Perspectives on the Civil War in Mozambique, 1976–1992*, edited by Eric Morier-Genoud, Michel Cahen, and Domingos do Rosario, 100–46. Oxford: James Currey, 2018.

————. *Les Bandits: Un historien au Mozambique, 1994.* Paris: Centre Culturel Calouste Gulbenkian, 2002.

————. "Les mutineries de la Machanga et de Mambone (1953): Conflits sociaux, activisme associatif et tensions religieuses dans la partie orientale de la 'zone vandau.'" Paper presented at the International Meeting of Social Sciences Specialists on Portuguese-speaking Africa, Bissau, April 1991.

————. "L'état nouveau et la diversification religieuse au Mozambique, 1930–1974. I. Le résistible essor de la portugalisation catholique (1930–1961)." *Cahiers d'Études Africaines* 158 (2000): 309–50.

————. "The Mueda Case and Maconde Political Ethnicity: Some Notes on a Work in Progress." *Africana Studia* 2 (1999): 29–46.

————. "Nationalism and Ethnicities: Lessons from Mozambique." In *Ethnicity Kills? The Politics of War, Peace and Ethnicity in Sub-Saharan Africa*, 163–87. Basingstoke, UK: Macmillan 2000.

Cann, John P. *Counterinsurgency in Africa: The Portuguese Way of War, 1961–1974.* Wesport, CT: Greenwood Press, 1997.

Canu, J. *Religious Orders of Men.* New York: Hawthorn Books, 1960.

Capela, José. *O imposto de palhota e a introdução do modo de produção capitalista nas colonias.* Oporto: Afrontamento, 1977.

————. "Para a história do 'Diário de Moçambique.'" *Arquivo: Boletim do Arquivo Histórico de Moçambique* 6 (1989): 177–80.

————. "Preface." In *Moçambique pelo seu povo: Selecção prefácio e notas a cartas de Voz Africana*, edited by José Capela, 7–11. Porto: Afrontamento, 1974.

Cardoso, Ribeiro. *O fim do império: Memória de um soldado português; o 7 de Setembro de 1974 em Lourenço Marques.* Lisbon: Alfragide, Caminho, 2014.

Carvalho, Rita. "Salazar e a concordata com a Santa Sé." *História* 19, no. 31 (1997): 4–15.

Castelo, Claudia. "Colonial Migration to Angola and Mozambique: Constraints and Illusions." In Morier-Genoud and Cahen, *Imperial Migrations*, 105–26.

————. *"O modo português de estar no mundo": O luso-tropicalismo e a ideologia colonial portuguesa (1933–1961).* Oporto: Afrontamento, 1998.

Cava, Ralph della. "Financing the Faith: The Case of Roman Catholicism." *Journal of Church and State* 35, no. 1 (1993): 37–59.

Cem anos de presença das irmãs de S. José de Cluny em Moçambique, 1890–1990. Maputo, [1990].

CEM (Conférencia Episcopal de Mogambique). *Cartas pastorais: Documentos CEM.* Oporto: Humbertipo, 1985.

————. "'Comunicado da Conferência Episcopal de Moçambique às Comunidades Cristãs' (8 May 1977)." In *Comunicações e notas pastorais*, edited by CEM. Oporto: Humbertipo, 1984.

————. *Comunicações e notas pastorais.* Oporto: Humbertipo, 1984.

————. "Viver a fé no Moçambique de hoje." In *Cartas pastorais: Documentos CEM*, edited by CEM, 3–42. Oporto: Humbertipo, 1985.

Cerqueira, Silas. "L'église catholique portugaise." In *Les églises chrétiennes et la décolonisation*, edited by Macel Merle, 464–501. Paris: Armand Colin, 1967.

Cerqueira Gonçalves, Joaquim. "Sabedoria e arte de ser Franciscano." In *Actas do I–II Seminário: O Franciscanismo em Portugal*, 79–84. Lisbon: Fundação Oriente, 1996.

Chabal, Patrick, with David Birmingham, Joshua Forrest, Malyn Newitt, Gerhard Seibert, and Elisa Silva Andrade. *A History of Postcolonial Lusophone Africa*. London: Hurst, 2002.

Charles, Pierre. *Prayer for All Men* [La prière de toutes les heures]. Translated by Maud Monahan. London: Sands, 1925 [first French edition 1923; first Portuguese edition 1934].

Cheza, Maurice. "Le franciscan Placide Tempels, un pasteur." In Jacquin and Zorn, *L'altérité religieuse*, 179–89.

Chichava, Sérgio Inácio. "Unlike the other Whites? The Swiss in Mozambique under Colonialism." In Morier-Genoud and Cahen, *Imperial Migrations*, 147–65.

Chirenje, J. Mutero. "Portuguese Priests and Soldiers in Zimbabwe, 1560–1572: The Interplay between Evangelism and Trade." *International Journal of African Historical Studies* 6, no. 1 (1973): 36–48.

Christie, Iain. *Samora: Uma biografia*. Maputo: Ndjira, 1996.

Chung, Fay. *Re-Living the Second Chimurenga: Memories from Zimbabwe's Liberation Struggle*. Stockholm: Nordic Africa Institute, 2006.

Cidade da Beira: Projecto de urbanização; Memória justificativa. Beira: Empresa moderna, 1951.

Cita-Malard, Suzanne. *Religious Orders of Women*. New York: Hawthorn, 1964.

Clarence-Smith, William Gervase. *The Third Portuguese Empire, 1825–1975: A Study in Economic Imperialism*. Manchester: Manchester University Press, 1985.

Comaroff, Jean, and John L. Comaroff. "Christianity and Colonialism in South Africa." *American Ethnologist* 13, no. 1 (1986): 1–22.

———. *Of Revelation and Revolution*. 2 vols. Chicago: University of Chicago Press, 1991, 1997.

Conselho dos Presbíteros da Beira. *Mensagem do Conselho de Presbíteros da Beira*. Beira: Centro Tipográfico da Beira, 1971.

"Constituição de República Popular de Moçambique." In *Datas e documentos da história da FRELIMO: De 1960 a 1975, ano da independência de Moçambique*, 2nd ed., edited by Armando Pedro Muiuane, 531–47. Maputo: Edição da Impresa Nacional, 1975.

Cooper, Fred. *Colonialism in Question: Theory, Knowledge, History*. Berkeley: University of California Press, 2005

———. "Possibility and Constraint: African Independence in Historical Perspective." *Journal of African History* 49, no. 2 (2008): 167–96.

Correia, P. M. Alves. *Missões franciscanas portuguesas de Moçambique e da Guiné*. Braga: Tipografia das Missões Franciscanas, 1934.

Costa, Ernesto Gonçalves. *Chamados à missão e desenvolvimento integral do homem.* Braga: Editorial Franciscana, 1996.

———. *De Inhambane para Beira.* Beira: Centro Tipográfico da Beira, 1975.

———. "Radio Pax—emissora católica de Moçambique: Obra dos missionários franciscanos." In *Franciscanos em Moçambique: Cem anos de missão, 1898–1998,* edited by Carlos Azevedo, Manuel Marques Novo, José A. Correia Pereira, and Américo Montes Moreira, 103–12. Braga: Editorial Franciscana, 1991.

Couto, Fernando Amado. *Moçambique 1974: O fim do império e o nascimento da nação.* Maputo: Ndjira, 2011.

Cox, Harvey. *The Secular City: Secularization and Urbanization in Theological Perspective.* London: Macmillan, 1965.

Creary, Nicholas M. *Domesticating a Religious Import: The Jesuits and the Inculturation of the Catholic Church in Zimbabwe, 1879–1980.* New York: Fordham University Press, 2011.

Creuzen, Joseph. *Religious Men and Women in Church Law.* 6th ed. Milwaukee: Bruce, 1958.

Cruz, Lopes da. *Anuário católico de Portugal 1941.* Lisbon: Tip. da Revista Renascença, 1940.

Cruz Correia, Francisco Augusto da. "Moçambique (1498–1975)." In Azevedo, *Dicionário de história religiosa,* 4:242–46.

———. *O método missionário dos Jesuítas em Moçambique de 1881 a 1910: Um contributo para a história da missão da Zambézia.* Braga: Livraria Apostolado da Imprensa, 1991.

Cruz e Silva, Teresa. "Igrejas protestantes no sul de Moçambique e nacionalismo: O caso da Missão Suíça (1940–1974)." *Estudos Moçambicanos* 12 (1992): 19–39.

———. *Protestant Churches and the Formation of Political Consciousness in Southern Mozambique (1930–1974).* Basel: P. Schlettwein, 2001.

Cruz Pontes, José Maria da. "Tomismo." In Azevedo, *Dicionário de história religiosa,* 5:294–97.

Cunha, Amadeu. *Jornadas e outros trabalhos do missionário Barroso.* Lisbon: Agência Geral das Colonias, 1938.

Cyprien d'Alger. "Ordres mendiants." In *Dictionnaire de droit canonique: Contenant tous les termes du droit canonique, avec un sommaire de l'histoire et des institutions et de l'état actuel de la discipline,* edited by Raoul Naz, 1156–63. Paris: Librairie Letouzey et Ané, 1965.

Darch, Colin, and David Hedges. "Political Rhetoric in the Transition to Mozambican Independence: Samora Machel in Beira, June 1975." *Kronos* 39, no. 1 (2013): 32–65.

Denis, Philippe. *The Dominican Friars in Southern Africa: A Social History (1577–1990).* Leiden: Brill, 1998.

Derluguian, Georgi. "The Social Origins of Good and Bad Governance: Reinterpreting the 1968 Schism in Frelimo." In Morier-Genoud, *Sure Road?* 79–102.

Desfois, G. "La répartition des pouvoirs dans l'église." *Pouvoirs* 17 (1981): 5–24.

Dhada, Mustafah. *The Portuguese Massacre of Wiriyamu in Colonial Mozambique, 1964–2013.* New York: Bloomsbury, 2016.

Dinerman, Alice. *Revolution, Counter-Revolution and Revisionism in Postcolonial Africa: The Case of Mozambique, 1975–1994.* London: Routledge, 2006.

Diocese da Beira. *Relatório Quinquenal.* Beira, 1982.

Diocese da Beira e Quelimane. *Regulamento dos missionários.* Cucujães: Escola Tipográfica das Missões, 1956.

Direcção Provincial dos Serviços de Estatística Geral. *Anuário estatístico 1964.* Lourenço Marques: Direcção Provincial dos Serviços de Estatística Geral, [1964].

Divisão adminstrativa da província de Moçambique. Lourenço Marques: Imprensa Nacional de Mocambique, 1964.

Dores, Hugo Gonçalves. *A missão da República: Política, religião e o império colonial Português (1910–1926).* Lisbon: Edições 70, 2015.

Duarte, Sandra. "Entre évangélisation et lutte politique: Les missionnaires comboniens au Portugal et au Mozambique dans le panorama historique de l'état nouveau (1947–1974)." *Histoire, monde et cultures religieuses* 14 (2010): 83–101.

Duffy, James. *Portuguese Africa.* Cambridge, MA: Harvard University Press, 1959.

Dunkerley, James. *Power in the Isthmus: A Political History of Modern Central America.* New York: Verso, 1988.

Ellis, Adam. *Religious Men and Women in Church Law.* 6th ed. Milwaukee: Bruce, 1958.

Etheringon, Norman. "Missionaries and the Intellectual History of Africa: A Historical Survey." *Itinerario* 7, no. 2 (1983): 116–43.

———, ed. *Missions and Empire.* Oxford: Oxford University Press, 2005.

Ferreira, António Matos. "A acção católica: Questões em torno da organização e da autonomia da acção da Igreja Católica (1933–1958)." In *O Estado Novo: Das origens ao fim da autarcia, 1926–1959*, vol. 2, edited by António Barreto and Maria Filomena Mónica, 281–302. Lisbon: Editorial Fragmentos, 1987.

———. "Acordo missionário." In Barreto and Mónica, *Dicionário de história de Portugal,* 7:38–31.

Ferreira, Eduardo de Sousa. *Le colonialisme portugais en Afrique: La fin d'une ère.* Paris: Presse de l'UNESCO, 1974.

Ferreira, Luciano da Costa. *Carisma vicentino em Moçambique: Memória e testemunho.* Cucujães: Tipográfica das Missões, 2003.

———. *Igreja ministerial em Moçambique: Caminhos de hoje e de amanhã.* Lisbon: Tipografias Silvas, 1987.

Fontes, Paulo Oliveira. "A acção católica portuguesa (1933–1974) e a presença da igreja em Portugal." *Lusitania Sacra* 6 (1994): 61–100.

———. "A acção católica portuguesa e a problemática missionária (1940–1974)." In *Actas do Congresso Internacional de História: "Missionação e encontro de culturas,"* vol. 1, 411–51. Braga: Universidade Católica Portuguesa, 1993.

Foy, Felician, ed. *Our Sunday Visitor's Catholic Almanac 1998.* Huntington, IN: Our Sunday Visitor, 1998.

Francis, E. "Toward a Typology of Religious Orders." *American Journal of Sociology* 55, no. 5 (1950): 437–49.

Franco, José Eduardo. "A visão do outro na literatura antijesuítica em Portugal: De Pombal à primeira república." *Lusitania Sacra* 12, 2a série (2000): 121–42.

Franzen, A. *Kleine Kirchengeschichte.* Freiburg im Breisgau: Herder, 1988.

Freitas, João da Costa. "Movimentos subversivos contra Moçambique." In *Moçambique Curso de Extensão Universitária, Ano Lectivo de 1964–1965,* 317–37. Lisbon: Instituto Superior de Ciências Social e Políticas Ultramarina da Universidade Tecnica de Lisboa, 1964.

FRELIMO (Frente de Libertação de Moçambique). *"Consolidemos aquilo que nos une": Reunião da Direcção do Partido e do Estado com os representantes das confissões religiosas, 14 a 17 de Dezembro 1982.* Maputo: INLD, 1983.

Furtado, Joaquim. *A guerra | colonial | do ultramar | de libertação,* episode 42, DVD. Lisbon: Rádio e Televisão de Portugal, Edições/Público/Lenoir, 2012.

Gadille, Jacques. "L''idéologie'des missions catholqiues en Afrique francophones." In *Églises et histoire de l'Église en Afrique: Actes du colloque de Bologne, 22–25 octobre 1988,* edited by Giuseppe Ruggieri, 43–61. Paris: Beauschesne.

———. "Les stratégies missionnaires des églises." In Mayeur et al., *Histoire du Christianisme,* 239–58.

Garcia, Álvaro Carbonell. "'Señor, en tu nombre echaré las redes . . .' (Lc.5.5.)." [Madrid], 2006.

Goddijn, H. P. M. "The Sociology of Religious Orders and Congregations." *Social Compass* 5–6 (1960): 431–47.

Goffman, Erving. *Asylums: Essays on the Social Situation of Mental Patients and Other Inmates.* New York: Anchor Books, 1961.

Gonçalves, Jaime Pedro. *A paz dos Moçambicanos.* Beira/Maputo: CIEDIMA, 2014

Goyau, Georges. *Une fondatrice d'Institut missionnaire: Mère Marie de la Passion et les Franciscaines missionnaires de Marie.* Paris: Editions Spes, 1935.

Gray, Richard. "Christianity, Colonialism, and Communications in Sub-Saharan Africa." *Journal of Black Studies* 13, no. 1 (1982): 59–72.

———. "Problems of Historical Perspective: The Planting of Christianity in Africa in the Nineteenth and Twentieth Centuries." In Baëta, *Christianity in Tropical Africa,* 18–33.

Guerra, João Paulo. *Memória das guerras coloniais.* Oporto: Edições Afrontamento, 1994.

Hall, Margareth, and Tom Young. *Confronting Leviathan: Mozambique since Independence.* London: Hurst, 1997.

Hanson, E. *The Catholic Church in World Politics*. Princeton, NJ: Princeton University Press, 1987.

Hastings, Adrian. "Vocation for the Priesthood in Eastern Africa." In *African Initiatives in Religion: 21 Studies from Eastern and Central Africa*, edited by David B. Barrett, 188–97. Nairobi: East African Publishing House, 1971.

———. *Wiriyamu*. London: Search Press, 1974.

Heimbucher, M. *Die Orden und Kongregationen der katholishen Kirche*. Munich: Verlag Schöningh, 1965.

Helgesson, Alf. "Church, State and People in Mozambique: A Historical Study with Special Emphasis on Methodist Developments in the Inhambane Region." PhD diss., Swedish Institute of Missionary Research, 1994.

Henriksen, Thomas H. *Revolution and Counterrevolution: Mozambique's War of Independence, 1964–1974*. Westport, CT: Greenwood Press, 1983.

Hill, M. *The Religious Order: A Study of Virtuoso Religion and its Legitimation in the Nineteenth-Century Church of England*. London: Heinemann, 1973.

Hostie, R. *Vie et mort des ordres religieux: Approches psychosociologiques*. Paris: Desclée de Bouwer, 1972.

Huyghe, Gérard. *Religious Orders in the Modern World: A Symposium*. Westminster: Newman Press, 1966.

Idowu, E. Bolaji. "The Predicament of the Church in Africa." In Baëta, *Christianity in Tropical Africa*, 417–37.

Ilundáin, José Antonio Izco. *Gozo y lágrimas (1954–1976): Los 22 primeros años de misión de 36 sacerdotes jóvenes y 6 laicos en Tete-Beira (Mozambique)*. Madrid: Editorial Mundo Negro, 2011.

———. *Proyección misionera del clero diocesano español: historia del Seminario de misiones-IEME*. Salamanca: Ediciones Sígueme, 1991.

Isaacman, Allen. *Cotton Is the Mother of Poverty: Peasant, Work and Rural Struggle in Colonial Mozambique, 1938–1961*. Portsmouth, NH: Heinemann, 1996.

———. *Mozambique: The Africanization of a European Institution, the Zambezi Prazos, 1750–1902*. Madison: University of Wisconsin Press, 1972.

Isaacman, Allen, and Barbara Isaacman. *The Tradition of Resistance in Mozambique: Anti-colonial Activity in the Zambezi Valley, 1850–1921*. London: Heinemann, 1976.

Isaacman, Allen, and Derek Peterson. "Making the Chikunda: Military Slavery and Ethnicity in Southern Africa, 1750–1900." *International Journal of African Historical Studies* 36, no. 2 (2003): 257–81.

Isaacman, Allen, and Richard Roberts, eds. *Cotton, Colonialism, and Social History in Sub-Saharan Africa*. Portsmouth, NH: Heinemann, 1995.

Isaacman, Allen F., and Barbara S. Isaacman. *Slavery and Beyond: The Making of Men and Chikunda Ethnic Identities in the Unstable World of South-Central Africa, 1750–1920*. Portsmouth, NH: Heinemann, 2004.

Jacquin, Françoise, and Jean-François Zorn, eds. *L'altérité religieuse: Un défi pour la mission chrétienne, XVIIIè–XXè siècles*. Paris: Karthala, 2001.

Jardim, Jorge. *Moçambique: Terra Queimada*. Lisbon: Editorial Intervenção, 1976.

Jerónimo, Miguel Bandeira, ed. *O império colonial em questão (sécs. XIX–XX): Poderes, saberes e instituições.* Lisbon: Edições 70, 2013.

———. *A diplomacia do império: Política e religião na partilha de África (1820–1890).* Lisbon: Edições 70, 2012.

Keese, Alexander. "Bloqueios no sistema: elites africanas, o fenómeno do trabalho forcado e os limites de integração no estado colonial português, 1945–1974." In Jerónimo, *O império colonial,* 223–49.

———. *Living with Ambiguity: Integrating an African Elite in French and Portuguese Africa, 1930–61.* Stuttgart: Franz Steiner Verlag, 2007.

Kuhn, Thomas S. *The Structure of Scientific Revolutions.* 2nd ed. Chicago: University of Chicago Press, 1970.

Lacouture, Jean. *Les Jésuites: Une multibiographie,* vol. 2. Paris: Éditions du Seuil, 1992.

Landau, Paul. *The Realm of the Word: Language, Gender and Christianiy in a Southern African Kingdom.* London: James Currey, 1995.

Lavado, Maria Ludovina de Seixas. *Franciscanas missionárias de Maria: 100 anos em Moçambique, 1897–1997.* Maputo: Provincia Portuguesa do Instituto das Franciscanas Missionárias de Maria em Moçambique, 1997.

Laweki, Lawe. "A crise de 1968 no 'Instituto Moçambicano' na Tanzania." *Canal de Moçambique* (Maputo), October 6, 2011.

———. "Sérgio Vieira mente sobre o Instituto Moçambicano e sobre o Padre Mateus Pinho Gwenjere." *Canal de Moçambique* (Maputo), April 28, 2010.

Le Goff, Jacques. *Saint François d'Assise.* Paris: Éditions Gallimard, 1999.

Legrand, M. *Colonisation portugaise et discours religieux.* Louvain: Centre de Recherches Socio-religieuses, 1974.

Leite, António. "Enquadramento legal da actividade missiónaria portuguesa." *Bróteria* 133, no. 1 (1991): 36–52.

Leite, Joana Pereira. "Colonial, política." In Barreto and Mónica, *Dicionário de história de Portugal,* 7:355–57.

———. "La formation de l'économie coloniale au Mozambique." PhD diss., École des Hautes Études en Sciences Sociales, 1989.

Léonard, Yves. *Salazarisme et fascisme.* Paris: Éditions Chandeigne, 2003.

———. "Salazarisme et Franc-Maçonnerie." Unpublished paper, n.d.

Lesegretain, Claire. *Les grands ordres religieux: Hier et aujourd'hui.* Paris: Fayard, 1990.

Liesegang, Gerhard. "A obra autogiográfica do Missionário Jesuíta M. Thoman (1788) e o problema das Missões Católicas no Século XVIII em Moçambique." In *Actas do seminário "Moçambique: Navegações, comércio e técnicas,"* edited by Faculdade de Letras da Universidade Eduardo Mondlane de Maputo and Comissão Nacional para as Comemorações dos Descobrimentos Portugueses, 37–66. Lisbon: Comissão Nacional para as Comemorações dos Descobrimentos Portugueses, 1998.

———. "Sofala, Beira e a sua zona (c. 900–1894)." *Arquivo: Boletim do Arquivos Histórico de Moçambique* 6 (1989): 21–64.

Liesegang, Gerhard, and Joel Tembe das Neves. "Subsídios para a história da UDENAMO e FRELIMO: Da fundação e dos planos de fusão da UDENAMO e MANU à revolta da base da UDENAMO em Junho de 1962 e o resurgimento deste partido em 1963: Um plano e primeiros resultados da recolha de fontes para permitir uma leitura sociológica." Unpublished paper, 2005. https://www.academia.edu/9800597/Da_Udenamo_a_Frelimo.

Lima, A. Carlos. *Aspectos da liberdade religiosa: Caso do bispo da Beira.* Lisbon: Diário do Minho, 1970.

————. *Caso do Bispo da Beira: Documentos.* Oporto: Civilização, 1990.

Linden, Ian. *The Catholic Church and the Struggle for Zimbabwe.* London: Longman, 1980.

————. *Catholics, Peasants, and Chewa Resistance in Nyasaland 1889–1939.* Berkeley: University of California Press, 1974.

————. "Chewa Initiation Rites and Nyau Societies: The Use of Religious Institutions in Local Politics at Mua." In Ranger and Weller, *Themes in the Christian History of Central Africa*, 30–45.

————. *Global Catholicism: Diversity and Change since Vatican II.* London: Hurst, 2009.

Lloyd, Christopher. *The Structures of History.* Oxford: Blackwell 1993.

Lopes, Félix. *Missões franciscanas em Moçambique, 1898–1970.* Braga: Editorial Franciscana, 1972.

Löwy, Michael. *The War of Gods: Religion and Politics in Latin America.* New York: Verso, 1996.

Lucena, Manuel de. "Adriano Moreira." In Barreto and Mónica, *Dicionário de história de Portugal*, 8:531–44.

Luzia, José. "A igreja das Palhotas: Génese da igreja em Moçambique, entre o colonialismo e a independência." *Cadernos de Estudos Africanos* 2, no. 4 (1989).

————. *A igreja das Palhotas: O renascer da igreja católica em Moçambique; Os ministérios dos Animadores Leigos; Sementes de futuro.* Rev. and exp. ed. Prior Velho, PT: Paulinas Editora, 2017.

————. *Manuel Vieira Pinto: O visionário de Nampula.* Prior Velho, PT: Paulinas Editora, 2016.

Mabuiange, Pe. "União dos Sacerdotes Negros de Moçambique." In USAREMO, *1a Reunião dos Sacerdotes e Religiosos Negros*, 1–2.

Mabunda, Abel. "A C. E. M. na luta armada de libertação de Moçambique." Unpublished paper, n.d.

MacGonagle, Elizabeth. *Crafting Identity in Zimbabwe and Mozambique.* Rochester: University of Rochester Press, 2007.

Machado Pires, António. "Messianismo." In Azevedo, *Dicionário de história religiosa*, 4:195–97.

MacNamara, J. *Sisters in Arms: Catholic Nuns through Two Millennia.* Cambridge, MA: Harvard University Press, 1996.

Majeke, Nosipho. *The Role of the Missionaries in Conquest.* Johannesburg: Society of Young Africa, 1952.

Malheiro da Silva, Armando. "Tradicionalismo." In Azevedo, *Dicionário de história religiosa*, 5:297–303.

Mandelbaum, Jonna-Lynn K. *The Missionary as a Cultural Interpreter*. New York: Peter Lang, 1989.

Marcum, John A. *Conceiving Mozambique*. London: Palgrave Macmillan, 2018.

Marime, Benedito. *Arquidiocese do Maputo: Sessenta anos de história (1940 a 2000)*. Maputo: Cegraf, 2002.

Marques, A. H. de Oliveira. *A maçonaria portuguesa e o Estado Novo*. 3rd ed. Lisbon: Dom Quixote, 1995.

———. *Breve história de Portugal*. Lisbon: Editorial Presença, 1995.

Marques, Álvaro B. "Anexo A. Dados biograficos [Interview with Miguel Buenida]." In *Quem Matou Samora Machel?* edited by Álvaro B. Marques, 209–34. Sacavem, PT: Ulmeiro, 1987.

Martin, Malachi. *The Jesuits: The Society of Jesus and the Betrayal of the Roman Catholic Church*. New York: Simon and Schuster, 1987.

Martin, Phyllis M. *Catholic Women of Congo-Brazzaville: Mothers and Sisters in Troubled Times*. Bloomington: Indiana University Press, 2009.

Martins, Helder. *Porquê Sakrani? Memórias dum médico duma guerrilha esquecida*. Maputo: Editorial Terceiro Milénio, 2001.

Mateus, Dalila Cabrita. *A PIDE /DGS na guerra colonial (1961–1974)*. Lisbon: Terramar, 2004.

Matos, Luís Salgado de. "Os bispos portugueses: Da concordata ao 25 de Abril—alguns aspectos." *Análise Social* 29, no. 125–26 (1994): 319–83.

Matos Ferreira, António. "A Accão Católica: Questões em torno da organização e da autonomia da acção da Igreja Católica (1933–1958)." In *O Estado Novo: Das origens ao fim da autarcia, 1926–1959*, vol. 2, edited by António Costa Pinto, 281–302. Lisbon: Editorial Fragmentos, 1987.

———. "La péninsule ibérique." In Mayeur et al., *Histoire du Christianisme*, 402–50.

Mayeur, Jean-Marie, Charles Pietri, Luce Pietri, André Vauchez, and Marc Venard, eds. *Histoire du Christianisme des origines à nos jours, Tome XII "Guerres mondiales et totalitarismes (1914–1958)."* Paris: Desclée-Fayart, 1990.

Mbembe, Achille. "Rome et les églises africaines." *Pro Mundi Vita Dossiers* 2–3 (1986): ch. 4.

McKensie, John. *The Roman Catholic Church*. New York: Holt, Rinehart and Winston, 1969.

McNamara, Joann Kay. *Sisters in Arms: Catholic Nuns through Two Millennia*. Cambridge, MA: Harvard University Press, 1996.

"Memória: A bandeira do Macúti" [interview with Fernando Marques Mendes and Joaquim Teles Sampaio]. *Visão* (Lisbon) (June 5, 2003): 106–8.

Meneses, Filipe Ribeiro de, and Robert McNamara. "The Origins of Exercise ALCORA, 1960–71." *International History Review* 35, no. 5 (2013): 1113–34.

Meneses, Filipe Ribeiro de, and Robert McNamara. *The White Redoubt, the Great Powers and the Struggle for Southern Africa, 1960–1980.* London: Palgrave, 2018.

Meneses, Maria Paula, and Bruno Sena Martins, eds. *As guerras de libertação e os sonhos coloniais: Alianças secretas, mapas imaginados.* Coimbra: CES/Almedina, 2013.

Middlemas, Keith. *Cabora Bassa: Engineering and Politics in Southern Africa.* London: Weidenfeld and Nicolson, 1975.

———. "Twentieth Century White Society in Mozambique." *Tarikh* 6, no. 2 (1979): 30–45.

Moises, Francisco. *Daring to Survive.* London: Austin Macaulay, 2015.

Molina, Antonio Molina. "Domination coloniale et évangélisation au Mozambique." BA Honors thesis, Institute Lumen Vitæ, 1972.

Mondlane, Eduardo. *The Struggle for Mozambique.* London: Penguin, 1969.

Montes Moreira, António. "A restauração da província franciscana de Portugal em 1891." *Itinerarium* 39, no. 146–47 (1994): 163–234.

———. "Bibliografia dos franciscanos em Moçambique no século XX." In *Actas do Congresso Internacional de História, Missionação Portuguesa e Encontro de Culturas,* vol. 2 ('Igreja, sociedade e missionação'), 29–38. Braga: Faculdade de Teologia, 1993.

———. "Franciscanos." In Azevedo, *Dicionário de história religiosa,* 2:273–80.

Morier-Genoud, Eric. "Alberto Cangela de Mendonça. Visão sobre a religião e o desenvolvimento do Estado." Paper presented at the conference for the celebration of the twentieth anniversary of the Mbuzini Disaster, Instituto Superior Politécnico e Universitário (ISPU), Maputo, September 10, 2006.

———. "Archives, historiographie et églises évangéliques au Mozambique." *Lusotopie* 7 (2000): 621–30.

———. "The Catholic Church, Religious Orders and the Making of Politics in Colonial Mozambique: The Case of the Diocese of Beira, 1940–1974." PhD diss., State University of New York at Binghamton, 2005.

———. "Of God and Caesar: The Relation between Christian Churches and the State in Post-colonial Mozambique, 1974–81." *Le Fait Missionnaire* 3 (1996), 80p.

———. "José Capela e a Igreja Católica." *Africana Studia* 27 (2016): 143–51.

———. "Review of Pedro Ramos Brandão, *A igreja católica e o 'Estado Novo' em Moçambique.*" *Lusotopie* 13, no. 2 (2006): 185–87.

———, ed. *Sure Road? Nationalisms in Angola, Guinea-Bissau and Mozambique.* Leiden: Brill, 2012.

———. "The Vatican vs. Lisbon: The Relaunching of the Catholic Church in Mozambique, ca. 1875–1940." Basler Afrika Bibliographien Working Papers no. 4, 2002.

————. "Y-a-t-il une spécificité protestante au Mozambique? Discours du pouvoir post-colonial et histoire des églises chrétiennes." *Lusotopie* 5 (1998): 407–20.

Morier-Genoud, Eric, and Pierre Anouilh. "The Catholic Church in Mozambique under Revolution, War, and Democracy." In *Religion and Politics in a Global Society: Comparative Perspectives from the Portuguese-Speaking World*, edited by Paul Christopher Manuel, Alynna Lyon, and Clyde Wilcox, 185–203. Lanham: Lexington, 2012.

Morier-Genoud, Eric, and Michel Cahen, eds. *Imperial Migrations: Colonial Communities and Diaspora in the Portuguese World*. Basingstoke: Palgrave Macmillan, 2012.

Morier-Genoud, Eric, Michel Cahen, and Domingos M. do Rosário, eds. *The War Within: New Perspectives on the Civil War in Mozambique, 1976–1992*. Oxford: James Currey, 2018.

Morozzo Della Rocca, Roberto. *Mozambique de la guerre à la paix: Histoire d'une médiation insolite*. Paris: L'Harmattan, 1997.

Moulin, Léo. "Aux sources des libertés européennes: Réflexions sur quinze siècles de gouvernement des religieux." *Les Cahiers de Bruges* 2 (1956): 97–140.

————, ed. *Churches as Political institutions/Les Églises comme institutions politiques*. 2 vols. Brussels: Institut Belge de Science Politique, 1970.

————. *Le monde vivant des religieux: Dominicains, Jésuites, Bénédictins . . .* Paris: Calmann-Lévy, 1964.

————. "Le pouvoir dans les ordres religieux." *Pouvoirs* 17 (1981): 129–34.

————. "Les origines religieuses des techniques électorales et délibératives modernes." *Revue internationale d'Histoire politique et constitutionnelle* (1953): 106–48.

————. "Pour une sociologie des ordres religieux." *Social Compass* 2 (1960): 145–70.

Mussanhane, Ana Bouene, ed. *Protagonistas da luta de libertação nacional*. Maputo: Marimbique, 2012.

Nardin, G., and G. Rocca. "Unione internazionale delle Superiore Generali (UISG)." In Rocca, *Dizionario degli Istituti di Perfezione*, 1556–57.

Naz, Raoul, ed. *Dictionnaire de Droit Canonique*. Paris: Librairie Letouzey et Ané, 1935–65.

Ncomo, Barnabé Lucas. *Uria Simango: Um homem, uma causa*. Maputo: Edições Novafrica, 2003.

Neill, Stephen. *A History of Christian Missions*. 2nd ed. London: Penguin Books, 1986.

Neil-Tomlinson, Barry. "The Mozambique Chartered Company, 1892 to 1910." PhD diss., University of London, 1987.

Neto, Vítor. *O Estado, a Igreja e a Sociedade em Portugal (1831–1911)*. Lisbon: Imprensa Nacional Casa da Moeda, 1998.

Neuhouser, Kevin. "The Radicalization of the Brazilian Catholic Church in Comparative Perspective." *American Sociological Review* 54, no. 2 (1989): 233–44.

Neves, Joel das. "The State, Missionary Education, Child Labour and Migration in Manica, 1930–1960." Paper presented at the African History Seminary, School of Oriental and African Studies, London, February 19, 1997.

Neves, Joel M. das. "Economy, Society and Labour in Central Mozambique, 1930–c. 1965: A Case Study of Manica Province." PhD diss., University of London, 1998.

Neves, Manuel Carreira das. *São Franciscao de Assis: Profeta da paz e da ecologia.* Petropolis: Vozes, 1992.

Newitt, Malyn. *A History of Mozambique.* Johannesburg: Witwatersrand University Press, 1995.

———. *Portugal in Africa: The Last Hundred Years.* London: Hurst, 1981.

———. *Portuguese Settlement on the Zambezi.* Harlow: Longman, 1973.

Nóbrega, Pedro Filipe de Góis. "A Congregação das Irmãs Franciscanas de Nossa Senhora das Vitórias: Antes e depois do Concílio Vaticano II." MA thesis, Portuguese Catholic University, 2013.

Nolan, Frank. *The Departure of the Missionaries of Africa (The White Fathers) from Mozambique in 1971.* Rome: Missionaries of Africa Society, 2017.

Nunes, Inácio António. "50 anos da Frelimo: Inácio Nunes [interview]." Video, 2012. Accessed June 12, 2012. http://macua.blogs.com/moambique_para_todos/2012/06/50-anos-da-frelimo-ina%CC%81cio-nunesvideo.html.

Oliveira, Miguel de. *História eclesiástica de Portugal.* Mem Martins, PT: Publicações Europa-América, 1994.

O'Malley, John W. *Vatican I: The Council and the Making of the Ultramontane Church.* Cambridge, MA: Belknap Press of Harvard University Press, 2018.

Opello, Walter C. Jr. "Internal War in Mozambique: A Social-Psychological Analysis of a Nationalist Revolution." PhD diss., University of Colorado, 1973.

———. "Pluralism and Elite Conflict in an Independence Movement: FRELIMO in the 1960s." *Journal of Southern African Studies* 2, no. 1 (1975): 66–82.

Orradre, Rafael Janín. "Origen y evolución historica del IEME." *Misiones Extranjeras: Revista de Missionologia* 82–83 (1984): 381–95.

"Os principais acontecimentos da Igreja em Moçambique nos ultimos dez anos." *Tempo* (Lourenço-Marques), May 19, 1974.

Pacheco, António. "A paz na rota dos irmãos franciscanos desde 1983." *Savana* (Maputo), September 20, 1996, 16–17.

Panzer, Michael G. "The Pedagogy of Revolution: Youth, Generational Conflict, and Education in the Development of Mozambican Nationalism and the State, 1962–1970." *Journal of Southern African Studies* 35, no. 4 (2009): 803–20.

Pasquier, Abel. "Lavigerie et le renouveau du catéchuménat." *Bulletin de Littérature Ecclésiastique* 95, no. 1–2 (1994): 89–106.

Pedro, Albano Mendes, ed. *Anuário católico do ultramar português 1960.* Lisbon: Junta de Investigação do Ultramar, Centro de Estudos Políticos e Sociais, 1962.

———, ed. *Anuário católico do ultramar português 1964.* Lisbon: Junta de Investigação do Ultramar, Centro de Estudos Missionários, 1965.

Pedro, Eusébio André. "A missionação jesuíta em Moçambique: As relações com a sociedade e com o poder político em Tete, 1941–2011." MA thesis, University of Oporto, 2013.

Pélissier, René. *Naissance du Mozambique.* 2 vols. Orgeval: Author's edition, 1984.

Pereira, José António Correia. *D. Ernesto Gonçalves Costa: Bispo e irmão.* Braga: Editorial Franciscana, 2002.

Pereira, Victor. "A economia do império e os planos de fomento." In Jerónimo, *O império colonial,* 251–85.

Pereira, Zélia. "Jésuitas em Moçambique (1941–1974): a construção do modelo imperial do Estado Novo." MA thesis, Instituto Universitário de Lisboa, 1998.

———. "Les Jésuites et la formation d'élites au Mozambique, 1961–1974." *LFM. Social Sciences and Missions* 14 (2004): 75–116.

———. "Os Jésuitas em Moçambique: Aspectos da acção missionária portuguesa em contexto colonial (1941–1974)." *Lusotopie,* no. 7 (2000): 81–105.

Perez, Father. "Memórias dos missionários de Africa em Moçambique. Segunda Parte—desde 1975." Unpublished paper, n.d.

Peterson, Derek R. "Conversion and the Alignments of Colonial Culture." *Social Sciences and Missions* 24, no. 2–3 (2011): 207–32.

———. *Creative Writing: Translation, Bookkeeping, and the Work of Imagination in Colonial Kenya.* Portsmouth: Ohio University Press, 2004.

———. *Ethnic Patriotism and the East African Revival.* Oxford: Oxford University Press, 2012.

Peterson, Derek, and Jean Allman. "Introduction: New Directions in the History of Missions in Africa." *Journal of Religious History* 23, no. 1 (1999): 1–7.

Pinheiro, Francisco Maria. *Na entrega do testemunho 1975: Acção missionária portuguesa em Moçambique.* Torres Novas, PT: Paróquia de S. João de Deus, 1992.

Pinto, Manuel Vieira. "Como ser Cristão na Revolução Socialista." In Borges, *D. Manuel Vieira Pinto,* 91–103.

———. "Dez meses de presença apostólica na Beira: Alguns acontecimentos, algumas reflexões." Beira, May 1, 1971.

Pinto Rema, Henrique. "A actividade missionária de Portugal nos séculos XIX e XX: I. A missionação portuguesa em geral." *Itinerarium* (Braga) 43 (1997): 251–332.

———. "Padre Albano Emílio Alves, OFM. Professor, filólogo e missionário." *Itinerarium* (Braga) 45 (1999): 249–66.

Pitcher, Anne. "From Coercion to Incentives: Portuguese Colonial Cotton Policy in Angola and Mozambique, 1946–1974." In Isaacman and Roberts, *Cotton, Colonialism, and Social History*, 119–43.

———. "Sowing the Seeds of Failure: Early Portuguese Cotton Cultivation in Angola and Mozambique." *Journal of Southern African Studies* 17, no. 1 (1991): 43–70.

Pitcher, Anne M. *Politics in the Portuguese Empire: The State, Industry and Cotton, 1926–1974.* Oxford: Clarendon Press, 1993.

Porter, Andrew. "'Cultural Imperialism' and Protestant Missionary Enterprise, 1780–1914." *Journal of Imperial and Commonwealth History* 25, no. 3 (1997): 367–91.

———. *Religion versus Empire? British Protestant Missionaries and Overseas Expansion.* Manchester: Manchester University Press, 2004.

Prudhomme, Claude. "Mission et religions: le point de vue catholique (1939–1957)." In Jacquin and Zorn, *L'altérité religieuse*, 347–73.

———. "Probématiques missionnaires catholique du XIXè siècle." In *Actas do Congresso internacional de História, Missionação Portuguesa e Encontro de Culturas*, vol. 1, "Cristandade Portuguesa até ao século XV: Evangelização interna, Ilhas Altlântica e Africa Oriental," 131–66. Braga: Faculdade de Teologia, 1993.

Rademaker, Cornelius I. M. *Called to Serve: History of the Congregation of the Sacred Hearts of Jesus and Mary (1800–1988).* Dublin: Fathers and Brothers of the Sacred Hearts, 1988.

"Rádio Pax—posto emissor da Beira." *Igreja e Missão* (Cucujães, PT) 28 (October–December 1967): 824–25.

Ranger, Terence, and John Weller, eds. *Themes in the Christian History of Central Africa.* Berkeley: University of California Press, 1975.

Reese, Thomas. *Inside the Vatican: The Politics and Organization of the Catholic Church.* Cambridge, MA: Harvard University Press, 1996.

Rego, António da Silva. *Alguns problemas sociológico-missionários da África negra.* Lisbon: Junta de Investigação do Ultramar, Centro de Estudos Políticas e Sociais, Estudos de Ciências Políticas e Sociais, 1960.

———. *Le patronage portugais de l'orient: Aperçu historique.* Lisbon: Agência Geral do Ultramar, 1957.

———. *Temas sociomissionológicos e históricos.* Lisbon: Junta de Investigação do Ultramar, Centro de Estudos Políticas e Sociais, Estudos de Ciências Políticas e Sociais no. 58, 1962.

Rego, Lobiano do (Father Albano). *Pátria morena: A vista da Maior Epopeia Lusíada.* With a letter and preface by Gilberto Freyre. Lisbon: Edition LAIN, 1959.

Reis, Bruno Cardoso. "A concordata de Salazar? Uma análise a partir das notas preparatórias de Março de 1937." *Lusitania Sacra* 2, no. 12 (2000): 185–220.

———. "Portugal e a Santé Sé no sistema internacional (1910–1970)." *Análise Social* (Lisbon) 36, no. 161 (2002): 1019–59.

————. *Salazar e o Vaticano*. Lisbon: Imprensa de Ciências Sociais, 2006.

Renault, François. *Le Cardinal Lavigerie, 1852–1892: L'église, l'Afrique et la France*. Paris: Fayart, 1992.

Rennie, Keith John. "Christianity, Colonialism and the Origins of Nationalism among the Ndau of Southern Rhodesia, 1890–1935." PhD diss., Northwestern University, 1973.

Resende, Sebastião [Soares de]. *O sacrifício da missa em D. Frei Gaspar do Casal*. Oporto: Tavares Martins, 1941.

————. *Profeta em Moçambique*. Lisbon: Difel, 1994.

Ribeiro, Jorge. *Inhaminga: O último massacre*. Oporto: Edições Afrontamento, 2015.

Riccardi, Andrea. *As políticas da igreja*. Lisbon: Paulus, 1998.

Rocca, Giancarlo, ed. *Dizionario degli Istituti di Perfezione*. Vol. 9. Rome: Edizione Paoline, 1997.

————. "La fabrication d'une sociologie des ordres religieux dans le Dizionario degli istituti di prefezione." *Social Compass* 48, no. 2 (2001): 279–97.

Rocha, Ilídio. *A imprensa de Moçambique: História e catálogo (1854–1975)*. Lisbon: Livros do Brasil, 2000.

Rodrigues, Manuel Augusto. "Teologia." In Azevedo, *Dicionário de história religiosa*, 5:276–81.

Rodriguez, Saturnino. "Sintesis y evaluacion del sondeo realizado en el I. E. M. E. en 1974." *Misiones Extranjeras: Revista Bimestral de Missionologia* 34–35 (1976): 487–93.

Rosas, Fernando. *História de Portugal, vol. 7 O Estado Novo*. Lisbon: Editorial Estampa, 1998.

Said, Edward W. *Culture and Imperialism*. London: Chatto and Windus, 1993.

————. *Orientalism*. London: Routledge and Kegan Paul, 1978.

Sampaio, Teles. "Interview." In *A guerra de África, 1961–1974*, vol. 2, edited by José Freire Antunes, 791–98. Lisbon: Circulo de Leitores.

Santos, Eduardo dos. *O Estado Português e o problema missionário*. Lisbon: Agência-Geral do Ultramar, 1964. (Translated by Jean Haupt as *L'état portugais et le problème missionnaire*. Lisbon: Junta de Investigações do Ultramar, 1964.)

Santos, João Afonso dos, Carlos Adrião Rodrigues, António Pereira Leite, and William Gerard Pott. *O julgamento dos padres do Macúti*. Oporto: Afrontamento, 1973.

Sardica, José M. "150 Anos da regeneração: A politíca depois da era das revoluções." *História* 23, series 3, no. 36 (2001): 20–31.

Schebesta, Paul. *Portugals Konquistamission in Südost-Afrika*. St. Augustin, DE: Steyler Verlag, 1966. [Portuguese version published as *Portugal: A missão da conquista no sudeste da África; história das missões da Zambézia e do reino Monomotapa (1560–1920)*. Lisbon: Missionários do Verbo Divino, 2011.]

Schneidman, Witney W. *Engaging Africa: Washington and the Fall of Portugal's Colonial Empire*. Lanham, MD: University Press of America, 2004.

Schubert, Benedict. *A guerra e as igrejas: Angola 1961–1991*. Basel: P. Schlettwein, 2000.

Seguy, Jean. "Une sociologie des sociétés imaginées: monachisme et utopie." *Annales* 26, no. 2 (1971): 328–54.

Seidler, John, and Katherine Meyer. *Conflict and Change in the Catholic Church.* New Brunswick, NJ: Rutgers University Press, 1989.

Seixas Lavado, Maria Ludovina de. *Franciscanas Missionárias de Maria: 100 anos em Moçambique, 1897–1997.* Maputo: Provincia Portuguesa do Instituto das Franciscanas Missionárias de Maria em Moçambique (no centenário da Provincia), 1997.

"Seminário de S. João de Brito do Zóbuè." *Miraduro: Revista dos alunos do Seminário Maior de S. Pio X* (Namaacha) 11 (1970): 145–47.

Serapião, Luis B. "The Catholic Church and Conflict Resolution in Mozambique's Post-Colonial Conflict." *Journal of Church and State* 46, no. 2 (2004): 365–87.

————. "The Preaching of Portuguese Colonialism and the Protest of the White Fathers." *Issue: A Quarterly Journal of Africanist Opinion* 2, no. 1 (1972): 34–41.

Serrão, Olga M. L. Iglésias Neves. "Contributos para a história da Maçonaria em Moçambique." In *Actas do seminário 'Moçambique: navegações, comércio e técnicas,'* edited by Faculdade de Letras da Universidade Eduardo Mondlane de Maputo and Comissão Nacional para as Comemorações dos Descobrimentos Portugueses, 285–95. Lisbon: Comissão Nacional para as Comemorações dos Descobrimentos Portugueses, 1998.

Servais, Emile, and Francis Hambye. "Structure et signification: Problème de méthode en sociologie des organisations claustrales." *Social Compass* 18, no. 1 (1971): 27–44.

Sheldon, Kathleen. "'I Studied with the Nuns, Learning to Make Blouses': Gender Ideology and Colonial Education in Mozambique." *International Journal of African Historical Studies* 31, no. 3 (1998): 595–625.

Silva, António da. *Mentalidade missiológica dos Jesuítas em Moçambique antes de 1759: Esboço ideológico a partir do núcleo documental.* 2 vols. Lisbon: Junta de Investigação do Ultrama, 1967.

————. "Ocupação missionária de Moçambique." In *Moçambique: Curso de extensão universitária, ano lectivo de 1964–1965, 673–95.* Lisbon: Instituto Superior de Ciências Sociais e Política Ultramarina, [1964].

Silva, Maria da Conceição Tavares Lourenço da. *As missões católicas femininas.* Lisbon: Junta de Investigação do Ultramar, 1960.

Simpson, Duncan. *A igreja católica e o Estado Novo Salazarista.* Lisbon: Edições 70, 2014.

Soares Tomás, Maria Helena. *Irmãs franciscanas missionárias da Mãe do Divino Pastor em Moçambique.* Braga: Livraria Apostolado da Imprensa, 1998.

Soullard, R. "Le pouvoir des religieux dans l'église." *Pouvoirs* 17 (1981): 119–28.

Sousa, Fernando de. *As franciscanas missionárias de Nossa Senhora em Portugal (1868–1992).* Oporto: [Simão Guimarães], 1992.

Sousa, Gabriel de. "A conferência nacional dos institutos religiosos." In *I Congresso nacional de religiosos: Trabalhos apresentados ao congresso, Lisboa 8 a 13 de abril de 1958.* [1958]: 683–87.

Sousa, José Augusto Alves de. *A igreja e a paz em Moçambque. Síntese Histórica: 1979–1994,* Maputo: Edibosco, 1995.

———. *Memórias de um jesuíta missionário em Mocambique: 1960–2004 quarenta e quatro anos de compromisso na igreja e na sociedade moçambicana; uma nova face da missão.* Braga: Editorial Apostolado da Oração, 2015.

———. *Os jesuítas em Moçambique, 1541–1991: No cinquentenário do quarto período da nossa missão.* Braga: Livraria Apostolado da Imprensa, 1991.

Sousa, José Augusto Alves de, and Odilo Congil, eds. *Arquidiocese da Beira: Resenha Histórica.* Braga/Beira: Editorial A. O. 1988.

Sousa, José Augusto Alves de, and Francisco da Cruz Correia. *500 anos de evangelização em Moçambique.* Maputo: Paulinas, 1998.

Souto, Amélia Neves de. *Caetano e o ocaso do "império": Administração e guerra colonial em Moçambique durante o Marcelismo, 1968–1974.* Oporto: Edições Afrontamento, 2007.

Spencer, Leon P. *Toward an African Church in Mozambique: Kamba Simango and the Protestant Community in Manica and Sofala, 1892–1945.* Luwinga, MW: Mzuni Press, 2013.

Stiff, Peter. *The Silent War: South African Recce Operations, 1969–1984.* Alberton, ZA: Galago, 1999.

Systermans, H., and M. Gendrot. "Unione dei Superiori Generali (USG)." In Rocca, *Dizionario degli Istituti di Perfezione,* 1586–88.

Tajú, Gulamo. "Dom Sebastião Soares de Resende, primeiro bispo da Beira: Notas para uma cronologia." *Arquivo: Boletim do arquivo histórico de Moçambique* 6 (1989): 149–76.

———. "O projecto do engenheiro Jorge Jardim." MA thesis, Instituto Superior Pedagogico, 1990.

———. "RENAMO: Os factos que conhecemos." *Boletim do Departamento de História da Universidade Eduardo Mondlane* 1 (November 1988): 5–44.

Taveneaux, René. "Le catholicisme post-tridentin." In *Histoire des religions,* vol. 2, edited by Henri-Charles Puech, 1049–146. Paris: Gallimard, 1972.

Teixeira, Francisco Nunes. *A igreja em Moçambique na hora da independência (1955–1975).* Coimbra: Grafica de Coimbra, 1995.

Tembe, Joel das Neves. "Uhuru na Kazi: Recapturing MANU Nationalism through the Archive." *Kronos* 39, no. 1 (2013): 257–79.

Tembe, Joel das Neves, and Napoleão Gaspar. "O contexto colonial e a génese do movimento nacionalista." In *História da Luta de Libertação National,* vol. 1, edited by Joel das Neves Tembe, 9–84. Maputo: Ministério dos Combatentes, Direcção Nacional de História, 2014.

Tembe Ndelana, Lopes. *From UDENAMO to FRELIMO and Mozambican Diplomacy.* Terra Alta: Headline Books, 2016.

Tempo. "Interview with Miguel Murrupa." *Tempo* (Lourenço Marques), December 13, 1970.

Tiberondwa, Ado K. *Missionary Teachers as Agents of Colonialism.* Lusaka: Kenneth Kaunda Foundation, 1978.

Trindade, Manuel de Almeida. *Memórias de um bispo.* Coimbra: Gráfica de Coimbra, 1993.

União dos Sacerdotes e Religiosas de Moçambique (USAREMO). *1a Reunião dos Sacerdotes e Religiosos Negros de Moçambique,* 1974.

Universidade Eduardo Mondlane (Departamento de História). *Moçambique no auge do colonialismo, 1930–1961.* Vol. 2, *História de Moçambique.* 2nd ed. Maputo: Livraria Universitária, 1999.

Urresti, J., ed. *Structures of the Church.* New York: Herder and Herder, 1970.

Vail, Leroy. "The Making of an Imperial Slum: Nyassaland and Its Railways, 1895–1935." *Journal of African History* 16, no. 1 (1975): 89–112.

———. "Mozambique's Chartered Companies: The Rule of the Feeble." *Journal of African History* 17, no. 3 (1976): 389–416.

Vail, Leroy, and Landeg White. *Colonialism and Capitalism in Mozambique: A Study of Quelimane District.* London: Heinemann, 1980.

———. "The Struggle for Mozambique: Capitalist Rivalries, 1900–40." *Review: Fernand Braudel Center* 3, no. 2 (1979): 243–75

Valler, Vito. *In Africa con Francesco d'Assisi: 50 anni dei Cappucini di Trento in Mozambico.* Bologna: Editrice Missionaria Italiana, 1998.

van Dijk, Willibord C. "Le franciscanisme comme contestation permanente dans l'église." In *Churches as Political Institutions/Les églises comme institutions politiques,* edited by Léo Moulin, 241–58. Brussels: Institut Belge de Science Politique/Association de Science Politique, 1970.

Vasconcelos, Evaristo de. *Religiosos: Selecção sobre os institutos religiosos masculinos existentes em Portugal.* Braga: Edição do Mensageiro do Coração de Jesus, 1957.

Veloso, Agostinho. *D. Teodósio Clemente de Gouveia: Paladino de Portugal ao serviço de Deus,* vol. 1. Lisbon: Agência Geral do Ultramar, 1965.

"Venha o inimigo donde vier, nós o puniremos: President Samora Machel no 1º de Maio." *Tempo* (Maputo) 488 (May 13, 1979): 34.

Vergote, Antoine. "Folk Catholicism: Its Significance, Value and Ambiguities." *Philippine Studies* 30, no. 1 (1982): 5–26.

Vines, Alex. "'No Democracy without Money': The Road to Peace in Mozambique." *CIIR Briefing Paper.* London: Catholic Institute for International Relations, 1994.

———. *RENAMO: Terrorism in Mozambique.* London: James Currey, 1991.

Voodrow, Alan. *The Jesuits: A Story of Power.* London: Geoffrey Chapman, 1995.

Vorreux, Damien. "Les Franciscains." In *Les Ordres Religieux: La vie et l'art,* vol. 2, edited by Gabriel le Bras, 227–373. Paris: Flamarion.

Weber, Max. *Sociologie des religions.* Paris: Édition Gallimard, 1996.

Wellens, S. *La Société des Missionnaires d'Afrique.* Louvain: Publications Universitaires de Louvain, 1952.

Wenzel, Bernhard Josef. *Portugal und der Heilige Stuhl: Das portuguesische Konkordats- und Missionsrecht; ein Beitrag zur Geschichte der Missions- und Völkerrechtswissenchaft.* Lisbon: Âgencia-Geral do Ultramar, 1958.

Wheeler, Douglas. "'Estado presente de tranquilidade' posto en causa: Portugal observado e analisado no contexto internacional de 1958–1959." In *Humberto Delgado: As eleições de 58*, edited by Iva Delgado, Carlos Pacheco, Telmo Faria, and Nair Alexandra, 448–71. Lisbon: Vega, 1998.

White Fathers. "Mozambique: Une église, signe de salut . . . pour qui?" (Mimeographed documents). Rome: Société des Missionnaires d'Afrique, 1973.

Wilde, Melissa J. *Vatican II: A Sociological Analysis of Religious Change*. Princeton, NJ: Princeton University Press, 2007.

Willis, Justin. "'Men on the Spot,' Labor, and the Colonial State in British East Africa: The Mombasa Water Supply, 1911–1917." *International Journal of African Historical Studies* 28, no. 1 (1995): 25–48.

Wilson, Monica Hunter. *Religion and the Transformation of Society: A Study in Social Change in Africa*. Cambridge: Cambridge University Press, 1971.

Wittberg, Patricia. *The Rise and Decline of Catholic Religious Orders: A Social Movement Perspective*. Albany: State University of New York Press, 1994.

Woodrow, Alan. *The Jesuits: A Story of Power*. New York: Geoffrey Chapman, 1995.

Zengazenga, António Disse. *Memórias de um rebelde: Uma vida pela independência e democracia em Moçambique*. AmazonCreatespace, 2013.

Index